CHINA'S
Nonprofit
Sector

CHINA'S Nonprofit Sector

PROGRESS AND CHALLENGES

Chien-Chung Huang, Guosheng Deng,
Zhenyao Wang, and Richard L. Edwards, editors

Routledge
Taylor & Francis Group

LONDON AND NEW YORK

First published 2014 by Transaction Publishers

2 Park Square, Milton Park, Abingdon, Oxfordshire OX14 4RN
711 Third Avenue, New York, NY 10017

Routledge is an imprint of the Taylor & Francis Group, an informa business

First issued in paperback 2017

Copyright © 2014 Taylor & Francis

Library of Congress Catalog Number: 2013012463

Library of Congress Cataloging-in-Publication Data

China's nonprofit sector : progress and challenges / Chien-Chung Huang, Guosheng Deng, Zhenyao Wang, and Richard L. Edwards, editors.
    pages cm
 Includes bibliographical references and index.
 ISBN 978-1-4128-5296-8
 1. Nonprofit organizations—China. 2. Nongovernmental organizations—China. I. Huang, Chien-Chung, 1968-
 HD2769.2.C6C45 2013
 338.7—dc23
                                                      2013012463

ISBN 13: 978-1-4128-5296-8 (hbk)
ISBN 13: 978-1-138-50813-2 (pbk)

Contents

Preface

Dezhi Lu

Thirty-two years have passed since the implementation of China's Reform Era policies. Since that time, the number of nonprofit organizations in China has grown substantially. However, these organizations are still in a nascent stage of development and civil society has not yet fully recognized their potential. For the majority of Chinese people, nonprofit organizations are new and unfamiliar—distant entities discussed only in academic or technical settings. The public typically associates nonprofit organizations with charity and volunteer work, which has fueled the misconception that nonprofit employees should always act as self-sacrificing, uncompensated, moral role models. In turn, the public holds nonprofit organizations and their staff to extremely high ethical standards. Unfortunately, the laws regulating nonprofit organizations in China are also in the earliest stages of development, and do not provide a sufficient framework to ethically guide and support these organizations. These circumstances have led to divergently evolving expectations between the general public, and those in the nonprofit sector.

The good news is that the nonprofit sector has benefitted substantially from rapid developments in China's political, economic, and cultural systems. Some organizations are directly engaged in public service, while others are focused on research and advocacy. In this way, current organizations are not only improving their systems of management and governance but also reshaping public conceptions of the nonprofit sector. Widespread use of technology and social media, most notably Weibo (a microblog site that is somewhat of a hybrid of Twitter and Facebook) has certainly contributed toward this end. These platforms have made it possible to disseminate ideas about public service and charity, and encourage transparency among nonprofit organizations, on a much wider scale. Most importantly, the public has developed a new passion for public service, which has positively impacted the development of civil society in China. These new systems have involved close cooperation between the government and the nonprofit sector.

Over the course of this process, the nonprofit sector has become a focus of academic research; current experts in the field include Dr. Ming Wang, Dr. Guosheng Deng, and Dr. Xijin Jia at Tsinghua University; Dr. Gongcheng Zheng and Dr. Xiaoguang Kang at China People's University; Dr. Zengzhi Shi and Dr. Jinping Jin at Beijing University; Dr. Xiulan Zhang and Dr. Zhenyao Wang at Beijing Normal University; and Dr. Jun Tang and Dr. Tuan Yang at the Chinese Academy of Social Sciences. These individuals have made tremendous contributions to research pertaining to Chinese nonprofit organizations, and the field of study is quickly expanding. An increasing number of Chinese universities have recently established programs and courses related to the nonprofit sector, which has widened the pool of professionals qualified to train, supervise, and manage. In light of this growing capacity, and within the broader context of China's economic and social developments, the nonprofit sector is likely nearing a period of rapid development.

The Huamin Research Center at Rutgers University is an academic institution established and supported by the Huamin Charity Foundation. It is the first research institution of its kind, established overseas by a Chinese foundation. The Huamin Research Center conducts research on issues of social welfare and philanthropy affecting China and the United States. This book is comprised of articles written by well-known scholars in the field, whose research and analysis offer an important introduction to the practices and theories related to China's nonprofit sector. The purpose of this book is to facilitate and strengthen exchange and cooperation in nonprofit practices and research between China and the West. In the coming years, the growth of China's nonprofit sector will become increasingly important. China's history spans 5,000 years. The establishment and development of a new, modern sector will surely involve many challenges, but I am confident that it will also produce many important opportunities.

Acknowledgments

With gratitude and pleasure, we would like to acknowledge the many people whose diverse perspectives and technical expertise have contributed to this undertaking. This book could not have been completed without the generous support of the Huamin Charity Foundation. We warmly thank the Huamin Charity Foundation Chairman, Dr. Dezhi Lu, for his unfailing support and encouragement. Thank you also to the support staff who have dedicated their time and energy to make this book possible. These include Rocky Citro, for his invaluable editing and layout contributions; and Huamin Research Center staff Shuang Lu and Juliann Vikse for their exceptional translation efforts.

Introduction

Chien-Chung Huang, Guosheng Deng,
Zhenyao Wang, and Richard L. Edwards

Much has been written about the economic changes that have taken place in China over the past few decades, but another area of Chinese society has largely escaped the attention of scholars—the nonprofit sector. From government-affiliated organizations to private charitable foundations to small social groups, nonprofit organizations abound in the country. Since China began its shift to a market economy, the nonprofit sector has gone from a relatively minor industry to an integral part of the nation's social fabric. Organizations have been established to address environmental protection, poverty relief, women's rights, rural development, transportation, education, and a range of other social issues. Funding sources, which historically have been limited in China, have begun to branch out in recent years, moving beyond the government and international foundations to local private foundations, college alumni associations, and with the growth in corporate social responsibility, for-profit corporations as well. Organizations are now forming strategic alliances to strengthen funding streams and programmatic efforts. Recognizing the sector's growing capacity, the government has even entrusted private organizations with some of its public services.

However, these accomplishments have not come easily. For much of the Reform Era, the government controlled nonprofit activity through preferential treatment for certain organizations and policy restrictions for others. For many years it was difficult for private organizations to even register for legal status and the government controlled the registration process and influenced the flow of donations. In addition to policy barriers, funding sources have not always been abundant. Nonprofit organizations have added to these difficulties with a lack of organizational structure, and at times, accountability. And while most nonprofit actors have struggled toward establishing the sector's identity, building its capacity, and earning the public's trust, some organizations have damaged the sector's reputation with a range of donation scams, embezzlement scandals, and kickbacks. The media had a field day with several high-profile scandals; the barrage of negative reporting throughout the year of 2011 rocked the public's confidence in private organizations, adding another hurdle as the nonprofit sector continues its development. The general lack of oversight and transparency in the sector has added to the public's growing suspicion of charitable foundations and nonprofit organizations.

Given the recent scandals, perhaps it is not surprising that the number of new nonprofit organizations and the amount of donations grew more slowly in 2011. But the story runs deeper than that. The year of 2011 also saw a lull in natural disasters, so new organizations and donations grew without one of its biggest areas of need. Adding to this, another trend was quickly making fundamental changes to the nonprofit sector. The past couple of years have been marked by a boom in *microphilanthropy*—that is, donations collected by individuals or small groups through microblogging and social media websites. Microphilanthropy is an exciting new development in the industry and the people have responded quickly to the opportunity to take donations into their own hands. This has caused a noticeable shift in the flow of donations, which used to go almost exclusively to formal organizations.

So are nonprofit organizations thriving or stagnating in China? What is really driving the rates of individual donations and the establishment of new organizations? Going forward, how will nonprofit organizations regain some of the trust that they have lost with the public? As private organizations continue to expand their role in social services, what role should the government play in the registration, administration, and oversight of these organizations? Does a lack of regulatory standards help or hurt the growth of foundations and organizations? Given the current policy and social contexts, what are the logistical next steps to advance the nonprofit sector's development? What is the next stage of development in terms of organizational structure and management? Is microphilanthropy a sustainable funding source? Will they take over traditional donation methods? How can they be better organized? It may be that China's nonprofit sector faces more unanswered questions today than ever, but a few things are clear from the country's short but highly active history. The birth and continued growth in private foundations and organizations have demonstrated that nongovernmental charitable donations and social work are here to stay in China. The burgeoning popularity in microphilanthropy has also demonstrated the people's desire to donate, especially when they have control over and more faith in where their donations will go. Indeed, microphilanthropy may be the apotheosis of the shift from government to private control in the nonprofit sector.

In general though, the nonprofit sector in China is in an early stage of development and is not well understood. A look at the figure below provides a brief glimpse into the diversity of China's nonprofit sector today. As the sector evolves, scholarly discussion will be instrumental in better understanding how nonprofit organizations can effectively develop their organizational structures, improve the efficiency of their services, and make larger and more positive impacts in Chinese society. The essays in this book take on the difficult and important questions above to begin the scholarly discussion and provide timely and important context for scholars, policy makers, professionals, donors, and the public (Figure 1).

Figure 1
The Nonprofit Sector in China

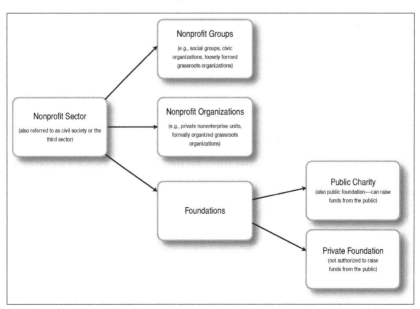

This tour through China's quickly evolving nonprofit sector begins with Guosheng Deng's overview of the most recent era of development in the sector. In the past two decades, NGOs have gone from a little-known social phenomena to a basic part of Chinese society. Grassroots NGOs have emerged and have begun to better organize their operational and management structures. Over time, they have learned to improve their capacity building and strengthen their funding base. They have also realized the power of working together—by creating networks of like-minded organizations, grassroots organizations have begun to impact local policy and create societal change. In contrast to the growing autonomy of grassroots NGOs, government-affiliated NGOs are struggling to achieve independence because they remain reliant on government funding and because the government tends to influence or control their decision making and services.

In Chapter 2, Xiufeng Chen and Li Li tackle corporate social responsibility in China. They discuss corporate participation in social philanthropy as a precondition and basis for cooperation between corporations and charitable foundations. The cooperation between the two is a win-win situation. For corporations, participating in philanthropy can expand their social impact, enhance their public image, increase their economic and societal benefits, and eventually meet their profit goals. For charitable foundations, incorporating corporations into their charity work gains them more resources for philanthropy and models the values of love and harmony for society. In reality, however, the interaction between corporations and charitable foundations is hindered by corporations' lack of motivation to donate to charity and prioritize social responsibility, foundations' lack of charitable marketing strategies, poor fund-raising abilities, and the government's unreasonable tax policies. China needs an improved strategy to facilitate the win-win situation of corporate-charitable partnerships.

In Chapter 3, Jiangang Zhu provides an analysis of the development of NGOs and civil society in China's Reform Era. Zhu views grassroots NGOs as a fundamental influence in shaping the civic community at the local level. Establishing stable funding structures, building trust with society, training volunteers, and dealing effectively with shortages in resources and staff are common issues faced by grassroots NGOs. As Zhu argues, however, what they lack in resources they make up for with a strong spirit of volunteerism. Perhaps it is this perseverance and loyalty to their core values that has inspired a growing public trust in grassroots NGOs, while scandals have rocked the public's trust in larger, more established organizations. Moving forward, the question becomes how grassroots organizations can maintain their spirit while expanding in scale and scope.

In Chapter 4, Xiaoyong Huang and Liqiang Cai delve into the effects of bureaucracy on the nonprofit sector. Once part of a highly constrictive, bureaucratic system, nonprofit organizations have now become one of the primary mediums of public management. This trend, coupled with vast improvements in the state of social resources in the country, helps to explain why the development of nonprofit organizations has gone from a snail's pace to new and unprecedented opportunities for growth. To capitalize on these opportunities, nonprofit organizations will need to establish more stable and effective management structures and build credibility with the public, which with the growing attention to nonprofit organizations in mainstream and social media, has quickly become a central issue in their development.

In Chapter 5, Peifeng Liu aims to analyze nonprofit legislation in China, as part of a broader examination of the development of civil rights. Liu points out that the centralization of political power in China has led to somewhat contradictory policies and laws surrounding nonprofit management and governance. The "centralized registration" system features strong regulations that serve to tightly control the establishment, expansion, and development of nonprofit organizations and groups. Alternatively, the "dual-oversight" system has led to somewhat lenient government oversight of nonprofit operations. Liu not only outlines the current systems in place, but also suggests ways the Chinese government might effectively reform nonprofit legislation and encourage the development of a strong, healthy civil society in China.

Outside China, nonprofit organizations strongly influence and contribute to national economies and societies. The effects of these organizations in China, however, have been relatively unexplored. Using nationwide questionnaires, Chapter 6 analyzes the current status, characteristics, and contributions of nonprofit organizations in China for the first time. Guosheng Deng's analysis reveals that China's nonprofit organizations are now facing a crossroads in their development, which is increasingly influenced by public policy and participation at the individual level. The study also demonstrates that, compared with less organized nonprofit groups, nonprofit organizations make greater contributions to employment and economic development. What the more established organizations lack, however, is a strong connection to the public. The development of nonprofit organizations in China will require a prolonged, joint effort by government, organizations, and society.

The growing participation of individual people in China's nonprofit sector is discussed by Zhenyao Wang and Huajun Gao in Chapter 7 on recent trends in charitable donations. Consistent with the larger shift away from government-affiliated organizations to organizations run by individuals and groups, donations have been flowing increasingly to non-governmental charities. This trend has become clear with the declining success of government-run local fundraising days. Wealthy individuals have begun to start their own foundations, and amid growing distrust of official organizations due to recent scandals, the people have turned to social media to have more control over their donations, often directing them to nongovernmental charities. The authors continue their analysis by breaking down the top contributors and recipients of charitable donations in the country and analyzing recent trends with corporate donations and the professionalism and normalcy of individual donations.

In Chapter 8, Huajun Gao develops China's newly emerging charity industry network. Gao explains how donations flow and the internal and external supports to the network. The network is still taking shape but is quickly facing critical questions. How exactly should donations be processed? What does the emergence of social media and other new fund-raising platforms mean for future directions in the charity industry? Gao also discusses the important issues of oversight, evaluation, staff development, and online and off-line interagency communication.

Chapter 9 moves from social media to a more complete discussion of the media's role in the development of China's nonprofit sector, including television stations and print media. Gaorong Zhang and Zhenyao Wang provide an insightful analysis of the frequency and scope of the media's coverage of philanthropy work. Fueled at times by disasters and scandals, increased media coverage of philanthropy issues has taken philanthropy work from a little-known phenomenon to a household name in China. Additionally, Zhang and Wang describe how the media has helped raise awareness about social issues, has functioned as a means for the public to provide a level of oversight to nonprofit organizations and founda-tions, and has even been directly involved in planning, implementing, and funding philanthropic events.

In Chapter 10, Yongguang Xu applies path dependence theory to the transformation of public foundations in China. Public foundations have gone from nonexistent to playing a powerful role in shaping public welfare and culture. Public foundations today continue to face the issue of government bureaucracy and control, and a continuing core issue is who exactly should and will control public resources and funds. In an environment of continued corporate and government control over donations and growing scandals of established donations, Xu points us to the growth of grant-giving foundations and special funds as hopeful and promising directions in the field.

In Chapter 11, Li Feng and Xiaoguang Kang point to another new direction—microphilanthropy. Individuals have always found small ways to help each other, but with the advent of social media, people can now do this on a larger scale than ever before. And in China, the ability to make a donation or forward a message of hope has a special significance—in a society where issues of freedom and control are paramount, the people have quickly taken to their ability to make personal decisions about their contributions to philanthropy. Social media has allowed individuals to work together as small groups and large coalitions to help others and even influence policy and social change. The genuinely altruistic spirit of individual efforts inspires others and the platform of social media can spread that inspiration in moments. Whether it is providing free lunches to students in low-income schools or giving rides to would-be passengers stranded in an airport, the people have shown that they can and will come together as a powerful force. The authors take new steps in the literature by classifying three types of microphilanthropy, exploring the benefits and limitations of each, and analyzing the future potential and likely directions of microphilanthropy in the country.

In the final chapter, Kam-tong Chan uses a competing values framework to examine the nature and characteristics of the evolving third sector in mainland China, particularly as it stood before the 2008 Sichuen earthquake disaster. Drawing upon case studies, Chan shows how the structure and dynamics of civil society organizations in the third sector can be understood from the perspectives of the open system, the rational-goal system, the natural system, and internal process. The findings suggest that, owing to its historical trajectory, the third sector in China is following a top-down route that stands in contrast to the bottom-up approach typical of Western countries. Given the ambiguities and difficulties of this alternative model, Chan concludes that Western concepts relating to the third sector should be applied cautiously to the Chinese context.

With China's shift to a market economy, the government and corporate sectors have undergone substantial change. Similarly, the nonprofit sector has experienced a radical transformation in the country, especially over the past three decades. Private nonprofit organizations and foundations have gone from almost nonexistent to core components of Chinese society. Like all societal change, the development of China's nonprofit sector has not been without its challenges, in part because the government has tried to hold onto some measure of control of public services, in part because a handful of high-profile nonprofit scandals have caused the people to distrust the sector as a whole, and in part because the government and society are figuring out how to incorporate this new system into public life. Even in this early stage of development though, the nonprofit sector has demonstrated resourcefulness in designing and implementing programs, recruiting staff, locating funding, and inspiring action among the people. When bureaucratic restrictions made it difficult to create formal organizations, the people still came together in grassroots efforts in their local communities and, recently, online through the microblogosphere. This resilience makes one thing clear—the Chinese people have a passion for helping others, and as the country continues to move forward and redefine itself in all spheres, the people will be taking an active role in this relatively new but thriving third sector.

Part I

The Development of the Nonprofit Sector in China

1

The Development of China's Nonprofit Sector since 1995

*Guosheng Deng**

Nongovernmental organizations (NGOs) in China have gone through four phases of development since 1949. During the first phase—the emerging phase (1949–1966)—many academic, arts, and other large public organizations were founded, such as the Federation of Industry and Commerce and the China Association for Science and Technology. In the second phase—the lag phase (1966–1978)—the Cultural Revolution slowed the activities of most organizations to a near halt and prevented new organizations from forming. Next, in the redeveloping phase (1978–1995), a large number of NGOs, particularly industrial associations and foundations, sprang up and developed rapidly in response to the demands of China's Reform Era. Unlike these earlier phases, NGOs in China have changed substantially in the last phase (1995–present). During this time, NGOs have begun to play new roles in the country's economy and political development.

This article focuses on NGOs founded after 1995. The discussion covers changes in NGOs in China and transitions in the relationship between the government and society. I also attempt to explain the motivations and barriers of NGO reform, and finally attempt to predict future trends in NGO development.

* Translated by Shuang Lu, Research Fellow, Huamin Research Center, School of Social Work, Rutgers University.

3

The Increasing Autonomy of NGOs

Many scholars—especially Western scholars—believe that there are no true NGOs in China because they do not function independently from the government. This might have been true before 1995, but since then NGOs have progressively become more autonomous.

The Rise of Grassroots NGOs since 1995

In 1995, many civic groups, scholars, and government officials in China attended the NGO Forum at the World Conference on Women, during which they began to contact and build relationships with NGOs outside China (hereafter, foreign NGOs), especially grant-giving NGOs. The conference and related media reports not only raised awareness about NGOs, but also inspired people to find new NGOs or modify existing NGOs to follow the international model. Since then, grassroots NGOs have increased in number and have become more active in China. Overall, the development of Chinese grassroots NGOs has consisted of three phases since 1995.

The Emergence of Grassroots NGOs, 1995–2000

The first generation of Chinese grassroots NGOs emerged from 1995 to 2000. During this time, grassroots NGOs were primarily located in Beijing and Yunnan Province. These organizations worked on issues such as environmental protection, women's rights, and poverty alleviation. Most of these organizations were founded and led by important members of society, who tended to be older in age, such as Congjie Liang from Friends of Nature, Xingjuan Wang from the Maple Women's Hotline, Lihua Xie from Rural Women, and Xiaoyi Liao from Global Village, among others. Funding for these grassroots NGOs mostly came from grants from other countries. For Friends of Nature and the Maple Women's Hotline, for instance, 70 to 90 percent of funding was from foreign donations. Of course, some organizations, especially the lesser known ones, were supported by individual organization leaders. These NGOs were generally small in size, their expenses were mostly related to transportation and communication, and they relied on volunteer efforts. For example, the Green Friends Association had no formal funding and relied exclusively on donations from its founder and volunteers in its early stages of development.

Before 2000, the majority of grassroots NGOs did not have a board of directors, and the organizations' founders had a high level of authority and the power to make decisions. Generally speaking, the government did not influence the administrative decisions in these organizations, especially in NGOs that were registered as industrial or commercial organizations or were not registered at all. At the same time, foreign funders did not intervene in the organizations' decisions. Therefore, for the most part, these NGOs were able to make decisions independently.

Most organizations did not need to ask for government approval before conducting their activities, mainly because they were not registered with the Ministry of Civil Affairs. Another reason was that organizations purposely chose nonpolitical activities to avoid conflict with government institutions. Therefore, local governments managed these organizations with the Three-No policy (no recognition, no intervention, and no publicity). However, although government impact on these organizations was very less, a few of them experienced high levels of intervention from their international funders, particularly organizations that relied too heavily on one or two funders. Because a precondition for receiving program grants was that the program would coincide with the supporting agency's interests and strategies, many NGOs had to adjust the planning, design, and implementation of their programs and activities. Overall though, these NGOs had some level of autonomy in terms of their staffing, finances, decision making, and activities.

The Steady Development of Grassroots NGOs, 2000–2008

The success of the first-generation grassroots NGOs motivated others to find new NGOs and obtain foreign financial support. After 2000, grassroots NGOs spread to thirty-one cities nationwide, and their activities expanded to serving migrant populations, serving people with AIDS, providing legal aid, and working as civil think tanks. After 2000, a significant characteristic of the development of Chinese grassroots NGOs was the rise of capacity building, which led to the founding of several capacity-building centers. For example, the China Association for NGO Cooperation founded a training center with grants from the Evangelischer Entwicklungsdienst Church Development Service. From 2003 to 2006, the center trained 843 people 1,081 times for 521 grassroots organizations. The Institute for Environment and Development and the NGO Information Center continually provide NGO training and consulting services with the grants they receive from foreign NGOs.

Influenced by the capacity-building trend, some grassroots NGOs began to develop organizational strategies, and some even developed a board of directors. Although most of the strategies and boards were not run effectively, these efforts still signified the beginning of a process of institutionalization and normalization for Chinese grassroots NGOs.

Around 2003, Chinese grassroots NGOs experienced a wave of organizational secession. Some founders or key members left Global Village, Rural Women, the Maple Women's Hotline, and other first-generation grassroots NGOs, to start new organizations. Some organizations were broken into four or five new organizations. In general, the organizational departures were good for the development of Chinese NGOs because they resulted in new organizations, but for some NGOs, the situation impeded their growth.

Meanwhile, another development trend was taking place: organizations were beginning to network with each other. Foreign NGOs, such as the Asia Foundation and the Misereor Foundation, encouraged NGOs that provided similar services to form informal action networks and oversight committees. One such network included the China Youth Development Foundation, the China Foundation for Poverty Alleviation, the Aider Foundation, and the Enjiu Information Center. Another NGO, the Beijing Stars and Rain Organization, started a network of child-autism NGOs. An anti-domestic violence network was run by the China Law Society. The Civil-Society Network on Chinese Trade, Environment, and Development was formed by various environmental-protection NGOs and colleges. Another network was the Participatory Rural Appraisal Network, which spanned over Yunnan and Guizhou. These networks greatly improved the ability of grassroots NGOs to work together, advocate for policy, and impact society. For example, the network of environmental-protection NGOs played a significant role in impacting local government policy and temporarily preventing the construction of a dam in Nujiang.

Instead of relying on the charismatic leaders from the first-generation grassroots NGOs, a new generation of leaders emerged. The shift in leadership was away from elites and toward young people from modest socioeconomic backgrounds. In particular, college graduates began to take leadership roles, which greatly improved the professionalization and specialization of grassroots NGOs. For example, Chinese environmental-protection NGOs moved from more traditional activities such as observing birds, planting trees, and cleaning up trash to activities such as environmental evaluation, advocacy, and public participation.

Additionally, the funding sources of grassroots NGOs diversified after 2000. While the portion of foreign grants continually decreased, the portion of national grants continually increased. For instance, the portion of international grants for Friends of Nature and Global Village fell from 70 to 90 percent to under 50 percent. One of the primary causes of the decrease in international funding was that corporate social responsibility became a hot topic in society, and consequently, Chinese corporations began to be an important funding source for grassroots NGOs. Additionally, new regulations for foundations were enacted in 2004 that favored private foundations, making them another major funding source for grassroots NGOs.

Since 2008, Accelerated Development of Chinese Grassroots NGOs

The 2008 Wenchuan earthquake was another milestone in the development of Chinese grassroots NGOs. Since then, Chinese grassroots NGOs have developed rapidly.

First, the legal environment for the development of grassroots NGOs has improved significantly. Government and public understanding of volunteers and grassroots NGOs increased greatly because of their outstanding disaster-relief efforts; therefore, 2008 is also often referred to as "the first year of civil society" in China. Since then, provincial and local governments began to have a new attitude toward NGOs; for instance, Guangdong Province enacted a policy to strengthen the management of nonprofit organizations and loosened restrictions on the registration of grassroots NGOs. In particular, community organizations that focus on economic, technological, public service, urban, and rural issues can register at their local civil affairs office directly, without needing permission from the applicable governmental oversight department. Normally, Chinese law dictates that NGOs may register with their local civil affairs office only after obtaining approval from their local oversight department. Due to difficulties in being approved by this department, grassroots NGOs cannot usually become legally registered organizations. Therefore, the Chinese government's treatment of NGOs is also referred to as a "dual-oversight system." In an attempt to provide a more comfortable environment for NGO development, the central government is also amending laws on registering associations, managing foundations, and registering and managing private nonprofit enterprises.

Second, the trend toward local funding sources for grassroots NGOs has become increasingly prevalent. The 2008 Wenchuan earthquake inspired people to donate to public causes, and that year Chinese public donations exceeded ¥100 billion for the first time. In the same year, China held the Olympics, and international funding declined substantially. Within this context, China's Red Cross Foundation, the China Foundation for Poverty

Alleviation, the China Women's Development Foundation, and other large domestic private foundations began to fund programs run by grassroots NGOs. At the same time, private domestic foundations, such as the Narada Foundation and the SEE Foundation, have been making a greater effort to support grassroots NGOs. As a result, grassroots NGOs are gradually diversifying their funding sources by adding local resources to their budgets, which have traditionally relied heavily on international resources.

As noted above, since 2008, local governments have begun to increase their support for NGOs. Many local governments have created programs dedicated to fostering and supporting the development of grassroots NGOs; examples include the Charity Organization Incubator in Shanghai, the Social Organization Service Base in Guangzhou, and the Social Organization Incubator in Chengdu. Meanwhile, the government has also allocated more money to purchasing NGO services, which has in turn diversified NGO funding sources.

Finally, after 2008, a new development trend has taken place among Chinese grassroots NGOs. Some NGOs that used to completely rely on external funding began turning into "social enterprises," such as the Beijing One-Plus-One Cultural Development Center for People with Disabilities and the Workers' Home. These organizations have attempted to solve the problem of financial instability and enhance NGOs' autonomy and sustainability.

The discussion up to this point shows that, since 1995, Chinese grassroots NGOs have increased in number and have evolved substantially. How can the rise of grassroots NGOs be explained?

First, in terms of demand, since 1992, China has continued its conversion to a market economy. Due to the high costs of providing public services, the government—especially at the local level—has relied on societal resources to provide many services. After implementing the market economy system, vulnerable groups had to protect their own benefits by organizing their resources.

Second, in terms of supply, the public has growing resources and freedom to initiate nonprofit activities. Meanwhile, in addition to greater funding from foreign NGOs and the United Nations, China's grassroots NGOs have begun to attract attention and financial support from international development-aid agencies and international corporate donors because of their growing focus on aid efforts. Additionally, the sudden growth of the middle class and a difficult job market for college graduates have created a human resource pool for China's grassroots NGOs. (Figure 1.1)

Figure 1.1
A Supply-and-Demand Theory of the Development of Grassroots NGOs

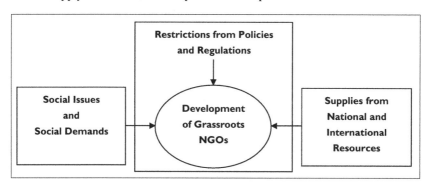

The Increasing Autonomy of Government-Affiliated NGOs

Since 1995, China's NGOs have experienced a revolution, and this has been especially true for NGOs that were officially founded in order to apply for international funding and collaborate with international organizations. At first, these organizations were mainly headed by government officials or individuals appointed by the government. Although they were registered as NGOs, they were actually government departments. Indeed, their identity as an arm of the government superseded their identity as NGOs. In China today, some NGOs are still run (to varying degrees) by government departments; these NGOs are customarily referred to as official or government-affiliated NGOs. Through collaborations with international agencies, leaders in government-affiliated NGOs have obtained many opportunities to communicate, train, and engage with international funding agencies. After witnessing successful cases of grassroots NGOs, these leaders began to form their own organizations around their own interests. Most of these NGOs were registered in local civil affairs offices; were authorized as independent, legal entities; and were funded by international agencies rather than the government. Therefore, they could hire and fire staff, manage finances, and make other decisions independent of the government. Meanwhile, local governments relied on these NGO leaders, who were known by national and international agencies, to obtain more funding for public services.

Among government-affiliated NGOs, foundations had the most independent footing and demand. Unlike foundations in developed countries, China's foundations are normally official fund-raising agencies founded by the government. They have diverse funding sources, including indirect policy support from the government and direct financial support from the public, corporations, and international agencies. Funding is used to operate programs. Thanks to the advantages in funding sources, foundations do not have to rely on the government; therefore, they enjoy a high degree of autonomy in designing and managing their programs and activities and in making executive decisions. However, for the same reason, the local government oversight department has stricter control over foundations; for instance, the boards of directors and secretary-generals of government-affiliated NGOs are appointed by the government. Foundations also need authorization from their local oversight department to conduct large-scale programs and activities. Under these circumstances, reforms have been made in some of China's foundations since 1995. Foundations that have sufficient funding or that are in a good financial situation have generally begun to strive for a higher degree of autonomy by utilizing media publicity and expanding their popularity in the global arena. In China, the more popular an organization's leader, the more considerations will be taken when the government department intervenes with the organization; consequently, the organization tends to have more autonomy in staffing and decision making.

People have been calling for the reform of professional associations. For instance, in January 2002 Shanghai government issued a regulation that stated that,

> as a starting point of professional association reform, the division of government and professional associations should be facilitated. Government departments should be separated from professional associations in structure and staffing. An administrative body of professional associations cannot merge with government departments. Leaders in professional associations, who are mainly business owners, should be elected by people other than government officials.

Professional associations in other areas are also making efforts to facilitate reform. The core mission of the reform is to separate professional associations from the government and promote the self-service, self-governance, and self-development of these associations.

After 1995, the issue of improving independency and autonomy has also been raised in a special type of NGO unique to China—"people's organizations"—which are civic organizations that send representatives to the Chinese People's Political Consultative Conference. These organizations consist of the Labor Union, the Women's Federation, the Communist Youth League, and the Association for Science, among others. According to the Registration of Social Organizations ordinance, people's organizations do not have to register with the Ministry of Civil Affairs. They can still register with the department if they prefer; for instance, the Women's Federation requested to register with the Ministry of Civil Affairs in order to attend the World Conference on Women in 1995. The Association for Science has also begun to discuss how to decrease dependency on the government, how to strengthen relationships with its members, and how to provide its members with better service.

In conclusion, China's government-affiliated NGOs have been reforming since 1995. What has driven this reform? First, it was pushed by the reforms within the government. For a long time, government-affiliated NGOs were inefficient and redundant institutions; in other words, many of these NGOs performed no unique function or almost no function at all. To alleviate this problem and to reduce the financial burden on the government, the idea of reducing the government's role in administrating social service organizations was advanced in the early 1990s. Among other changes, all social service organizations founded after 1985 were supposed to take charge of their own fundraising, staff recruitment, and program design (for more information, see Xiumei Zhao's 1,000 Survey and Analysis on Beijing Environmental Protection NGOs in Ming Wang's case study of Chinese NGOs). Although it was not implemented effectively, the policy encouraged government-affiliated NGOs to seek a new development model. For example, the China Foundation for Poverty Alleviation was one of the earliest NGO "de-administration" efforts. Since the late 1990s, the foundation initiated positive reforms, leaving out governmental staffing and administrative ranking. In China, many government-affiliated NGO leaders are given an institutional administrative rank and therefore are able to enjoy government benefits, and many NGO staff members also belong to governmental institutions and receive corresponding benefits. Second, the reform was also pushed by the implementation of a market economy and the country's participation in the WTO, which increased NGOs' needs to communicate with and engage organizations on an international level.

Meanwhile, the pull factor of reform stemmed from the transfer of government functions to social service organizations, which gave organizations more influence in public services and thus laid the groundwork for the autonomy of government-affiliated NGOs. In addition, NGOs enjoyed more access to social and market resources after the transition to a market economy, which in turn encouraged NGOs to charge for services and build their fund-raising capacity. Finally, the advanced management models and abundant resources of international NGOs also stimulated NGO reform within the country.

During the reform of government-affiliated NGOs, although the government has had to facilitate NGOs' development and thus reduce its financial burden by decentralizing power, the government still also wants to control that development and maintain a stable political environment. Additionally, some governmental oversight offices have resisted giving up their power in government-affiliated NGOs out of self-interest. Therefore, the reform is taking shape slowly due to insufficient policy push factors. In the meantime, China has not developed a strong culture of donations and volunteerism; furthermore, the NGO sector as a whole still has relatively low public credibility. For these reasons, it is difficult for government-affiliated NGOs to obtain funding and volunteers from national corporations, the public, or international agencies. Additionally, the reform of the social security system is not yet finished. As a result, the pull factor for government-affiliated NGO reform is inadequate as well.

In summary, the reform of government-affiliated NGOs—even for those that had obtained some level of independence—has been passive so far. On the one hand, these NGOs want autonomy in staffing, finances, and decision making in general; on the other hand, they expect to continue receiving stable grants, policy benefits, and executive administration power from the government. Therefore, these organizations face a dilemma. Additionally, some organizations have not begun to establish their independence because they do not have other reliable funding resources, prefer having ties with the government, or even aspire to become a government agency (Figure 1.2).

Figure 1.2
The Push-Pull Theory of the Reform of Government-Affiliated NGOs

The Increasing Capacity and Social Impact of NGOs

The Increasing Capacity of NGOs

Since 1995, the capacity of China's NGO sector has greatly increased. Three trends have been apparent throughout these years.

Expansion and Diversification of the NGO Sector

Before 1995, only a few NGOs operated successfully or were influential in the sector. Two examples were the China Youth Development Foundation (a government-affiliated NGO) and Friends of Nature (a grassroots NGO). After 1995, however, many new organizations found success as well; some examples include the China Foundation for Poverty Alleviation, China Children and Teenagers Foundation, and China Charity Federation. Some organizations were able to raise anywhere from ¥10 million to nearly billions in 2011. Among grassroots NGOs, Friends of Nature, the Global Environment Research Institute, Shanxi Women's Marriage and Family Seminar, Rural Women, the Fuping School, and other organizations have become active in various areas of societal need. Since 1990, their annual fundraising has rapidly increased from less than ¥1 million to millions and even tens of millions of Yuan. Certainly, the developments in the capacity of NGOs have been facilitated by exposure in the media, the examples set by successful international NGOs, improvements in integrative competencies, and increased communication among organizations.

Forming Strategic Alliances

China's NGOs have greatly increased their internal communication and cooperation since 1995. Organization leaders have used three main communication approaches. The first approach is to hold conferences, such as Global Village's annual national conference for environmental-protection NGOs, the annual national conference on gender and development among NGOs serving women, and the annual national forum on professional development held by private foundations. The second approach is to conduct seminars, such as the monthly seminar on environmental protection held by Green Home Volunteers, the monthly seminar on gender and development held by Social Gender and Development Collaborators Group, NGO study seminars among young staff, and the monthly seminar of local international NGOs in Yunnan Province, among others. Finally, the third approach is to establish networks. For example, the NGO Stars and Rain founded the Heart Association to promote collaboration among grassroots NGOs in the area of autism, and Green-Net was established to connect environmental-protection volunteers across the country. Although the improvement of information technology has been very successful in promoting communication and cooperation, NGOs commonly face challenges such as integrating resources, reducing costs, reinforcing coalitions, and extending their impact as a way to improve their negotiation leverage with the government, corporations, and grant-giving agencies.

Comprehensive Capacity Building

China's NGOs have been through two phases of capacity building since 1995. In the first phase, which spanned 1995 to 1999, Chinese NGOs began to incorporate advanced modes of program management from other countries and build their own brands through international communication. In the second phase, which began in 2000, the focus has shifted from program management to organizational capacity building. With the help of international agencies, some NGOs started to discuss and formulate development strategies. Some organizations have even asked professional research institutes to help with their competency assessments or accountability evaluations. Moreover, professional training opportunities for NGO managers have begun to take place in China during recent years, including long-term and short-term training provided by colleges and intermediary institutes. These developments indicate that China's NGOs have entered a new stage of capacity building.

International agencies have also been playing a noticeable and significant role in the capacity-building efforts of China's NGOs. Capacity building is highly valued and encouraged by various international NGOs and the World Bank. Meanwhile, national and international competition has urged China's NGOs to improve their core competencies. In recent years some foreign NGOs, which are mainly funded by foreign foundations located in China, have begun to compete with local NGOs for talent and funding. It is not surprising that China's participation in the WTO has intensified this competition.

The Increasing Social Impact of NGOs

Before 1995, the concept of an NGO was unfamiliar to the Chinese people. Such organizations had very little social impact, and few academic studies had been done on the subject. But the situation has changed substantially since 1995.

First, various national and international conferences are now held by the NGOs, and this has created a new environment for NGO development on the macro level. Since the first conference on NGOs and China's Development, which was held by Tsinghua University in July 1999, large international NGO conferences have been held in China more than twice a year. Additionally, many small international and national conferences on government-affiliated NGOs and grassroots NGOs are held throughout the country every year.

Second, NGOs have increased their impact on government policies through various approaches. Some government-affiliated NGOs make proposals to government departments directly by using their relationship with their department of oversight (which approves and oversees the operations of NGOs in each service area, such as child welfare and poverty relief), whereas grassroots NGOs tend to influence government policies through mass media. For instance, in 1998, Chongqing Green Volunteers Association reported the deforestation in Sichuan Province on China Central Television, which got the central government's attention and ultimately pressured the Sichuan government to ban deforestation. Grassroots NGOs also take the approach of making proposals at the annual sessions held by the National People's Congress and the Chinese People's Political Consultative Conference; one method of doing this is to have NGO leaders make policy suggestions to representatives from democratic parties. Under these circumstances, some government departments have even begun to ask NGOs to propose and discuss relevant laws or regulations.

Third, NGOs have increased their social impact through mass media. After 1995, reports of NGOs, especially grassroots NGOs, have become much more frequent in the Chinese media. Since the first philanthropic newspaper appeared in 2001 (*China Philanthropy Times*), more than ten philanthropy-focused newspapers and magazines have emerged, including *Charity Reports*, *China Philanthropist*, *China Fortune*, *Global Philanthropy*, and *New Philanthropy*, among others. Some widely distributed and influential print media have also created a philanthropy column, including the *Beijing Times*, *Beijing Youth Daily*, and *Southern Metropolis*. Media reports have helped NGOs significantly. Some grassroots NGOs have obtained legitimacy in society and essential resources, such as volunteers and materials, through these reports. Media publicity has also increased the public's awareness of and knowledge about NGOs in China. Indeed, some grassroots NGOs were initially inspired by reports of successful NGOs.

Finally, scholars and government leaders have begun to value the role of NGOs in China's economic development. Before 1995, no research institutes specialized in this area, and few academic studies had been conducted on the subject. After 1995, the professional NGO research institute at Tsinghua University was founded, and similar institutes have been established at Peking University, Fudan University, Sun Yat-Sen University, and Renmin University. It has become more popular to conduct research on NGOs, and books and papers on the subject are increasing. Additionally, the government has begun to pay attention to the roles that NGOs play, especially in the areas of environmental protection, poverty alleviation, industrial management, and community development.

Development Trends of NGOs in China

The changes in China's NGOs since 1995 indicate two developmental trends for the nonprofit sector. First, grassroots NGOs are in an early stage of development that is similar to but not exactly the same as pluralism. In this pattern of development, although grassroots NGOs have not obtained legal status (except for some individual provinces that have already reformed, such as Guangdong), the government has allowed them to conduct nonpolitical, public activities. Historically, this pattern can help grassroots NGOs maintain a high level of autonomy, which is beneficial for different groups. Overall, the relationship between grassroots NGOs and the government is neither confrontational nor collaborative.

Second, government-affiliated NGOs are developing in a corporatist pattern. That is, in addition to promoting the autonomy of government-affiliated NGOs with a policy of self-fund-raising, self-recruiting, and self-decision-making, the government has also tried to obtain the cooperation and loyalty of NGOs by giving NGOs sole control of certain public services. This tactic may help build alliances between the government and civil society while maintaining a united and stable society. This trend, however, does little to encourage government-affiliated NGOs to seek funding and resources beyond the government, and consequently, hardly promotes independence or autonomy.

Overall, grassroots NGOs are rapidly developing and becoming increasingly influential in China, but they are still limited in number, size, and impact. Furthermore, although government-affiliated NGOs have reformed more quickly since 1995, the majority have been passive in terms of reform. In conclusion, both the first and second development patterns are still in emerging stages.

Development Trends of Grassroots NGOs in China

The development of grassroots NGOs since 1995 has primarily been influenced by the public's need for NGO services, the availability of resources to them, and government policies and the legislative environment. Therefore, the future development trends of grassroots NGOs can be inferred by predicting these variables.

Regarding public need, the current social transition should take a long time given China's gradualist approach to reform. In addition to existing social issues, such as rural poverty, environmental pollution, women's rights, school dropout, and ethnic-minority issues, certain new issues, such as migration, unemployment, and HIV/AIDS, will be on the rise. Thus, active grassroots NGOs will be needed by both the government and vulnerable groups in society.

With respect to the supply of resources, international groups have been establishing NGOs in China. Since joining the WTO, China has been more open to the idea of international NGOs operating in the country. The government is drafting new legislation to adjust to the situation. In a few years, more and more international NGOs will be able to operate in China with formal legal status. In the meantime, with the rapid development of the Chinese economy, social donations are increasing rapidly, which has resulted in spikes in local resources. In addition, grassroots NGOs have already been staffed due to the maturation of young NGO leaders and unfavorable employment situations in recent years, which have led more people to seek opportunities in the nonprofit sector.

Regarding government policies, it is widely believed that the dual-oversight system has restricted the development of grassroots NGOs, and in response, NGOs have called on the government to abolish this policy. After more than ten years of advocacy, the dual-oversight system has already been abolished in some developed coastal cities, and the conditions for eliminating the system nationally are already present. In the future, grassroots NGOs in these areas will have new opportunities for development, and this development may take a quasipluralistic form. In this pattern, although grassroots NGOs will have a certain degree of autonomy, the government will still restrict the activities in which they can participate by controlling their legal status and limiting their role in public service. The government may even increase grassroots NGOs' dependency on the government by purchasing their services. Finally, grassroots NGOs will continue to strive for more influence in public services by engaging in nonpolitical, nonconfrontational public activities.

Development Trends of Government-Affiliated NGOs in China

In the early 1990s, the government raised the idea of separating government administration from NGO management. The government attempted what it called the Three-Self policy, but the legislation proved inefficient in stimulating NGO reform. However, in 1998, the government was restructured for the seventh time, and these changes were both more drastic and effective than the first six reforms. The restructuring extended to local governments in 2001, and the central government pursued a comprehensive reform of public institutions in 2012. Government-affiliated NGOs can expect to be the next target, and they should be prepared for a stronger push to reform than they have ever experienced. Meanwhile, as the market economy continues to take more prominence in China, domestic and international market pressures will accelerate the reform of government-affiliated NGOs in China. Additionally, recent scandals, such as the Meimei Guo scandal and similar incidents in 2011, revealed long-existing issues in government-affiliated NGOs in China, particularly the issue of inadequate social credibility. In response, public opinion has generated substantial advocacy and pressure to reform government-affiliated NGOs. This social pressure should also advance the reform of government-affiliated NGOs, particularly those that were involved in or impacted by the incidents.

Regarding pull factors for development, the preliminary reform of China's social security system will be completed in a few years. After solving the problems of health provision, medication, insurance, unemployment, and housing, professional mobility will increase sharply, which might be the strongest pull factor for the reform of government-affiliated NGOs. Another factor may come from the current government's policies on purchasing services, which can provide an institutionalized funding source for government-affiliated NGOs after they become autonomous. Finally, international communication and resources may also be pull factors for the reform of government-affiliated NGOs in the future.

Within the context of these push and pull factors, China's government-affiliated NGOs will slowly but surely be separated from the government, and as a result they will experience increasing autonomy and independence. However, government-affiliated NGOs in China will develop in a European style of corporatism, which might be the main trend in NGO development in China over the long term due to the government's limitations in the areas of management and governance. In this type of development, the government exchanges its monopoly on certain activities for help from NGOs in conducting those activities, while NGOs enjoy autonomy to certain extent.

2

The Rise of Corporate Social Responsibility and Charitable Foundations in China

Xiufeng Chen* and Li Li

The Origin and Development of Corporate Social Responsibility

At the end of the twentieth century, the role of corporations in society became a hot topic amid a budding era of globalization. The origins and development of the concept of corporate social responsibility match this trend. Corporations are aware that they must build a corporate value system that promotes mainstream values for societal progress and makes them socially responsible corporate citizens. Furthermore, this moral compass for corporate activity runs through all aspects of strategic planning and marketing operations. This focus not only promotes the healthy and sustainable development of corporations but also advances the partnerships between corporations and public philanthropy.

The concept of corporate social responsibility originated with improving the understanding of the relationship between society and corporations. The recognition of the relationship between society and corporations originated from Adam Smith's idea of the invisible hand. The traditional view is that society's needs and wants are best determined by the market. If a corporation can profit by responding to market need, the constant pursuit of profit will bring whatever society needs. In this way, the invisible hand thus turns the corporate benefit into societal benefit. That is, it is not the

---

* Translated by Xunjing Wu, graduate student, the Edward J. Bloustein School of Planning and Public Policy, Rutgers University.

corporations that deal with societal problems but the free markets that adjust and solve the problems through unlimited activities.

In the beginning of the twentieth century, when the industrial economy was booming, the tide of corporate mergers resulted in many industrial giants. Large multinational corporations created monopolies and limited competition, increased unemployment, broadened the gap between the rich and the poor, sharply decreased resources, rapidly deteriorated the ecological environment, and led to the frequent occurrence of economic lawsuits. As more and more corporations failed to meet ethical standards, people started to wonder whether corporations existed solely for profit, thereby causing environmental pollution, business fraud, fake and shoddy goods, or unemployment. People began to realize that it was important for corporations to take on social responsibility. In the beginning of the twenty-first century, the Enron and Arthur Andersen scandals made the public doubt the trustworthiness of corporations, which led corporate social responsibility and business ethics to resurge as hot topics.

Many scholars have studied corporate social responsibility. Among them, Carroll (1979) has given a relatively clear definition of the concept: a corporation's responsibility to society is a combination of its responsibility to the economy, the law, ethical standards, and self-determination. Management expert Peter Drucker also points out that "a healthy business cannot co-exist with a sick society." As members of society, corporations have countless connections with society. Corporations need a sound societal environment to survive and thrive. In return, corporations have a responsibility to respond to the needs and expectations of the social system in which they operate. The relationship between society and corporations is not simply economic but also ethical, moral, legal, and cultural. In other words, corporations exist not only for profit but also for social justice and equality, economic and social development, environmental protection, and social welfare. With great power comes great responsibility. As corporations become more powerful, the public expects them to better utilize their resources and power for the public good. In their research on the fit between societal needs and the corporate response, American scholars Keith Davis and Robert Blomstrom (1966) explained what they called the "iron law of responsibility." That is, in the long run, those who do not use power in ways that society considers responsible will tend to lose it. This not only framed the relationship between corporations and society but also initiated an era of corporate participation in social welfare.

Since then, concepts such as corporate citizenship and cause marketing have developed. For the purposes of this article, *cause marketing* is defined as the marketing of a corporation's philanthropic activities. At the end of the twentieth century, the new international term *corporate citizenship* gained importance, as it integrated the ideas of citizenship and corporate social responsibility. According to the definition by the Boston College Center for Corporate Citizenship, *corporate citizenship* means combining basic societal values with the company's strategies and operating practices. A corporate citizen thinks that the success of the corporation is closely related to the health of society. Therefore, the corporation will take all its stakeholders—employees, customers, communities, suppliers, and natural environment—into thorough consideration. In short, corporations are not just economic units of society but also citizens with social rights and obligations. They should make a larger impact on humanistic values.

With the rise of corporate social responsibility and corporate citizenship, modern corporations have paid more attention to connecting their public image with their profits. To achieve this, companies began using cause marketing. Philanthropy marketing is concerned with social progress and promotes a corporate brand by engaging in social welfare. As a result, cause marketing yields social benefits and thereby influences customers' preferences for the company's products or services. As a type of sensibility marketing, cause marketing taps into customers' emotions instead of just their consumer preferences to show that corporations do business for a good cause. This process humanizes their marketing efforts.

Methods and Outcomes of Corporate-Charitable Partnerships in China

The value that corporations place on social responsibility did not happen spontaneously; it evolved over a long history of give and take between corporations and nonprofit organizations (NPOs), such as various environmental organizations and charitable organizations. Since the 1990s, corporations' increasing awareness of NPOs led many to strategically cooperate with charitable foundations as a way to give back to society and establish their commitment to social values.

Motivations behind Corporate-Charitable Partnerships

Corporate participation in charity creates a win-win situation for society and corporations. Corporations are motivated not only by altruism but also by the prospect of increased sales, lower tax levels, improved social image, and increased organizational cohesion, ultimately helping them realize their profit goals. For society, corporate participation can help expand resources for charity development, improve communities, and embody the values of love and harmony. Therefore, corporations have two main motivations to partner with foundations: social responsibility and cause marketing. In reality, these motivations are intertwined.

For corporations, charitable donations are an opportunity for cause marketing. Even though it has only existed for just over twenty years, cause marketing has been widely used by manufacturers outside China to incorporate charity into their corporate goals. They have focused their donations in areas where they have operations or sales. Jim Campbell, vice president of General Motors Foundation, said that, before 1994, they donated only out of altruism, but later realized the need to balance both altruistic and strategic donations and take both societal and corporate benefits into consideration. Indeed, *Business Week* magazine has characterized cause marketing as "one of the hottest trends in charity." As more and more people call for corporate citizenship, it is easier for corporations with a stronger sense of social responsibility to stand out in today's business world of increasingly homogeneous products and services. Additionally, supporting charitable foundations can also make corporations more attractive to stakeholders.

Types of Corporate-Charitable Partnerships

Corporations partner with charitable foundations in four main ways. The first way is to give in-cash and in-kind donations. Monetary donation, the most traditional and common way for corporations to contribute to charity, has become a part of the annual budget of many corporations. Many internationally known corporations, such as IBM, GE, HP, Motorola, and Coca Cola, donate large sums of money to NPOs and foundations to support community development.

The second way of partnering is to collaborate on projects. Many corporations choose to partner with large foundations on charitable projects. Corporations not only achieve their goal of giving back to society but also advance their business strategy through advertising, promoting, and implementing these charitable projects. From a corporate perspective, a successful project should have both social and economic benefits.

The third way of partnering is to provide technical support, such as by helping charitable foundations build their organizational capacity and recruit talent. For example, in 1998 Nissan Motor Company initiated its

Nissan-Nonprofit Organization Learning Scholarship Program. Selected recipients—mainly undergraduates and graduates—receive hourly compensation for their work at NPOs. In this way, the program encourages young people to participate in various forms of charity work.

The fourth way is volunteer work. Corporations encourage their employees to volunteer for charitable activities and community development projects. Corporations even allow their employees to take paid leave to do so.

Benefits to Corporations

First, partnerships broaden corporations' social impact. Because foundations work at the grassroots level, they keenly understand the need for social services and have the professional knowledge, skills, response time, efficiency, and innovative spirit to address social problems and meet demands. By partnering with foundations, corporations diversify their methods of participation in charitable activities and strengthen their impact on society.

Second, by cooperating with charitable foundations, a corporation can send the message that it is socially responsible. Corporations can use cause marketing to build consumer trust and loyalty and influence consumer behavior. No other marketing method can have this result.

Third, in addition to enhancing their public image, partnerships can increase corporations' profits. A good public image and high profit usually come together. With more profit, corporations can make greater contributions to society. Therefore, corporations should view profits as a way of furthering their partnerships with charitable foundations.

Fourth, corporate-charitable partnerships benefit society and the environment. By advocating charity and focusing on societal and environmental benefits, a corporation can make long-term, positive impacts on social values and ideology. Partnerships also increase a corporation's organizational cohesion and employees' sense of belonging and thus allow for expanded corporate development in society.

Benefits to Charitable Foundations

Charitable foundations benefit from partnerships in several ways. First, foundations can receive considerable financial support from corporations, which helps to compensate for insufficient governmental funding and public donations. These contributions diversify foundations' capital resources and minimize reliance on government funding and avoid government control. For example, Motorola donated over $4.2 million to the Hope Project (a project by the China Youth Development Foundation). As a result, over seventy "Hope" schools have been built, 13,000 students have been enrolled in school, 700 Hope teachers have been trained, and 500 hundred students in Hope Star classes have been provided with financial aid.

Second, corporations can help foundations address social problems by supporting their research, communication, marketing, and recruitment of professional talent. Motorola requires its public relations department to be engaged in the entire process, right from project selection and up to project completion. A corporation utilizes its information technology, marketing tools, and social resources in the foundation's project operations, all of which contribute greatly to the foundation's social impact and quality of work.

Third, foundations can learn from and apply corporate marketing techniques, financial management, strategic planning, career planning, and human resources management and training. All of this experience can help foundations operate more effectively and sustainably.

Fourth, partnerships with corporations can expose foundations to new means of evaluating project outcomes. This is important because many foundations lack systems and standards to account for project costs and performance. For example, Motorola invited an independent third-party organization to evaluate the Hope Project and track its performance to improve its effectiveness.

The Difficult Reality of Corporate-Charitable Partnerships in China

Lack of Corporate Commitment to Philanthropy and Social Responsibility

Although corporations should be in the financial position to donate in general, the commitment to donate is equally important. In China, corporations still often demonstrate an unwillingness to engage in philanthropy or to donate. It is inevitable that corporations will lack this willingness while the country's economic system is in transition (Lu, 2001). *Corporate citizenship* is not yet part of the corporate vocabulary in China, especially for local corporations, which still have not adopted the concepts of environmental and social responsibility. Recently, a research survey on corporate citizenship in China by the School of Management at Fudan

University showed that 72.4 percent of respondents expressed respect for corporations that contributed to the wealth of society. Respondents identified the three most important elements of corporate citizenship as practicing business ethics, providing secure and trustworthy products and services, and taking care of employees. Respondents also cited paying taxes, protecting the environment, and supporting community service. The results revealed that corporations, customers, and employees attracted more attention than other stakeholders in today's practice of corporate citizenship. Societal factors contributed the most to the corporations' lack of commitment to philanthropy, but this varied case by case. For example, a 3,400-employee, state-owned building materials company established in 1953 stated that corporate philanthropy is unnecessary. The company argued that the primary mandate for large, state-owned enterprises is simply to survive. These enterprises have already contributed substantially to the public good by paying taxes. Therefore, corporate profits can be considered an indirect benefit to society. Corporate donations actually create an imperfect market economy. The reasons behind this opinion are obvious. First, many state-owned enterprises still regard employee welfare as important for society, but they think that by paying for those benefits they are shouldering the country's responsibility for welfare. Second, philanthropic activity is organized by the government, which gives people the impression that making a charitable donation is essentially supporting the government (Lu, 2001). Corporations can prosper in many ways in the short term, but sustainable corporate growth can only be attained by applying the values that have been developed by humankind over thousands of years. After China joined the WTO, many corporations sought a competitive advantage and ignored basic social morality and responsibility. When financial benefits conflict with social responsibility, some corporations only focus on the former. The relatively weak sense of corporate citizenship has limited the development of philanthropy in China.

Lack of a Cause-Marketing Strategy in the Market Economy

In a mature market economy, corporate philanthropy is mutually beneficial for corporations and charitable foundations. Corporate philanthropy is an important supplement to the market and to the government's redistribution of resources. This approach also grants donors more autonomy. Corporations make in-cash and in-kind donations, and in return they gain prestige and connections, as well as a sense of pride and worth. For corporations, philanthropy is an investment that yields economic and other benefits. Alongside economic development, corporate donations in China have been increasing for over ten years. Corporate donations are often spontaneous. To become more active contributors, corporations must incorporate comprehensive strategies for cause marketing into their core identity. Local corporations in China, probably influenced by traditional Chinese philosophy, seem to share the view that charity work should be performed quietly, without drawing too much public attention. In light of this, many corporations donate purely out of a sense of social responsibility and fail to consider the potential benefits of good cause marketing. From a corporate standpoint, donations benefiting social welfare should be made publicly. At the same time, limited by outdated public relations strategies, some local corporations fail to effectively market themselves through charity, either by missing opportunities or by engaging in blatant self-promotion. These missteps create a negative public perception that these corporations' motives are disingenuous. In summary, Chinese corporate philanthropy has traditionally been motivated by empathy rather than rationality. Few corporations create a long-term, comprehensive strategic plan for philanthropy because most are unaware of—or simply disregard—its practical benefits.

Preferential Tax Policy Deters Corporate Philanthropy

The lack of commitment to corporate donations in China is due in part to the country's unreasonable preferential tax policy. The popular practice abroad is for governments to allow corporations exemptions or deductions if they make charitable donations. Sometimes, the amount of the exemption is even higher than the amount of the donation, which of course encourages corporations to participate in charity. The US government stipulates that a corporation can receive a 10 percent tax deduction if its total annual donations exceed 10 percent of its pretax income. If total donations do not exceed 10 percent, then the tax deduction is equal to the percentage of taxable income donated. According to China's corporate tax code, if the amount of donations to social welfare programs does not exceed 3 percent of the company's annual taxable income, the corporation will receive a tax deduction of that same amount. If the amount of donations is higher than 3 percent of the corporation's taxable income for that year, the excess amount is still taxable. This tax policy impedes corporate donations. In addition, the Department of Finance and the State Administration of Taxation stipulate that a full tax refund will be given for donations to only eleven organizations: China Health Express Foundation, the Sun Yefang Foundation, the China Charity Federation, the China Legal Aid Foundation, the China Foundation for Justice and Courage, the Soong Ching Ling Foundation, the China Welfare Institute, the China Welfare Fund for the Disabled, the China Foundation for Poverty Alleviation, the China Coal Miner Pneumoconiosis Treatment Foundation, and the China Environmental Protection Foundation. In reality, however, because a full exemption is limited to these eleven organizations and because the exemption application procedure is very complicated, this policy does not encourage corporations to donate. One manager, who had a history of donating, complained that applying for tax exemptions was too complicated. Corporations were expected to calculate the amount of deductible tax, modify detailed tax forms, and complete up to ten kinds of paperwork that took at least two months. These requirements discouraged corporations from making donations.

Limited Fund-Raising Ability and Opportunity for Charity Foundation

Most foundations in China have to raise their own funds, which they generally obtain from individuals and nongovernmental organizations. Fundraising is therefore critical for continued survival.

In general, the fund-raising situation in China is rather bleak. According to case studies of Chinese NPOs conducted by the NPO Research Center's School of Public Policy and Management at Tsinghua University, around 90 percent of NPOs in China spend under ¥500,000 per year, and fewer than 2 percent spend over ¥1 million per year. The China Charity Federation and the China Legal Aid Foundation, which raise the most money, raise under ¥80 million per year. These statistics reveal that foundations in China are short on money.

Fund-raising efforts struggle for several reasons. First, foundations do not usually diversify their funding sources. Foundations need to better understand and meet requirements set by corporate donors. However, many foundations serve highly specific target populations, so the services they provide are not comprehensive enough to meet most corporations' donation requirements. In general, unfavorable internal and environmental factors limit foundations' ability to fund their social services. The for-profit purpose of capital and the nonprofit nature of charity are fundamentally at odds. Additionally, difficulties in tracking how foundations spend their funds make the public and corporations worry that their donations won't be used as expected, so many of them do not bother donating in the first place.

Second, the process of soliciting donations is highly politicized. In China, because public and private foundations are treated very differently, public foundations have an unmistakable fund-raising advantage over most grassroots private foundations. Public foundations have generally been monopolized since their establishment because most of them were part of the government before becoming foundations. Therefore, most foundations are NPOs that receive government grants and subsidies. This system fails to stimulate competition—which would improve the efficiency of those organizations—and leads to a highly inefficient fund-raising market. For example, the government requires some departments to solicit donations for disaster-relief efforts, which discourages voluntary donations from the public and corporations.

Third, most foundations do not have clearly defined, effective standards for soliciting donations. This can sometimes lead to donation scams, wasting public resources that are limited to begin with. Additionally, foundations should have specialized companies or professionals handle their fund-raising efforts, because it is such a labor-intensive process. Unfortunately, many foundations do not seem to recognize the importance of defining and streamlining their fund-raising strategies and methods, which in turn leaves many corporate and social resources unutilized.

Choosing a Path: How to Achieve Win-Win Results in Corporate-Charitable Partnerships

Corporate Social Responsibility and Corporate Citizenship

Corporate social responsibility is becoming an international trend. With economic globalization, the relationship between corporations and society has been redefined. Society expects corporations to balance corporate and societal benefits by being responsible corporate citizens and participating in public service. Furthermore, with increasing public awareness of environmental and social problems, many corporations now have to pay more attention to social responsibility to protect their public image. As China continues its key societal transition, the public needs corporations that respond to the market, comply with economic regulations, drive the economy forward, become voluntary corporate citizens, and maintain their sense of corporate citizenship. That is, corporations should use their resources to participate in philanthropy and should promote a moral, ethical, and stable societal environment to foster the development of charitable foundations.

When working with charitable foundations, corporations should develop a donation strategy that will reinforce their commitment to social responsibility while allowing them to still achieve their profit objectives, boost their public image, enhance corporate cohesion, and cultivate customer loyalty. Meanwhile, we can learn from the cause marketing of multinational companies. Multinational companies often choose charitable projects that are consistent with their corporate strategy, values, culture, and products or services so that value conflicts are prevented from the outset. For example, Microsoft's charitable projects Unlimited Potential and Partners in Learning provide money and software to people who live in remote areas to narrow the digital divide. These projects are related to Microsoft's products and are consistent with its strategy of finding new markets. Additionally, many corporations let as many people as possible, from managers to ordinary staff, participate in the philanthropy process. This approach promotes internal agreement about the company's philanthropy objectives, generates employee pride in the company's social responsibility, and fosters a corporate culture that is supportive of charity.

Making the Tax Policy Favorable to Donations

Perhaps the most prohibitive factor to corporate philanthropy is that donations to foundations and organizations are taxable. Since September 2003, the Department of Finance and the State Administration of Taxation have stipulated that any enterprise, institution, organization, or individual who donates to the eleven charitable organizations mentioned earlier in this chapter (e.g., the China Charity Federation) will receive a tax deduction equal to the amount of the donation on that year's taxable income. That is, if corporations donate to any charitable organizations other than the eleven listed above, the portion of their donations that exceeds 3 percent of their pretax income is taxable. The more corporations donate, the more they are taxed, which discourages them to donate. In many countries outside China, donations are fully tax deductible. Moreover, foundations and other charitable organizations can generate funds from revenue and receive monetary contributions from the public, both of which are tax exempt.

China's tax policy needs to do much more to encourage corporate donations. To accomplish this, two very important issues need to be addressed. First, China should allow all foundations and NPOs to benefit from tax-deductible donations and should increase exemptions and deduction amounts. Second, a complete and straightforward procedure is needed for tax exemptions and deductions. Regardless of whether the donations are made in cash or in kind, a complete regulation should exist for soliciting the donations, accepting them, processing them, doing the accounting for them, and claiming tax reimbursements. Additionally, illegal activities should be investigated seriously and eliminated to protect those who are obeying the law in their charity work.

Foundations' Need for Philanthropy Marketing

Charitable foundations in China used to rest their funding hopes on government grants. As a result, foundations have failed to develop their own fund-raising systems. It is becoming common thinking that, as the market economy develops, cause marketing will expand the resources available to foundations. Philanthropy marketing includes market surveys, market segmentation, targeted market positioning, and appropriate marketing, and most importantly, the design and establishment of a fund-raising strategy.

United Way of America is an example of a good fund-raising system. Every year, the organization raises money from the government, companies, and individuals. These fund-raising efforts cover 70 to 85 percent of their operational expenses. At the beginning of every year, United Way of America surveys community needs and sets fund-raising goals for that year. The organization provides fund-raising training to volunteers and temporary staff, most of whom come from large companies that pay them to work for United Way for four to six months. This is done because several skills are needed to effectively solicit corporate donations. The comprehensive training includes information on how to contact and organize corporate employees, how to analyze specific corporations' donation records, and how to set the fund-raising goal for the year. Training lasts until the beginning of the large donation activities. Trained volunteers and temporary staff are grouped with people from other corporations to be responsible for soliciting donations. They try their best to let everyone participate. United Way of America has a fund-raising cabinet, which consists of leaders from the local corporations. After the fund-raising starts, cabinet members hold meetings regularly, encouraging their employees to participate in fundraising from a corporate standpoint. All these measures guarantee the success of the fundraising.

In summary, charitable foundations in China should effectively establish marketing and fund-raising plans; use marketing principles to analyze the characteristics of the environment, market, and customers; and evaluate the status of societal resources. By analyzing the market, resources, and objectives, foundations can build win-win partnerships with corporations to enhance their organizational efficiency and maximize their public utility.

3

The Open Era: Grassroots Organizations and the Development of Civil Society in China

*Jiangang Zhu**

Since the 1990s, Chinese society has seen the rise of numerous non-governmental and nonprofit organizations. Most of these organizations are dedicated to social welfare and social development, including charity work, environmental protection, education, women's empowerment, and child welfare. Meanwhile, globalization has ushered in a period of international nongovernmental organization (NGO) involvement in China. These organizations have carried out poverty relief, environmental protection, and social welfare projects. These nonprofit organizations belong to a sphere called the third sector, which exists alongside the government and market sectors. Many of these so-called third-sector organizations, some of which are affiliated with the government, seek recognition from the international community (particularly international financial institutions) by establishing themselves as independent entities. At times, they do so by disregarding the government restrictions placed on associations and private nonprofits. By identifying themselves as NGOs, these third-sector organizations are able to win greater support from the international community and distinguish themselves from the government-controlled organizations.

* Translated by Juliann H. Vikse and Shuang Lu, Research Fellows, Huamin Research Center, School of Social Work, Rutgers University; Jiabao Chen and Meng Shen, School of Foreign Studies, Nanjing University of Science and Technology.

However, the concept of NGOs is more vaguely defined in China than it is in Western countries. In general, official organizations such as the Communist Youth League and the Women's Federation, as well as unregistered, voluntary grassroots organizations, label themselves NGOs. This label includes more specific types of organizations, including government-affiliated NGOs (GONGOs) and grassroots NGOs. GONGOs, such as the China Youth Development Foundation, are either established by the government or are administered by government-appointed personnel. These organizations are usually officially registered, hold governmental status, mobilize volunteers through administrative programs, and enable volunteers to formally and legally participate in nonprofit work.

This article considers grassroots NGOs to be distinct from the powerful GONGOs. Grassroots NGOs are organized by civilians from the bottom up and engage in direct public welfare services and community mobilization. They tend to lack formal organization and suffer high turnover rates, but are strongly autonomous and in many cases, attract passionate volunteers. We will focus on these grassroots NGOs, which are often managed or staffed by volunteers. Because events and activities predominantly depend on extensive volunteer participation, the volunteer spirit is a critical factor that distinguishes these grassroots NGOs from other organizations.

The emergence of these grassroots NGOs is not singularly owed to civilian efforts. Since the 1990s, a movement initiated by the Chinese government has increasingly popularized the Western concept of volunteerism in urban China. Many nonprofit organizations were established directly by the government and its surrogate agencies; these organizations include volunteer associations and youth volunteer branches of the Communist Youth League. This movement also created healthy conditions for the development of grassroots NGOs, and many new organizations—usually informal and unregistered—were founded by the people. Whereas some grassroots NGOs carry out independent programs, they often affiliate with government volunteer associations or GONGOs for the sake of obtaining the government's approval or at least acquiescence. As grassroots organizations increasingly take on such roles and become involved in collaborative projects with GONGOs, the line between the two types of organizations is becoming blurred. Indeed, outside observers often confuse them. However, our research has found that these two types of organizations differ greatly with respect to operational philosophy and internal standards and policies. While the government places heavy restrictions on GONGOs, grassroots NGOs typically demonstrate higher levels of autonomy. When they are discussed collectively, it is easy to disregard the important differences—and even conflicts—that exist between them. Moreover, each organization makes a unique contribution to the reform of larger social structures. Consequently, we must clearly distinguish between the two kinds of organizations and analyze each separately. This article specifically explores how grassroots NGOs are establishing their own sets of norms and regulations, devising their own development strategies, and building their own organizational frameworks. The discussion places particular importance on how these organizations and their volunteers overcome difficulties and grow within the challenging environment of Chinese civil society.

I began researching Shanghai volunteer organizations and volunteer service programs in 1997, and over the course of my research, concurrently worked to establish and develop volunteer organizations such as the Students Legal Aid Center of Fudan University, Grassroots Community, and the Green Hope Network. Through organizational networks, I studied volunteer organizations that dealt with environmental protection, poverty relief, rural education, and public health. My analysis took on various forms: participatory observation, interviews, and reflections on my own work experiences. Additionally, these analyses helped me to achieve the mission of a practical anthropologist: exploring how to achieve social change through participatory academic research. Based on two case studies, this article will discuss the ways in which grassroots volunteer organizations have resolved some of the difficulties faced by China's civil society and the alternative approaches they have taken for development. The article is composed of three sections. The first section will introduce the theoretical framework of civil society, within which we will examine the development difficulties that Chinese civil society faces. In the second section, we will utilize our typology to analyze grassroots volunteer organizations, based on the two case studies from Grassroots Community and the Green Hope Network. The final section will analyze the important role of grassroots NGOs and the volunteer spirit they cultivate in building civil society.

Theoretical Background: The Dilemma of the Precivil-Society State

As a result of the growing focus on Chinese civil society, the people have been paying increasing attention to volunteer NGOs. According to modern Chinese theories on political development, civil society is considered as a new force, or mode, in social change, and widespread controversy has surrounded it. The concept of civil society stems from the individualism that emerged in early modern Enlightenment philosophy. Although the specifics of Enlightenment theories differ, a common theme is that civil society is a distinct sector, independent from traditional or state-imposed hierarchies, in which individuals may act autonomously. This concept not only respects the authority of the state but also emphasizes a space free from state interference. In this space, there are both public and private spheres. The public sphere is comprised of nongovernmental and other civil organizations, which together make up the nucleus of civil society (Habermas 1989). This theory of the public sphere is both descriptive and normative (Metzger 1998). The private sphere consists of individuals, their families, and the economic and cultural activities that they take part in (Held 1987; Maier 1987). Based on the theoretical contributions of Georg Hegel, John Locke, Karl Marx, and Alexis de Tocqueville, individualism is considered as the core concept of civil society.

This conceptualization of civil society can be considered as an interpretive model, although with respect to NGO operations, it also acts as a normative theory. The advocates of civil society propose strengthening the public sphere and developing civil society as a means to restrict state power, because they assume that civil society is a driving force behind Chinese democracy (He 1997). Other scholars hold that China's failure to accomplish political transformation is primarily due to its lack of civil society (Wasserstrom and Perry 1994). There is a widespread debate regarding the possibility of a genuine civil society developing under China's authoritarian system. Some scholars have argued that, in the wake of the Reform Era (beginning in 1978), civil society began to emerge as the nation's role faded (He 1997; Vermeer et al. 1998). Others claim that no true civil society or related organizations can exist under the current authoritarian system (Wakeman 1993; Sun 1994).

Amid this academic debate, the relationship between state and society in China has been changing at a rapid pace. An increasingly market-based economy and the forces of globalization have erected divisions between state and society and have weakened the state's control. These circumstances, along with an increasingly uncensored media, have sparked the development of China's civil society. At the same time, individuals and nongovernmental groups have been playing more active roles in addressing important social concerns, such as environmental protection and women's rights. In the process, they have developed initiatives such as Project Hope (a project that provides access to education in poor communities) and the Nu River Protection Project. Although GONGOs do take part in these projects, they typically cannot implement programs independently because of their strong government affiliation. Grassroots NGOs, such as Green River and Global Village, often collaborate with international NGOs to jointly coordinate projects. This helps them to promote the development of civil society in China. However, given their limited social impact, lack of resources, and externally imposed restrictions, these grassroots NGOs have been unable to develop a truly independent voice.

It is generally argued that civil society has not yet become an independent sector in China. The current state of Chinese civil society is rather unstable; it exists as a collection of independent NGOs that comprise what can only be considered a "precivil-society" state. These organizations do not operate within any political or legal framework, so they have remained loosely connected and somewhat fragile, often lacking resources. Additionally, no adequate social foundation exists to support civil organizations in their negotiations with the state.

Nevertheless, the concept of civil society has been increasingly recognized as part of the national development strategy. In 2001, for example, the term "NGO" was included for the first time in the National White Book of Poverty Relief. International institutes are also important supporters. Civil society in China is about to emerge. This emergence may not reflect the Western experience, however, for a number of reasons. For instance, many Chinese NGOs are financially dependent on the Chinese government and international funds. It is uncertain whether they will be able to establish a more independent civil-society sector. It is possible that the precivil-society state is a precursor to a period of expanded independence and subsistence.

Civil society in this early stage faces a number of challenges. While resources have been employed in establishing the civil-society sector, those resources are not renewable or sustainable. In this light, civil society will soon be reaching a crossroads regarding several issues, which are discussed below.

Legal Status

To attain legal status, an NGO must first be approved by the oversight department related to its service area. Organizations that do not have a close relationship with their respective departments are normally held to unduly strict requirements regarding funding and membership. Moreover, organizations of a similar nature are not permitted to operate in the same locality. These political regulations, which are characteristic of the Chinese corporatist system, often leave grassroots NGOs unable to register. In general, very few regulations exist to protect the legal rights of NGOs.

Lack of Human Resources

In China, the best and brightest seek job opportunities in government offices, the next tier of candidates typically end up in the corporate sector, and those who cannot obtain work in the first two sectors are relegated to other areas, such as the nonprofit sector. Oftentimes, those choosing to work in the nonprofit sector lack adequate capacity-building knowledge or skills. This situation has led to a dearth of skilled, talented staff in the nonprofit sector. Although NGO staff often demonstrates extraordinary passion and patience, it is commonly assumed that it possesses little expertise.

Funding Shortages

Civil society faces the tremendous obstacle of very limited funding for developing organizations. Many NGOs have a budget of no more than ¥10,000 annually and are in desperate need of financial support. Given the difficult and expensive process to become legally registered, as well as the narrow scope of many international funds, these organizations often experience financial troubles. When NGOs do manage to secure international funding, it tends to be very limited, and these organizations struggle to pay their staff, let alone hire a director or other high-level staff.

Lack of Creditability and Popularity

The concept of civil society is not yet familiar to most people in China. Moreover, its nascent development has been riddled with problems such as inefficiency, ineffectiveness, and low levels of transparency. These issues, magnified by people's preconceived assumptions that volunteer efforts are for show, have contributed to a certain degree of public skepticism about the nonprofit sector. Furthermore, problems facing the nonprofit sector hurt internal cohesion and employee morale.

Lack of Experience

The biggest difficulty facing Chinese NGOs is a general lack of relevant knowledge and technology, as organizations in China have no precedent to follow. Although there are some national NGO trainings, few employees take part in them. Moreover, many trainers do not fully understand the state of civil society and NGOs in China, which leads to ineffectual instruction. For this reason, many organizations lack effective operational plans, professional guidance, codes of standards and conduct, appropriate self-identification, organizational strategies, or some combination thereof.

There are certainly potential solutions to these problems. Social elites can advocate and lobby for legislative reforms, enterprises can contribute funding, and the international community can share its experiences and frameworks. This article focuses on the efforts of and challenges faced by grassroots NGO volunteers. Because they take a grassroots approach, they have limited power and tend to make a small social impact. However, they have laid the foundation for building a sustainable civil society in China, which has begun to change the very social structure of the nation.

Grassroots NGO: Two Individual Cases

Active grassroots volunteer organizations in China typically fall into three categories, according to the sources of their authority and membership. The first category consists of student volunteer organizations, which are staffed primarily by students, but some of these organizations staff professional social workers. In some cases, community-oriented student organizations are able to hire professional social workers to serve as their directors; examples include the Students Legal Aid Center of Fudan University and the Lighthouse in Guangzhou. The second category is comprised of independent organizations that operate under an official work unit or parent organization. These organizations include the Pine and Cypress group, an elder-care agency, and the Endeavourers group—both of which are affiliated with the organization Youth Volunteer Guangzhou. The Bone Marrow Donor Club, affiliated with the Red Cross Society of China, the Shanghai Branch, and certain branches of the World Wildlife Fund also belong to this categorization. This latter type of organization is technically considered to be a component, or branch, of an officially registered organization, but is allowed to implement programs independently. The third category is civic volunteer organizations. Although these are typically viewed as subdivisions of neighborhood committees, they often develop independent projects and initiatives. Additionally, these three types of organizations are based on different sources of authority and membership, but they are all nonprofit, independent, and based on collective action. Some organizations use a survival tactic called "one group, many names." This entails frequent adjustments to the name and mission of the organization to survive, and in some cases, to obtain diverse sources of funding. The following section will describe their process of growth based on a case example.

Grassroots Community

Grassroots Community is a volunteer organization located in Zhabei district, Shanghai. It promotes the idea "love your life and community" and is dedicated to aiding disadvantaged groups in the surrounding neighborhoods. The community seeks to improve people's quality of life by promoting community collaboration and creating opportunities for community members and groups to network and organize. Grassroots Community promotes volunteerism and is dedicated to creating an action network that connects community organizations and other civil organizations. The association has fifty-six members and over hundred long-term volunteers. In April 2004, it became an officially registered nonprofit organization.

The roots of this organization date back to 1995, when a group of students at Fudan University founded the Students Legal Aid Center. The purpose of this organization was to provide legal consultation to community members in need. This was the first student-run legal-aid organization in Shanghai and it sparked a volunteerism movement in the city. The students who volunteered for the center during college often sought to continue their work there following graduation. In 2000, the students who had been involved with the Students Legal Aid Center met at a reunion and decided to start a new volunteer organization, which they called the Pingmin County Workstation. The Workstation was founded on three core principles: (a) care for society, (b) put words into action, and (c) do everything to your best ability. At first, the group hoped to register as an independent nonprofit organization. After seeking counsel from a local governmental office, however, they realized it would be impossible to establish such an organization without celebrity participation, ample funding, or hired staff. The concept of an independent nonprofit organization was nonexistent at that time. Promoter Yonglong Liu pointed out that registering with the government would only provide the organization independent status. Given their limited funding, he suggested that they begin their unofficial work through community engagement, and the group began to develop their program of voluntary service for community members.

Most community residents felt hesitant about sharing personal challenges with this group of strangers; it took some time and hard work to gain their trust. Community residents tended to trust only the service programs that were related to well-known, formal organizations or organizations that were affiliated with the government. Otherwise, the organization would need to be introduced to the community by someone who could vouch for it—for instance, an influential person from the neighborhood. In this particular situation, the Pingmin County Workstation gained access to the community through an acquaintance of the community. As they began their work, many volunteers were shocked at the existence of such a poor community in Shanghai. Their first goal was to get to know the neighborhood committee, a small branch of the local government, and obtain its approval to work in the community. With the help of a mutual acquaintance, the process was relatively smooth. The committee secretary expressed worry about whether the services would actually be free and wondered why the group would provide a service at no cost. The members of the Workstation responded that they hoped to gain experience and emulate Feng Lei, a well-known Chinese historical figure known for leading a life of altruism. They also spoke about their volunteer experiences of providing legal aid during college and their organization's affiliation with Fudan University. The committee secretary finally agreed to allow the group to work in the community.

After gaining the residents' trust, the Workstation moved forward in its strategy to understand and meet the residents' needs. The government-initiated volunteerism movement and grassroots development movements had produced some unanticipated outcomes. Although volunteerism and community building were entirely new concepts, many people made incorrect assumptions about what they entailed. In particular, many people associated these terms with preexisting situations and programs that were already common to their communities. The human tendency to comprehend new concepts through personal experiences and customs was magnified by the central government being the primary channel through which the information flowed.

The neighborhood committee had become familiar with the terms *community* and *volunteer service* but did not fully comprehend their meaning. Consequently, the so-called volunteer organizations were assumed to be any organizations "working in the spirit of Feng Lei." For this reason, the residents soon accepted the Workstation. This established favorable conditions for the development of other volunteer organizations in the community. As they assessed the needs of the community, the volunteers noticed that many of the older residents, through their senior-citizen task force, had been studying China's Law on the Protection of the Rights and Interests of the Elderly. These community members wanted to better understand the law but they did not have the necessary expertise or access to a professional consultation. With mutual acquaintances acting as a bridge, the volunteers were able to offer legal aid and consultation services to these clients.

It is standard in China for a volunteer organization to hold a large celebration as an icebreaker before officially engaging in community affairs. Having discussed its plans with the local committee, the Workstation organized its welcoming event at Double Ninth, a prominent lecture and consultation service pertaining to rights for aging populations. This type of activity helped the Workstation gain acceptance later, when it began carrying out legal aid for environmental-protection programs in other communities. Once the Workstation began to provide consultations, most volunteers routinely divided programs into two stages. The first stage focused on outreach and community education, which were tailored to specific characteristics of the community. These efforts typically consisted of lectures, poster and leaflet distribution, public displays, and on-site consultation about various topics, such as the government's aggressive demolition of housing, neighborhood disputes, and rights awareness in general. The second stage focused on providing substantive legal aid, which in some cases involved litigation.

At first, community members were not very enthusiastic about these consulting services. The Workstation soon discovered the importance of engaging in community activities. They began to create "client profiles" to accurately assess the basic situation of vulnerable groups in the community and keep in regular touch with each client to establish bonds of trust. During this period of time, the Workstation participated in an important community festival to celebrate the beginning of a new millennium. Workstation volunteers gave scarves to everyone over the age of eighty, a gesture that was very well received. Following this festival, the Workstation enjoyed a stronger reputation and improved relationships with the community. When the government began to engage in widespread demolition efforts in Pingmin County (which would result in the forced relocation of residents), the community turned to the Workstation for legal support. In a coordination meeting jointly held by the local district office, the neighborhood committee, and demolition coordinators, the district office insisted that the neighborhood committee prevent the Workstation from filing a lawsuit on behalf of the residents. The Workstation was allowed to disseminate general information among residents but was prohibited from directly assisting them. Aware of its position in the community, the Workstation agreed to abide by these restrictions. It gave up its original plan to not only offer legal counsel but also get directly involved in negotiations between the residents and local government. As a result, the residents who approached the Workstation for help were provided general information but not services. Eventually, as the number of residents who requested information dwindled, the Workstation staff lost its momentum. Finally, only two Workstation members remained in the community: Yonglong Liu and Dong Qu. Although disappointed by their lack of support, Liu and Qu printed and distributed leaflets that contained information on legally fighting the demolition. "We felt like criminals," they said.

When the entire village had been demolished, the organization's work finally came to a close. Soon after, the group provided legal consultation to union laborers about defending their rights in a district office in another community. Without adequate funding or dependable staff, the Workstation had no other choice but to recruit volunteers, whose commitment would be premised on their own ideals. Subsequently, the primary goals of the organization were reformulated. In a meeting held in Huzhou, the Workstation was reconceived as Grassroots Community, an organization that would encourage a spirit of volunteerism in China. It would engage in community development and support those in need. These goals clarified the new mission of Grassroots Community and gained more political support in the process.

In its earliest stages, Grassroots Community's funding primarily came from small, private donations or member donations. By forming relationships with other institutions, such as the Swedish International Development Agency, Grassroots Community obtained its first contribution to its endowment. Although modest, this source of funding made it possible to staff an assistant. Still, members of Grassroots Community soon began to choose between efficiency and the volunteer spirit. Many volunteers held other jobs and would often procrastinate or fail to follow through on commitments. The organization's leaders came to realize that both efficiency and the volunteer spirit were of great significance but sought to ensure that the latter would define the organization as it moved forward. To this end, the organization established a core set of principles:

1. Staff will diligently and steadfastly perform services, rather than seek undeserved credit.
2. The organization will be democratic, meaning it will treat staff and clients equally. Meanwhile, Grassroots Community staff will recognize that

cooperation with both neighborhood committees and the government is essential to effective community development.
3. The organization will take root among the masses, focusing on small-scale, community-based change in daily life instead of large-scale political advocacy.

It was difficult for the organization to drastically shift its mission and policies, but soon after, these new regulations began to direct their new projects. As Grassroots Community was first and foremost a volunteer-based organization, funding shortages were not of the utmost concern. Rather, most of their efforts targeted volunteer programs and recruitment. In cooperation with the Shanghai Young Men's Christian Association, Grassroots Community organized the Youth Tea Party, which later became tremendously successful. At a series of these tea parties, many volunteers got to know Grassroots Community and the previous experiences of its founders with the Pingmin County Workstation, and they subsequently got onboard.

For three years, Grassroots Community was successful at recruiting volunteers and securing funding to sustain its momentum. It expanded its projects and scope and began to provide legal aid, engage in community environmental-protection projects, address poverty alleviation in Western China, and become involved in the Taiyanghua Project, which provided education to children of migrant workers. The Chinese government and society had also liberalized and Grassroots Community became an officially registered organization in April 2004. While it remained an independent nonprofit organization, it also established an affiliation with the Communist Youth League Committee.

Guangzhou Green Hope Network

Guangzhou Green Hope Network (GGHN) is a young nonprofit group that was founded in 2002 by several environmental-minded volunteers. Realizing early on the unlikelihood of obtaining official registration, the volunteers determined to focus on developing programs and engaging in outreach. Through a connection with a local environmental-protection office, GGHN became affiliated with the Guangzhou Green Hope organization, which was registered under the Ministry of Environmental Protection, and thereafter adopted its name.

The founding members of GGHN commenced operations in the office of the Green Community Research Institute of Sun Yat-Sen University and soon connected with an international conservation group concerned with the safety of genetically modified food in China. By working with its volunteer base, GGHN developed and launched a public education campaign. Online volunteer recruitment expanded the group's membership to 210, which included mostly students and community members. This made it possible to implement environmental-education programs in schools, communities, and local supermarkets. GGHN also became affiliated with the Ren'ai Social Service Center, and the two organizations jointly invested in a vehicle, which they named Little Tiger, to travel around Guangzhou and disseminate information about environmental protection.

Limited funding and difficulty in finding well-trained professionals were problems for GGHN, which primarily relied on volunteer efforts. The organization established a temporary steering committee and several work teams, which included a networking team, a media team, an education team, and an investigation team. These teams became very successful and active, despite the unpaid status of their volunteers. Volunteers provided both human capital and social resources. For instance, some volunteers who also worked as reporters helped to establish connections with the media. Government officials who volunteered with Green Hope helped to integrate the organization's programs into local communities.

Green Hope benefited the most from collaborations with international NGOs and some well-known Chinese NGOs. It collaborated with Greenpeace and Friends of Nature, launched Little Tiger in January, organized tours of organic farms, and participated in a community day in March. Through these collaborative programs, volunteers with Green Hope gained experience in program implementation and working with the media and earned promotions. Green Hope also established training camps to equip volunteers with a broad knowledge base. As a result, Green Hope was run at a low cost and enjoyed widespread media coverage. This helped to expand its social influence and attract more volunteers.

Green Hope continued to remain unregistered, which helped it to minimize costs. The organization focused its efforts on several core areas and placed volunteers accordingly. The efforts of these volunteers made it possible to achieve project goals and evaluate programs at very little cost. Green Hope's mission is to promote its objectives through direct action and not just public education. The organization's slogan is "action is hope." In 2003, Green Hope expanded its goals to include the promotion of local, sustainable development. This required the organization to incorporate the ecological community development as a core concept.

Discussion

These two case studies demonstrate that in the face of registration difficulties, limited legal protection, and political restrictions imposed on NGOs, grassroots volunteer organizations have been able to develop a unique working model within the framework of China's precivil society. In doing so, these organizations have promoted the advancement of the public sphere.

Regarding legal and political challenges, grassroots volunteer organizations in China have attached great importance to business ethics and to adhering to their core principles. They have mobilized volunteers in good faith and have carried out activities under difficult circumstances. In many cases, their actions have not been legally sanctioned; however, these grassroots volunteer organizations have managed to operate on small budgets and strengthen internal cohesion. During their early development, many grassroots volunteer organizations buckled under various pressures, which led to high rates of turnover. Those that remained, however, formed stronger bonds to withstand the social and political pressures. Grassroots Community and Green Hope remain unregistered but have persisted in pursuing their social goals. The spirit of volunteerism has, no doubt, contributed to these organizations' survival and sustainability.

Although they have faced shortages of talented, well-trained professionals, grassroots volunteer organizations have assigned very few volunteers to handle administrative affairs. Rather, they recruit volunteers from all walks of life to apply their professional skills to public service programs. Both Grassroots Community and Green Hope successfully tapped the expertise of their volunteers. For example, many Grassroots Community volunteers had worked in the field of law or for foreign companies. Because of their experience, they were able to provide guidance on system and performance evaluation. When engaged in projects, even in a small-scale community consultation, these volunteers were able to carefully and professionally plan, discuss, and evaluate. In light of this, Grassroots Community shifted its goals and operations to better conform to volunteer needs and expectations. This shift, along with the participation of more professionals and student volunteers, has substantially improved Grassroots Community's organizational capacity.

Funding shortages pose a minimal concern for grassroots volunteer organizations given the largely unpaid volunteer makeup of their staff. Unhampered by fundraising needs, these organizations have more time and energy to focus on program operations. The volunteer base of

Grassroots Community and the "go Dutch" strategy employed by Green Hope have allowed these organizations to sustainably operate despite funding concerns. Zero-cost or low-cost strategic plans allow grassroots volunteer organizations to focus more on program operations than on fundraising.

Trust is another major issue faced by grassroots volunteer organizations, particularly among staff and volunteers. Grassroots Community and Green Hope, however, have never experienced breakdowns due to corruption or authoritarian leadership. This is because these organizations are based on volunteer services, which do not lead to rivalries for power or resources. These organizations work directly with people in need and constantly provide services for the public good, which in turn builds their credibility within communities. In contrast to officially registered NGOs, grassroots volunteer organizations can more easily develop trusting relationships with those they serve.

Knowledge management and training pose key challenges for grassroots volunteer organizations and can only be addressed through hands-on learning. Volunteers with Grassroots Community and Green Hope initially engaged in training programs in Beijing and invested in learning materials. Before long, however, they realized that regional knowledge could only be fully absorbed through hands-on work. Operating on low budgets, these organizations stress service learning and regional study as the best possible means to attain a solid understanding of a region and the issues affecting it. To be sustainable, these organizations must learn to expertly address issues facing local communities; this requires a firm understanding of each respective community and its concerns. Initially, Grassroots Community had an advantage in terms of legal expertise and Green Hope made use of its knowledge of genetically modified food. Possessing both professional knowledge and regional expertise gives grassroots volunteer organizations the best chance of being accepted by local communities and the government.

Grassroots NGOs often face difficulties when they attempt expansion. Volunteers with these organizations will argue, however, that expansion is not necessary at all. Expanded bureaucracy, after all, is not necessarily the best means to effect social change. What these grassroots organizations lack in resources, they make up for in spirit—the spirit of volunteerism. What is more important is that they serve to cultivate a national civic awareness. As Robert Weller (1999) argued, even under democratic governments and market systems, the forces of individualism and modernity have not suppressed the growth of civil organizations. According to

Weller, these organizations do not create a new civil society; rather, they provide social capital and other resources for the transition to democracy. Grassroots NGOs exemplify this idea. However, Robert Putnam (1993) described democracy as having varied effects on different communities. In addition to local government policies, a primary factor that determines these effects is the extent of participation in the local civic community. According to Putnam, social groups and individuals comprise the social capital of democracy. This social capital helps to develop the network of civic participation, norms and regulations, and mutual trust. It is this social capital that makes collective social action possible. Grassroots NGOs in China are not necessarily a mainstream feature of civil society; however, they are a fundamental driving force behind the civic community of each neighborhood and region. They will therefore make very important contributions to civil society.

Alexis de Tocqueville observed that in democratic states, individual citizens, isolated from outside help, are powerless and dependent. They would not acquire power, he argued, until they had created a system of mutual assistance and support. In my opinion, in the face of many challenges, grassroots volunteer organizations can introduce important, alternative empowerment strategies at the community level. Certainly, it is not feasible for Chinese civil society to run only on the social capital generated by grassroots organizations. However, it is possible for these organizations to cultivate and hone China's sense of civic consciousness, and thereby spark a larger movement toward social change. Additionally, these organizations can foster and maintain the essence of civil society: the public's participation in volunteerism.

4

A Major Breakthrough in the Development of the Nonprofit Sector in China

Xiaoyong Huang * *and Liqiang Cai*

The year 2011 was the first year of the "Five-Year Plan for 2011–2015" in China. It was also a year in which public management and innovation became important development strategies in the country. The highly bureaucratic oversight system, which had long constrained the development of the nonprofit sector in China, made a significant breakthrough. The nonprofit sector had not developed much before this point, and its credibility suffered at times with society. However, China is entering an era in which the number of nonprofit organizations will boom, the quality of services will improve, and their influence on society will increase.

Development Status, Opportunity, and Challenges since 2010

The Status Quo of the Nonprofit Sector

In China, the nonprofit sector consists of three types of organizations: nonprofit groups (or social groups or organizations, *shehui tuanti*), nonprofit organizations (or private nonenterprise units, *minban fei qiye danwei*), and foundations. In this chapter, I use the term *nongovernmental organizations* (NGOs) to refer to all three of these organizations. In China, the line between governmental and nongovernmental is sometimes

* Translated by Mingyue Chang, doctoral student, Department of Nutritional Sciences, Rutgers University.

blurred, but for the most part, NGOs are nonprofit organizations that are not run by the government. The nonprofit sector has grown at a slow rate in recent years. In 2010 the growth rate was just 3.5 percent, a decrease from 4.1 percent in 2009 (see Figure 4.1). By the end of 2009 there were 431,000 NGOs in China, and in 2010 the number was 446,000. Since 2010, improvements in the NGOs registration system and other areas have been explored nationwide. One improvement has been to allow organizations to register for NGOs status, as opposed to having to obtain approval from a government department before registering. Other efforts have included loosening the requirements needed to register an NGO to create a good environment for the development of NGOs. Despite a gradually improving external environment for NGO development, the overall growth rate of NGOs still reached an unprecedented low. Therefore, to some degree it seems that removing the barriers to registration will not alone be able to hasten the development of NGOs.

Nonprofit group is a common term in Chinese political discourse that refers to groups of people working together on a common activity, interest, or goal. Such groups are often unofficial networks organized informally by individuals. Nonprofit groups have the slowest growth rate among all types of NGOs. The growth rate of nonprofit groups was in decline from 2006 to 2010 (see Figure 4.2). By the end of 2010 there were 245,000 nonprofit groups in China, an increase of 2.5 percent (from 239,000 organizations) from 2009. However, although the overall total increased,

Figure 4.1
Change in the Nonprofit Sector, 2002–2010

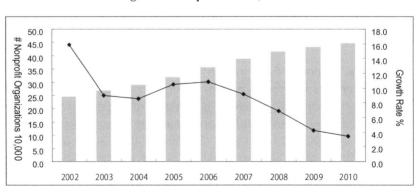

Source: Statistics Report of Civil Affairs Development (2002–2009); Statistics Report of Social Service Development (2010).

Figure 4.2
Change in Nonprofit Groups, 2002–2010

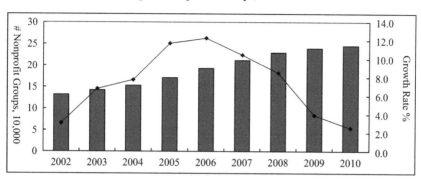

Source: Statistics Report of Civil Affairs Development (2002–2009); Statistics Report of Social Service Development (2010).

the growth rate in 2010 decreased by 1.4 percent from 2009, reaching its lowest growth rate since 2002. In addition, since 2009, nonprofit groups have had the lowest growth rate in the nonprofit sector—1.7 percent lower than nonprofit organizations and 16.9 percent lower than foundations. Moreover, these growth-rate gaps were higher than the prior year (0.5 and 11.5 percent, respectively).

China has about 1,810 national and interprovincial nonprofit groups, which accounted for 0.74 percent of all nonprofit groups by the end of 2010. Provincial nonprofit groups numbered 24,149 and accounted for 9.85 percent of all nonprofit groups. There were 64,169 prefecture-level nonprofit groups, which comprised 26.16 percent of all nonprofit groups. Finally, there were 166,128 county-level nonprofit groups, which accounted for 63.25 percent of all nonprofit groups (see Figure 4.3). All four types of nonprofit groups increased in number from 2009 to 2010, with growth rates of 0.56, 3.36, 1.79, and 3.05 percent, respectively. Although the growth rates were fairly balanced, the growth rate of provincial and county nonprofit groups was clearly faster.

Nonprofit groups provide services in several areas. In 2010, the proportions of agricultural-development and rural-development nonprofit groups were relatively high (19.46 and 13.35 percent, respectively; see Figure 4.4). Since 2007, these two nonprofit groups not only increased in number but also expanded in terms of their proportion of all nonprofit groups. Cultural, environmental, religious, professional, and occupational

Figure 4.3
Number and Percentage of Nonprofit Groups in Geographic Scope, 2010

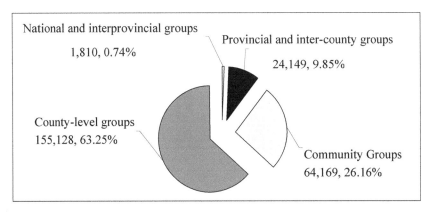

National and interprovincial groups
1,810, 0.74%

Provincial and inter-county groups
24,149, 9.85%

County-level groups
155,128, 63.25%

Community Groups
64,169, 26.16%

Source: Statistics Report of Social Service Development (2010).

nonprofit groups increased to different degrees in 2010, expanding their presence as well. Although sports and other nonprofit groups increased in absolute number, they represented lower proportions of all nonprofit groups. The number of industrial and commercial service nonprofit groups increased by 620, compared with that in 2009 and the percentage stayed almost the same. Scientific investigational, educational, health, law, and other international nonprofit organizations decreased from their numbers in 2009, as did their percentage shares.

The term *nonprofit organizations* refers to organizations that use nonstate assets and are formed by corporations, individuals, or groups. By the end of 2010 the total number of nonprofit organizations in China reached 198,000, a 4.2 percent increase from 2009. The growth rate of these units was 4.4 percent in 2009 but 4.2 percent in 2010. In other words, compared with the overall growth rate for NGOs in 2010, the growth rate for nonprofit organizations was 0.7 percent higher than the overall growth rate in 2010 and 0.3 percent higher than the overall growth rate in 2009. One reason why the growth rate of these nonprofit organizations was higher than the overall growth rate is that, in 2010, some regions in China experimented with direct registrations and relaxed registration requirements. However, the growth rate of nonprofit organizations decreased annually from 2002 to 2010 (see Figure 4.5), which indicates that China still has a long way to go to foster and develop NGOs and that loosening the registration requirement is not enough.

Figure 4.4
Number and Proportion of Nonprofit Groups in
Major Service Areas, 2010

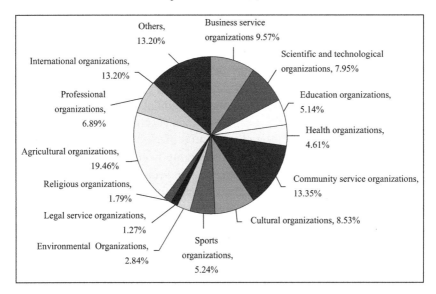

Source: Statistics Report of Social Service Development (2010).

Figure 4.5
Change of Nonprofit Organizations, 2002–2010

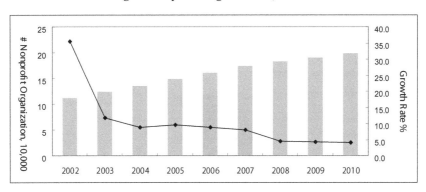

Source: Statistics Report of Civil Affairs Development (2002–2009); Statistics Report of Social Service Development (2010).

The three most active types of nonprofit organizations are educational, social service, and health organizations. In 2010, educational institutes comprised 49.47 percent of the total number of private nonprofit organizations, social service units made up 14.87 percent of the total, and health organizations accounted for 12.71 percent of the total (see Figure 4.6).

Foundations are nonprofit juristic persons who utilize the assets denoted by natural person, juristic person, or other organizations to improve the commonwealth. The growth rate of foundations remains high. By the end of 2010 the number of foundations reached 2,200; this was an increase of 357 from 2009 and an annual growth rate of 19.4 percent. The 2010 growth rate increased considerably from the 2009 rate of 15.4 percent. This relatively high growth rate is especially notable considering the trend toward lower overall growth rates for NGOs (see Figure 4.7). Foundations should maintain a high growth rate in the near future as the review and approval process decentralizes and enterprises' social responsibility strengthens.

In 2010 the number of public foundations increased to 1,101, accounting for 50.05 percent of all foundations; private foundations increased to 1,088 (including eleven international foundations), accounting for 49.45 percent of the total number. Seventy-two new public foundations

Figure 4.6
Number and Percentage of Nonprofit Organizations in
Major Service Areas, 2010

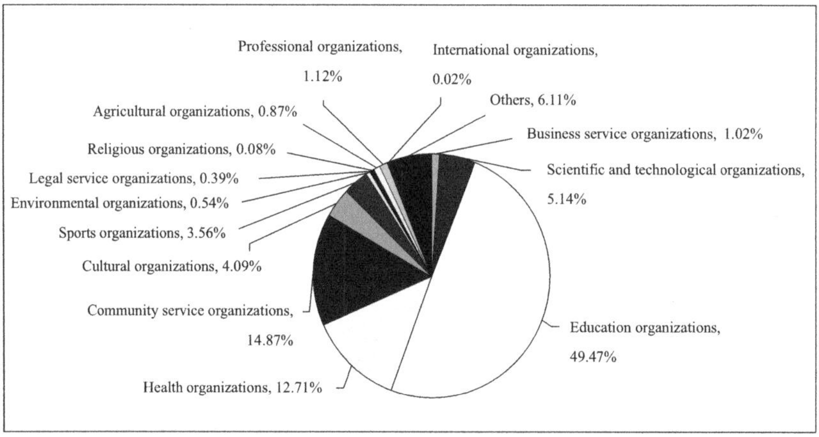

Source: Statistics Report of Social Service Development (2010).

Figure 4.7
Change in Foundations, 2004–2010

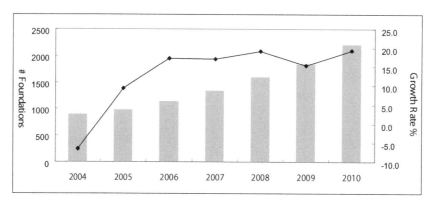

Source: Statistics Report of Civil Affairs Development (2004–2009); Statistics Report of Social Service Development (2010).

were established in 2010, and 288 private foundations were established. Because of the rapid growth of private foundations, its percentage expanded from 43.41 percent in 2009 to 49.45 percent in 2010. The percentage of public foundations shrunk from 55.83 percent in 2009 to 50.05 percent in 2010. In general, the percentage of public and private foundations only differed by 0.6 percent, and these two foundation types comprise almost all foundations in China (see Figure 4.8). The development trends of foundations indicate that private foundations are developing quickly and will exceed public foundations in percentage of total foundations.

Nonprofit Sector's Status in Society

An important economic index used to evaluate the status of the non-profit sector is the value that the nonprofit sector adds to the service industry. The added value in China increased fourfold from 2006 to 2010 (see Table 4.1). Additionally, between 2007 and 2009, the growth rate of the added value was much higher than the growth rate of the gross domestic product (GDP). In 2010, however, for the first time the increase in the growth rate of the nonprofit sector's added value was lower than the growth rate of the GDP, which was 10.3 percent. Still, in 2010 the nonprofit sector had fixed assets of ¥83.41 billion throughout the country and an astonishing growth rate. The sector's 2010 expenses totaled ¥119.52 billion; this represents an increase of 9.2 percent from

Figure 4.8
Foundation Constitution Diagram, 2010

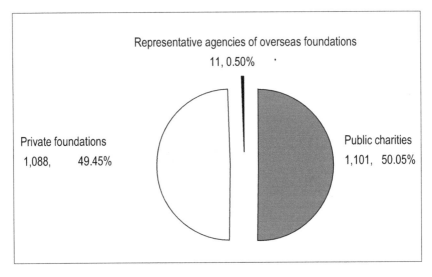

Source: Statistics Report of Social Service Development (2010).

the previous year and is a reflection of the ever-increasing activity of the sector in China's economy.

Two other general indices used to evaluate the function of the nonprofit sector in society are the number and growth rate of employees absorbed by nonprofit organizations. Overall, both figures have improved

Table 4.1
Annual Assets Growth, Growth Rate, and Percentage of Nonprofit Sector in Service Industry

Year	Annual assets growth (hundreds of millions ¥)	Annual growth rate (%)	Percentage of service industry (%)
2006	112.2	–	0.30
2007	307.6	173.9	0.32
2008	372.4	21.1	0.31
2009	493.1	32.4	0.35
2010	531.1	7.7	0.31

Source: Statistics Report of Civil Affairs Development (2006–2009); Statistics Report of Social Service Development (2010).

continuously. In 2010, the 446,000 NGOs throughout the nation employed 6.18 million people from all kinds of professions. These figures indicate that the economic and social influences of the nonprofit sector in China have spiked in recent years.

Unprecedented Development Opportunities

Public Management

Changes in public-management concepts have given the nonprofit sector a dominant position in the field of social services. The year 2011 can be called the "public management year" in China. Public management became the hot topic of the year, appearing frequently in government reports, academic research and discussions, and the media. Innovations in public administration have become an important strategy of the government and the Communist Party of China (CPC). Both stress that the long-term peace and stability of the nation should be guaranteed by updating to newer management models in design and practice, improving the execution of methods, and promoting public management.

The promotion of innovation in public management has stimulated great conversion about public management concepts. In terms of public management, it has been stressed that a transformation should be made from top-down administration by the government to a system of shared management. Modern public management not only includes the government's regulation of society through legislation but also society's governance of itself. Therefore, the government should enhance its abilities and efficiency in public management, and society should improve its self-governance as well. Based on the government's lead, all kinds of social powers should participate in self-governance, self-discipline, and regulation by and of others; the general public should be encouraged to use their positive and creative ideas to become active in public management, to join forces to promote coordinated social development, and to keep society safe and ordered. The nonprofit sector is no longer just being administrated by the government; rather, nonprofit organizations have become the main body of social self-governance and a cooperative management partner relied on by the government.

This transformation of public management ideas has promoted a change in the CPC's perspective of the nonprofit sector. The government's twelfth national Five-Year Plan gave nonprofit organizations and groups corresponding roles, assignments in social construction, and administration innovation, making the status and function of the nonprofit sector in society's development prominent.

In the process of making public management more innovative, the government is gradually shifting from its previous, top-down approach to public management and is trying to improve its ability and efficiency in administrating society. At the same time, the government began to attach great importance to nourishing and developing all kinds of nonprofit organizations and improving the self-governance of society by promoting the self-development of society. By stressing the primary leading role of government as usual, the government's flaw of overadministrating should be corrected. A public management system with Chinese characteristics is now coming into being in China—this system is social coadministration led by government.

In forming this system, it has become especially important to facilitate society's growth and ability to manage itself, both of which have been lagging. The coadministration system relies not only on the ability of the nonprofit sector to regulate itself, but it also relies on the sector's contribution to the government's regulation of society. This social synergy is intended to allow all types of nonprofit organizations to function fully, to integrate social administrative resources, to actively develop the government-society administrative network, and to foster interaction between the government and society to improve societal response to government policies. The government's synergistic power hinges on the nonprofit sector, which are the conduit through which citizens manage themselves and maintain public order.

Government-led innovation in public management makes party members at various government levels attach great importance to the function of the nonprofit sector in public management and take various actions to nurture and support the nonprofit sector, direct it toward self-development, and enhance its abilities to provide services to society to aid in self-governance. In this way, many innovative public management practices have come into being throughout the nation.

Breaking away from a Highly Bureaucratic Administrative System

The greatest system-level obstacle to the development of Chinese nonprofit sector is the dual-oversight system. In this system, organizations had to obtain permission from a government department to be able to register as a nonprofit group or organization, and that registration occurred with another department. Additionally, the second part of the registration process was complicated and contained stringent requirements, which made it difficult to register for many NGOs. Finally, the registration system involved strict license checks, which, like the stringent registration requirements, are typical in a top-down administration model.

The highly bureaucratic oversight system, which seriously obstructs the nonprofit sector, has received extensive criticism, but change has been slow. Before the CPC's seventeenth National Congress in 2007, the development of the nonprofit sector had long been restricted. Due to the urgent need for economic development in China, the requirements for registering an NGO were simplified because of their special role in society. For example, during the socialist process of rural development, the Ministry of Civil Affairs took measures such as enhancing the development and registration of rural professional economic associations, relaxing registration conditions, simplifying registration procedures, and clearly specifying which departments were in charge of the registration process. To progress toward a more harmonious socialistic society, the Ministry of Civil Affairs sends out notifications to promote the development of charity organizations, requiring that civil affairs offices at different levels take responsibility for supervising and managing charitable foundations. The Ministry of Civil Affairs is also responsible for managing the NGO registration process and has contributed considerably to revising what was previously a highly bureaucratic oversight system. In addition, community organizations and trade associations have overcome system constraints due to societal economic development, and the State Council has facilitated NGO registration by providing NGOs with informational documents on the process.

In general, a rather shortsighted thought process has guided the reform of the nonprofit sector, such as rural professional economic associations, charitable foundations, community organizations, and industrial commercial associations. Such thinking is characterized by treating only the symptoms and lacking in-depth attention to larger issues.

After the CPC's seventeenth National Congress, the reform of the NGO oversight system was a significant step in the development of the nonprofit sector. Some innovative practices with important systemic breakthroughs can be seen at local levels.

Since 2008, Shenzhen, the forerunner in the country's Reform Era policies, has tested a system of direct registration (without the need for approval from a separate government sponsor) for industrial and commercial NGOs, social welfare NGOs, and charitable foundations, igniting a wave of new NGO registrations. In February 2010 Beijing enacted the Zhongguancun National Independent Innovation Demonstration Regulations, which designated that the NGOs in the Zhongguancun demonstration zone could register directly as a truly independent NGO with no affiliation or attachment to the government. The regulation became the first local legislation to clearly allow NGOs to register directly with minimal conditions. In the first half of 2011 the requirements for registering an NGO were relaxed throughout Beijing, stipulating that industrial, commercial, and economic NGOs; social welfare NGOs; social service NGOs; and charitable foundations could register directly at the Ministry of Civil Affairs. At the end of 2011 a new regulation was enacted in Guangdong that stipulated that, beginning on July 1, 2012, the administrative departments of NGOs would be recategorized as instructional departments and that nonprofit organizations could apply directly to the Ministry of Civil Affairs without preapproval, except for special situations. The reform of the oversight system in Guangdong has essentially ended the bureaucratic oversight system in the province.

The brave exploration of a new oversight and registration system of these local governments received high praise and complete approval from the national Ministry of Civil Affairs. The leaders in the Ministry of Civil Affairs have publicized these local efforts and have called for reforming to the more innovative direct-registration system. At a press conference by the National People's Congress and the Chinese People's Political Consultative Conference in March 2011, Liguo Li, the head of the Ministry of Civil Affairs, announced that the key to successfully strengthening and innovating the public management system in Shenzhen was the reform of the registration process. Li hoped that the experience in Shenzhen could spread throughout the country. On May 3, 2011, Li said that the Beijing experience will be duplicated when Beijing conducts its periodic data collection and survey process. He also stated that, when the Ministry of Civil Affairs inspects nonprofit organizations, it should do so within the scope of current law and regulations and should also advance a system-level reform of nonprofit organizations by allowing charitable foundations and social welfare and social service NGOs to register directly at the Ministry of Civil Affairs. Finally, Li stated that the Ministry of Civil Affairs should speed up the government's purchase of NGO services, thereby supporting the development of the nonprofit sector.

On July 4, 2011, during the Annual Civil Work Analysis Conference, Li commented that the Ministry of Civil Affairs bears the responsibility of registering and managing public charity, social welfare, and social service organizations. This means that these charitable organizations can register directly with the Ministry of Civil of Affairs, which marks a big shift away from the dual-oversight system. On December 23, 2011, at the National Civil Work Conference, Li expressed that the Guangdong experience should be promoted, and direct registration and management systems for public charity, social welfare, and social service organizations should be instituted in locales that are developed enough to support them.

Judging from the brave exploration of some local governments and approval from the central government, no matter how the development of nonprofit groups, nonprofit organizations, and foundations proceeds, the reform of the NGO oversight system in China is poised to make a breakthrough. A revision of these regulations should entail a systematic shift toward supporting local organizations and giving them legitimacy on both the local and national levels.

Resources

The government has already improved its support of the nonprofit sector by incorporating them into its system of service provision. This has greatly reduced the scarcity of resources. The national government's twelfth Five-Year Plan, which indicated the state's goals and key objectives, stressed that economic NGOs, public charitable foundations, nonprofit organizations, and rural community organizations should have priority in receiving development assistance. A series of policies and measures has been put forth to foster the development of the nonprofit sector, for instance, creating more complete support policies, hastening the transfer of government functions to nonprofit organizations, opening up more public resources and fields to nonprofit organizations, and expanding tax benefits.

The national strategic plan has been carried out as concrete actions in various policy areas, such as services to older individuals and the poor, community development, health insurance, and employment. The nonprofit sector has been included in the government's administrative and work systems. The government leads these efforts but encourages the nonprofit sector to participate in public service and public management by purchasing their services and providing funding, among other ways.

According to the national council's newly promulgated plan for services to older individuals, all nonprofit organizations involved in this service area will have equitable and improved access to resources and will experience a friendlier operational environment. In its strategic plan the government clearly supported the development of this service industry.

At the beginning of 2011 the Chinese Center for Disease Control and Prevention in Changsha spent ¥50,000 to purchase services from the grassroots AIDS-prevention NGO Big Sunshine Working Group. Although the government did not buy much, the act was of great significance because it indicated that special government funds were becoming available to grassroots organizations. By the end of 2011, cancer-prevention NGOs were included in the government's National AIDS Action Plan. In doing so, the government will not only increase society's participation in AIDS-prevention work but will also improve communication with NGOs and volunteers, enhance training and support, and "provide funds and support to AIDS-prevention NGOs so that they can better perform their specialized functions."

While the national government has explored reforming the rules for nonprofit registration and oversight and has worked to create a more innovative public management system in general, all levels of government have increased their purchases and use of nonprofit services. For instance, the Department of Finance allocated ¥2 billion to support nonprofit organizations participating in social services for the first time. Additionally, local governments created systems for financial support and gradually increased funding. For example, a special fund was set up in Beijing. City and district governments spent ¥100 million on services from the nonprofit sector in 2010. That investment doubled to almost ¥200 million in 2011, and more than 600 public service projects were purchased from nonprofit organizations altogether.

Microphilanthropy

Microphilanthropy has thrived in China and is now taking a leading role in the development of charity work and inspiring enthusiasm for charity among the general public. Microphilanthropy received a great deal of attention in 2011, and the general public was the main source of donations. Additionally, nongovernmental charity figures inspired people to donate online, a powerful change in that it allowed for more donations in shorter periods of time. In 2011 official charity organizations encountered an unprecedented crisis in the public's trust, while in the same year microphilanthropy efforts quickly won the hearts and trust of the people. Thus, in China, the year 2011 is often referred to as the first year of social welfare or the first year of microphilanthropy.

Microphilanthropy is a new charity model that uses the Internet as a platform to promote the general public's participation in charity. The term *microphilanthropy* has two primary meanings. The first refers to donation efforts that use Sina Weibo (a Chinese microblogging website that is similar to Twitter) as a platform to mobilize potential donors. The second is to combine the individual power of common people to promote the practice of public charity projects. There are three main types of microphilanthropy: (a) providing small-scale material support (e.g., donations), which is often not much on the individual level, or donating personal items for auction; (b) giving spiritual or public opinion support (e.g., by forwarding news or comments to encourage individuals or companies to make donations); and (c) supporting causes through action (e.g., by taking part in volunteer activities).

Microphilanthropy efforts have four notable characteristics. First, they are a convenient, simple, and easy way of doing good deeds, which enables more people to get involved. Second, they are fast and efficient, which makes it possible to respond quickly to emergency events and offer rescue aid in the shortest time by using Weibo and other messaging services and social media. Third, microphilanthropy efforts take advantage of Weibo, QQ groups, forums, and other online venues to mobilize friends with shared charity interests. Fourth, microphilanthropy is a pleasant and relaxed way to donate compared with the ritualized and elitist charity activities common in the past.

Compared with traditional philanthropy efforts, microphilanthropy takes better advantage of the Internet's low threshold for participation, high-interaction rates, fast-spreading news, greater influence, and higher transparency. A microphilanthropy effort encourages everyone to participate, even if they can only make a small contribution. Contributions are not only confined to the monetary and in-kind donations that define traditional charities, but netizens can also participate in and contribute to charities by following, reading, and forwarding relevant information. Microphilanthropy greatly expands the possibilities for public charities by removing restrictions to participation and spreading the spirit of charity throughout society. Contributors to microphilanthropy efforts are usually common people, volunteers, media outlets, charity organizations, companies, and government officials, from which a diversification interaction could be found. Microphilanthropy is a new kind of model for charity with more diversified main body.

Microphilanthropy symbolizes a growing consciousness of the citizens' privilege and responsibility of participating in charity. The platform makes it easier for people to do good deeds and allows everyone to find a charity they can participate in. Microphilanthropy has forever changed the times when noted public figures and charity organizations shaped the charity industry, while ordinary people could only look on and do nothing.

Those who start a microphilanthropy effort include public figures, people who work for the media, and general citizens. Many microphilanthropy efforts are unofficial when they are first launched, but after gaining some influence in society, they are usually combined with the efforts of public charity organizations. For example, the Free Lunch program, which was started by Fei Deng, is operated by the China Social Welfare Foundation; Keqing Wang's Love Save Pneumoconiosis program is now affiliated with the China Social Rescue Foundation; and Shuxin Liang's Lunch Plan for Guizhou Rural Areas program is now part of the Youth Development Foundation in Guizhou and runs through a special fund called a microfoundation. Microphilanthropy programs gain legal status when they are affiliated with public foundations and special funds; this is an important step in assuring that public charity programs are able to receive donations from the public. Some microphilanthropy programs have been able to register directly as legal public charity organizations after operating for a period of time. Some examples are the Returning Veterans program initiated by Chunlong Sun, which gained legal status by setting up a special fund in Shenzhen, where the registration and regulation policies are relatively relaxed.

In addition to grassroots microphilanthropy, some formal public charity organizations, entrepreneurs, and media outlets have started microphilanthropy programs after noticing their power and influence. For instance, in June 2011, the Chinese insurance company Ping An came together with the China Youth Development Foundation to donate water to the Ping An Hope primary schools, which are located in drought areas. The theme of the donations passed around Sina Weibo and Tencent was "one bottle of water at one time." Shanghai Community Development Foundation launched a microphilanthropy donation program that aimed to provide children in poor areas with an egg every day. The China Mobile Henan Branch volunteer association initiated several microphilanthropy programs, including efforts to help poor college students, to provide assistance to orphans, and to help college students work part-time for tuition.

Microphilanthropy is still in an early stage of development, and it presently faces three challenges. The first challenge is to sustain development. Microphilanthropy is based on individual efforts, and volunteers often lose motivation or interest, which can quickly take away from the overall effectiveness of the effort. Microphilanthropy programs usually do not last long without professional organizations and operations. When microphilanthropy programs have been successful for a while, they should be taken over by professional institutes and personnel to propel the effort forward.

The second challenge is the regulation of microphilanthropy efforts. Most organizers of microphilanthropy programs will publicize donation amounts and details to attract the support of more netizens. But when microphilanthropy projects reach a certain scale, problems often arise with the transparency and appropriateness of the use of funds. The organizers of microphilanthropy programs should work to professionalize and standardize efforts to publicize and make transparent all efforts. Government officials should consider providing guidance in these areas by managing regulations or other parts of the process.

The third challenge for microphilanthropy is qualifying to collect public donations. By law in China, only formal charitable foundations and organizations can collect donations from the public, not individuals or informal institutes. If individuals or informal groups do collect donations, those donations are not protected or regulated by the laws that normally guide the donation process. Until they become a collaborative effort with formal charity organizations, most microphilanthropy efforts are not regulated by law.

With the growing and new potential problems presented by microphilanthropy, the government should take responsibility for inspecting and administering the qualifications for accepting donations, the process of collecting donations, and the utilization of funds, thereby legalizing and standardizing the process for all nongovernmental charities. Regardless, once microphilanthropy reaches a certain scale, the organizers should set clear guidelines for their finances and establish a system of program management. If possible, individuals involved in microphilanthropy should cooperate with formal charity organizations or set up formal corporate organizations to develop into an official donation program.

The Great Challenge Faced by NGOs in China

The Credibility of Public Charity Organizations

Credibility has been the major problem afflicting the nonprofit sector over the years. In the Chinese Nonprofit Sector Blue Book report in 2010, credibility was listed as the first of the three most prominent problems facing Chinese NGOs.

In 2011, several incidents contributed to a historic credibility crisis for the nonprofit sector: the Meimei Guo incident, which affected the

Red Cross; the Meimei Lu incident, which involved the China Youth Development Foundation's China-Africa Project Hope; and the Soong Ching Ling Foundation's real estate incident. Due to these incidents and the resultant public scrutiny, credibility became the lifeblood of a successful NGO.

In June 2011, a beautiful young woman in her twenties named Meimei Guo showed off her luxurious lifestyle on Sina Weibo. Her ID revealed that she was a manager for the China Red Cross Association. This attracted suspicion and irritated many people. The China Red Cross Association, a first-class organization with a centralized fiscal budget, is the largest humanitarian aid agency in China and enjoys the full financial support of the government and its employees, who are treated as civil servants as a pseudoadministrative institute. The China Red Cross Association is the only NGO that has had special laws and legal rights created directly for it. However, this highly influential and special public charity organization encountered the most serious credibility crisis in its history because of a short Weibo post from one young woman in the summer of 2011.

At the end of 2011, the Red Cross Society of China (RCSC) published an investigative report of what it called the "Meimei Guo incident." The report stated that Meimei Guo's wealth had nothing to do with the Red Cross, but there were indeed serious problems with the administration of the organization's finances. Several basic principles of charity organizations were being violated. The organization was found to have an incomplete management system for its finances, contracts, and projects; chaotic internal management; and suspiciously beneficial relationships with companies that collaborated with the organization on donation efforts. The RCSC decided to rescind the operational rights of the commercial branch of China Red Cross. The reason for the problems of the commercial branch was that the RCSC had a poor inspection and administration system in place to provide appropriate protection for the brand. The RCSC promised that they would strengthen the transparency, internal professional guidance, and operational and financial inspection system for local Red Cross organizations.

Looking back at the course of the Meimei Guo incident over the latter half of 2011, the most important question is not whether there is any relation between Meimei Guo and the Red Cross Society, but what to do about the transparency and operations of public charity organizations in general. The social dissatisfaction resulting from the Meimei Guo event has mainly revolved around the lack of transparency and operational procedures and concern that donations were being used for financial profit.

In the past, the lack of regulations for transparency meant that donors did not know if their donations were being used appropriately and effectively. When information about the Meimei Guo incident spread everywhere, the public became dissatisfied with the monopoly status of official charity organizations. People became concerned about their donations and began to suspect and reflect on the activities of public charity organizations. Consequently, public opinion not only propelled the reform of the Red Cross but also pushed for a major change and improvement of China's public charity organizations.

The pressure from public opinion caused by the Meimei Guo incident had a big impact on public charity organizations, severely shaking the monopoly status of official charity organizations and the lack of transparency. As a result, both official and unofficial public charity organizations realized that transparency and trust were important foundations of their survival and development. To some degree, the credibility crisis in 2011 sped up the transformation and regulatory reform of the transparency of public charity organizations.

Profit through Donation Fraud

The accumulation of wealth through disingenuous means has been around the nonprofit sector for a long time, but not until 2010 (and especially 2011) did this issue receive widespread attention from society. Three kinds of nonprofit organizations have been involved in this practice. The first type is legal, formally registered NGOs. Some examples include the China Economic Press Association, the Chinese Patriotic Engineering Federation, and the China News Culture Promotion Association. The second type is unregistered NGOs operating as registered NGOs. A typical example is the National High-Tech Association, which never registered with the Ministry of Civil Affairs. The group falsified forms, set up an illegal organization, and launched a series of activities to accumulate wealth by illegal means. The third type is "fake" NGOs, which register abroad and blur the line between NGO and commercial activity. For example, the Chinese Civil Entrepreneurs Association, registered in Hong Kong, swindled a great deal of money through bogus fund-raising causes and is in essence a branch of China's Harmonious Culture Group Limited. Fake NGOs have a few identifying characteristics. First, the brand name is usually misleading. They will often use a name from an existing Chinese organization and add the word *World*, *China*, or *International* to cause confusion. Second, they use the same staff hierarchy and operational style of the organization they are shadowing, except that their fund-raising efforts are really either partially or completely for commercial gain. Third, they register abroad to take advantage of a loophole in China's inspection regulations.

Although these three kinds of NGOs are not the same at first glance, they have one thing in common: obtaining unfair profits in the name of charity. These organizations primarily use two kinds of activities to generate profits. First, they often charge fees to individuals, companies, and organizations to get involved in their activities, such as conferences, forums, competitions, and so forth. Second, fraudulent NGOs profit by establishing branch organizations or selling associate positions. In addition to the two kinds of illegal profit methods discussed above, NGOs have several other ways in which they seek fraudulent commercial gain.

Illegal profit methods are relatively easy to uncover, but some fake NGOs are hard to recognize because they are very good at concealing their illegal activities and inspections aren't able to uncover enough information to officially classify them as fraudulent. A good example of this is the World Outstanding Chinese Businessmen Association. The association used the legal status and reputation of government offices, official agencies, and other well-known agencies and then, through media blitzes, legitimized its activities with the public. The association set up conferences, forums, and activities (e.g., the Ministerial Table Tennis and Fellowship Activity) at high-profile venues, such as the Beijing Conference Center, with famous presenters (e.g., Xiaoli Wu). The goal was to attract and make connections with influential political and business elites and social celebrities. The group's leaders would then invite these individuals to act as senior advisors, consultants, and vice presidents of the association to give it further legitimacy with the public. In cooperation with nationally renowned foundations, the association also launched public charity programs, such as Project Hope's humanitarian work in Africa. Altogether, the business status, the influential connections, and the high-profile events made the World Outstanding Chinese Businessmen Association a great "success."

In short, the World Outstanding Chinese Businessmen Association is an advanced multilevel marketing organization in need of further investigation. According to media reports, it might not seem clear that the association has committed a crime; however, its leaders took advantage of an environment with weak inspections to deceive the public by mixing commercial and charity behaviors. On its face, the association provides a service to politicians and businesspersons by holding conferences and forums that allow them to network. Additionally, it can be inferred that some legally registered NGOs did not function well as communication platforms. However, in addition to the benefits mentioned above, the association's connections with influential people give it yet another advantage: when the public began to suspect the organization's true intentions, it was able to hold a high-profile press conference to deny all accusations and state its intention to sue for defamation.

Management Standards and Service Ability

Relative to the widespread reports of the nonprofit sector's illegal activity and credibility, the ability of nonprofit organizations to manage their programs and provide professional services did not receive much attention from the media or the public. But the latter issues raise deeper questions about whether the nonprofit sector can grow healthily in China.

Ultimately, poor credibility and illegal behavior boil down to corrupt or nonstandard management structures and a lack of transparency with the public. To solve these problems, the nonprofit sector needs to have standardized management structures, provide more efficient services, be open to stronger inspections, and in general be more transparent in their activities. For now, these shortcomings cause public suspicion and criticism.

Similar to government-affiliated charity organizations, which tend to have a good reputation in society, some NGOs have gained positive reputations through their sound management system. The Environmental Entrepreneurs Foundation has a three-level management system that includes supervisors, an association committee, and a board of directors. By basing its operations in a strong, well-organized, standards-based management structure, the foundation has become the most popular and influential public environmental-protection charity organization.

At the end of 2010, after successfully registering to become a public charity foundation in Shenzhen, the One Foundation announced that its fees would comprise less than 5 percent of its budget and that the organization would be completely transparent to the public. The foundation's board of directors is accessible to donors and the media, and none of the directors receive any stipend from the foundation, not even travel compensation. The One Foundation uses very standard administrative methods and, as a result, has been improving its donations and influence within society. Additionally, in May 2011 the Heren Charity Foundation was founded in Beijing by Dewang Cao, a famous entrepreneur. It was the first foundation in China to be formed through a stock donation and is the public charity foundation with the most assets. The Heren Charity Foundation created its funding structure and management model, and four months after its establishment, the organization's founder retreated completely, resulting in the demise of the organization. However, while it was in existence, the Heren Charity Foundation set up benchmarks and models for stock donations and managerial structure and procedures, which will move the development of charity organizations forward in China.

It can be expected that, in an era of ever-increasing media attention and transparency, the development of all NGOs, especially public charity organizations, depends on creating and utilizing standardized management practices. The managerial practices and funding of NGOs have become two of the biggest transparency issues in China's nonprofit sector.

Part II

Environment and Challenges of China's Nonprofit Sector

5

Nonprofit Legislation in China

*Peifeng Liu**

In this new era of civil rights, legislative action is the most important means to meet citizens' needs and demands. Developing legislation to protect people's rights has become a universal ideal in China, but rights cannot be protected by law unless they are defined in the law. Legislation is not only used to affirm state power but also to form and regulate social relations according to the shared values of a people—particularly that of order. Order is imposed by the law, is influenced by the established social system, and ultimately responds to the demands of both. There-fore, both current legislation and cultural history are important factors in shaping civil rights and political order. The aim of this chapter is to analyze nonprofit legislation in China as part of a broader examination of the development of civil rights in the country.

Introduction

Nonprofit legislation in China has entered a new stage since the implementation of the Reform Era policies of 1978. Current legislation has fallen in step with historical trends. In the context of the sudden emergence, systematic reforms, and bourgeoning success of nonprof-its, government legislation has at times actively regulated and at other times passively reacted to them. Modern nonprofit legislation was born

* Translated by Juliann H. Vikse, Research Fellow, Huamin Research Center, School of Social Work, Rutgers University.

out of various crises in the 1970s. These crises, which included waning government legitimacy, failure of centralized rule, and lack of democracy, nearly led to China's collapse after ten years of upheaval during the Cultural Revolution. During that time, the Chinese people, to their benefit, realized the extent of corruption and the weaknesses of their political and economic systems. A highly centralized political and economic system would not lead to long-term social stability; instead, such a system would lead to social unrest and a paralyzed system of governance. Lingering civil strife and economic decline made social rehabilitation impossible and left the new government facing a crisis of legitimacy. These crises sparked the rise of civil society. The diverse nonprofit sector that emerged managed to rebuild social legitimacy, fill the gaps left by an ineffectual and corrupt central government, and encourage democratic participation. The emergence of nonprofits in the wake of these crises was, in many respects, a natural process. After the implementation of the Reform Era policies, people were able to manage their own resources independently, in a freer society. Thus, the development of a civil society to meet increasingly diverse needs should have been foreseeable. Many grassroots volunteer organizations were also established at this time.

The emergence of modern nonprofits occurred in response to both induced and spontaneous social changes. In some respects, the government effected change by taking a leading role in the evolution of nonprofits. Additionally, social vicissitudes contributed diversity and vitality to the sector. China's long history of statist rule and its efforts to develop a modern Chinese cultural identity have compelled the government to play a strong role in regulating the development of nonprofits. Vigorous government reforms have, at the same time, provided nonprofits a degree of autonomy and thereby influenced their development. Most nonprofits in China are corporatist (i.e., government-led) organizations. In the short term, Chinese nonprofits will not necessarily undermine government power but will more likely either contribute to or limit government power. Nonprofits exist at the secondary level of government, an intermediate sphere between government control and independence. Consequently, nonprofit reform can only take place within a framework of broader government reform. Social changes have given rise to new social problems and issues that have, in turn, determined nonprofits' path to reform. They have also determined the acceptance and normalization of democratic reforms. Only the rise of civil society and the subsequent emergence of political order and social participation can resolve the crises of waning legitimacy, the failure of centralized rule, and a lack of democracy. Only through this emerging civil society, can China establish a modern, integrated state and protect its people's civil rights.

Both induced and spontaneous social changes have influenced Chinese nonprofits to develop complex management models that most foreign nonprofits have never experienced. Government-affiliated nonprofits had to develop enough independence to become irreplaceable entities in the realm of public management. At the same time, private nonprofits needed to learn how to handle their position between the state and civil spheres. The most important aspect of nonprofit reform was to avoid being subsumed by the government. For grassroots organizations, which are a response to the lack of means for citizens to contribute to social and political endeavors, the most important goal was to achieve organized civil participation in social-reform movements. Only in this way could developing nonprofits positively influence interactions between the nation and civil society and effect social change and integration. In this way, nonprofit legislation established an important balance between control and freedom.

A General Review of Current Nonprofit Legislation

The legislation that currently pertains to nonprofits in China was formulated in the context of the rise of China's Socialist regime and the Reform Era policies of 1978. Nonprofits have been managed unsustainably; in some cases, strict supervision has led to organizational collapse, whereas insufficient supervision has led to chaos. This situation is primarily a result of three circumstances. First, China's long tradition of nationalism has created an uninhabitable environment for nonprofits. Second, individuals' social participation and free expression are less feasible in a poorly organized system. Finally, the rigid administrative system leaves no space for conflict management, particularly at the level of administrative management. The government's recent crisis of legitimacy and low levels of public trust have left it no choice but to impose stricter means of social control. Compared to China's increasingly market-based economy, its social-governance system continues to embody strong characteristics of a socialist planned economy.

The centralization of political power and China's concurrent societal transformations have led the government to enact statist legislation pertaining to nonprofits, while at the same time approaching nonprofit management with a relatively hands-off approach. Article 5 of the People's Republic of China (PRC) Constitution, issued in 1982, reads, "Citizens of the People's Republic of China enjoy freedom of speech, of the press, of assembly, of association, of procession, and of demonstration." Article 5 reads, "All state bodies, the armed forces, all political parties and public organizations, and all enterprises and nonprofits must abide by the Constitution and the law. No organization or individual is above the Constitution or the law." These laws ensure the legal status of nonprofits and define principles by which they can operate. In the general principles of the Civil Law of the PRC, issued in 1986, nonprofit groups are considered individuals under the law. This law established foundational procedures for establishing, registering, modifying, and disbanding nonprofits. Against the backdrop of an increasingly robust system of laws, nonprofit legislation became an important part of the agenda. In the late 1980s, a nonprofit law was drafted and civil administration departments exerted significant effort to implement it. However, for many reasons, the law was never formally adopted into the legislative agenda.

To offset the problems in the registration and oversight processes, the State Council commissioned the Ministry of Civil Affairs to draft a bill to regulate the registration of nonprofits. This piece of legislation went into effect on October 25, 1989, and was amended by the State Council in 1998. For some nonprofits, the State Council issued additional regulations. These included the Provisional Regulations for the Registration and Administration of Private Nonprofits (1998), the Regulations for Foundation Management (1988), and the Interim Provisions for the Administration of Foreign Chambers of Commerce in China (1989). To bolster these regulations, the Ministry of Civil Affairs and other government departments issued additional guidelines that influenced the management and governance of nonprofits. On February 26, 1998, the Communist Party of China (CPC) and the Ministry of Civil Affairs jointly released a circular pertaining to the establishment of CPC branches within nonprofit organizations. This document described its goal as promoting the healthy development of nonprofits by expanding the role of CPC organizations. It dictated that any permanent office whose professional staff included three or more CPC members must establish a grassroots party organization. This group would be responsible for fully integrating the party constitution and its objectives, supervising the nonprofit organization's leadership, and carrying out CPC policies. In 1994, the State Council General Office had issued a circular that banned state ministry officials from taking leadership roles in nonprofit organizations, and in 1998, the CPC General Office and the State Council General Office jointly issued a circular banning CPC members from holding such positions. In 2004, the government had also issued a document regarding funding regulations for civic organizations. Aside from minor adjustments, these regulations represented essentially no ideological shift from the 1950s.

Centralized Registration and Dual Oversight

China's centralized registration system requires nonprofit organizations to register with the Ministry of Civil Affairs and report to the local office of the government department related to their service area. In this system, nonprofits should enjoy the civil rights—and assume the responsibilities—of individual citizens. National organizations are registered by the Ministry of Civil Affairs and are governed by relevant departments within the State Council, whereas local organizations are registered by either the national or local Ministry of Civil Affairs, depending on their jurisdiction. Nonprofits that operate in multiple jurisdictions are registered by the lowest level department that is common to all its jurisdictions. The State Council and local government then authorize the oversight department that corresponds to the nonprofit's mission to oversee the nonprofit's operations.

Each registration department has the following responsibilities: (a) perform all registrations and keep information filed for every registered, modified, or disbanded organization; (b) assess each registered organization annually; and (c) handle any breach of the law and administer penalties. Alternatively, the oversight departments are responsible for (a) performing all registrations and keeping information filed for every application, registration, modification, and assessment; (b) ensuring that organizations comply with national laws and regulations and other applicable rules; (c) conducting intake assessments for new organizations; (d) supporting the institutions responsible for registration and any other entities involved in handling any breach of the law or regulations; and (e) cooperating with other institutions to guide organizations through the process of liquidation.

Once nonprofits register with the government, they acquire legal status. All nonprofits are deemed equal in terms of both status and rights; no nonprofit may subordinate or control another. This system of nonprofit oversight is characteristically Chinese, as it conforms to the planned economy. Although it is not perfect, this system is considered the best possible means for the government to oversee nonprofit operations.

The current systems of centralized registration and dual oversight create and maintain regional inequalities. The dual-oversight system also reflects the extent of state control in the nonprofit sector. Although the state encourages the development of nonprofits, it still attempts to control them and ensure that they do not overstep state-defined boundaries. In this way, these two systems conform to the patterns of the Socialist planned economy. In some ways, these types of oversight systems are appropriate in the Chinese context. Given China's insufficient administrative capacity, coupled with its vast territory, diverse cultures, and disparate levels of economic development across provinces, oversight at multiple levels of government is perhaps the most viable strategy. It is very important that dual oversight not be misinterpreted as doubly restrictive, as that would most likely prevent nonprofits from registering at all. Under such a restrictive system, competition among nonprofits would be limited, which in turn would obstruct the integration of a marketplace of free public goods, create divisions among organizations, and undermine the efficiency of resource allocation. At this early stage in their development, nonprofits are often plagued by disorganization and ineffective oversight. In light of these problems, registration and oversight by specialized departments may provide temporary sources of support. The Civil Affairs Department does not have the capacity to handle registration and oversight for all nonprofits; moreover, oversight by specialized departments allows nonprofits to serve as intermediaries. It is essential to employ the proper means to establish and sustain this system. As the present situation reveals, oversight has been too restrictive, and integration too rigid. Many regulatory agencies are operating far beyond their capacity.

Strict Registration Requirements, Lenient Oversight

Nonprofits must fulfill very strict qualifications to attain an official registration permit. Nonprofits that operate without this official permit do so illegally; their programs are not only unprotected by the law but are also at risk of being banned. China's registration process is more rigorous than in many other countries, where formal registration often only requires an initial, thorough assessment. In China, however, both the registration department and oversight department rigorously assess newly formed nonprofits. They impose strict measures to limit the development of the nonprofits in question. The dual-oversight system thereby acts as a means for the government to more tightly control civil society by eliminating antigovernment organizations. This results in red tape, wasted time, and potentially conflicting standards of assessment and censorship by the different authorities involved. The high costs of application and assessment are also burdensome for both the government and the nonprofits concerned. Another problem is that, at times, no relevant oversight departments are able to perform initial assessments, which leaves some nonprofits no choice but to operate illegally. When government authorities are unavailable or unwilling to perform assessments, or when institutions refuse to take responsibility for overseeing specific associations (to avoid controversy), access to legal registration is cut off.

In contrast with these tightly controlled registration processes, a more lenient approach is adopted to control nonpolitical, more loosely organized nonprofit groups, such as cultural and religious organizations, book clubs, and discussion forums. Although these groups do not technically qualify for legal registration, the government often treats them permissively and allows them to operate. This inconsistent application of the law often limits nonprofit programs to the short term. When circumstances become less politically stable, these groups are sometimes penalized or even outlawed. Registration standards are unjustifiably high, but there is little emphasis on overseeing their operations and implementation. Nonprofits, as members of China's civil society, must be transparent and develop solid internal management to grow; however, few regulations address these issues. Government officials place tremendous ideological importance on position; their perspective is that an individual or group's identity determines its behavior. As a result, most government efforts are focused on strictly regulating the registration process.

The government's strict registration requirements were intended to be a guide for the proper management of nonprofits. In reality, however, the inconsistent practices raise questions about the relationship between nonprofits and the government. Is the government capable of tightly regulating nonprofits, and if so, is such strict control necessary? How can we frame and understand the relationship between the government and nonprofits? Modern bureaucratic systems in China have allowed the government to control civil society. However, the complexities of China's pluralistic society are beginning to exceed the complexity of its governing structures. Given the state's limited resources and management capacity and the liberalization of Chinese society, achieving a totalitarian system will be impossible. Nonprofits were established to meet the needs of the people; the diverse and pluralistic nature of these organizations reflects the diverse needs of society. When nonprofits are limited, human development is subsequently limited. Both the government and nonprofits are essentially social organizations, and both are absolutely necessary to achieve a highly organized, modern society. The government, from its position of authority, provides public services through enforcement, whereas nonprofits offer public services through volunteerism. They are complementary to some extent; nonprofits are able to address the problems that the government has neglected or failed to address. With respect to social management, both governmental and nongovernmental efforts are necessary. The government maintains social stability and prosperity by force, whereas nongovernmental actors play an important role in achieving social order by shaping public opinion. A complex modern society requires the integration of efforts from both civil society and individuals.

Limiting Competition and Constraining Development

Oversight structures tend to limit competition and restrain development. This is certainly true of the Chinese system, and is reflected in existing regulations. China's *Regulations for Registration and Management of Social Associations* (1998) is a 5,000-word document that contains the term *shall* in thirty-four instances; *must* in eighteen instances; and *cannot* in eight instances while barely mentioning strategies for development. Although this document is apparently aimed at protecting the civil and legal rights of nonprofits and improving the registration processes, in reality its only detailed content pertains to limitations and prohibitions. Notably, it lacks information about protection and development. Article 13 explains that multiple nonprofits with similar objectives and programs cannot exist in the same geographical area and that the registration of any subsequent nonprofits in a given location must be rejected. Local authorities are also granted the power to "unregister" existing nonprofits or merge related nonprofits. This style of management assumes that competition is merely a cause of social instability. Additionally, an influx of nonprofits is considered undesirable, as it would potentially challenge the government's control over society. From the government's perspective, fierce competition among nonprofits could lead them to pursue resources at any cost, and in turn, deviate from their prescribed path. Article 19 describes regulations surrounding branches of large nonprofits, explaining that nonprofits do not have full legal status and that they, as well as nonprofit work units, are prohibited from establishing any additional branches. Nonprofits may only register in one location, and their operations are strictly limited to their registered location. Registration authorities oppose the establishment of multiple branches because they believe it would make the elimination of "unnecessary" nonprofits impossible. Moreover, authorities fear that, as nonprofits spread throughout provinces, counties, and towns and as new nonprofits follow suit, they will become uncontrollable.

These restrictive laws and regulations are technically effective; after all, the best way to solve a problem is to nip it in the bud. However, these regulations greatly inhibit the impact that nonprofits can make on society. Limited competition inevitably leads to abuses of power, and restricting the expansion of an organization undermines its potential effectiveness. In determining the legal status of a nonprofit, the Ministry of Civil Affairs requires that a nonprofit "meet the needs of society." This phrase is meaningless because the needs and the parties that determine those needs are not clearly defined. In theory, the government is a projection and representation of its people, so its standards and regulations should promote the needs of society. In reality, this is far from the truth—standards and regulations are designed to maintain government control over the services that nonprofits provide.

Inadequate Legislation and Outdated Ideas

In general, inadequate laws and outdated ideas are the key problems facing nonprofit legislation. Attributing problems only to inadequate laws and regulations would be an oversimplification. Legislation must be carried out in the context of broader political reforms, which shift the distribution of power and establish new systems of public management. Given the connection between power and vested interests, nonprofit legislation represents the reorganization and rearrangement of social benefits. Reforming management systems through legislation is essential to establishing a lawfully fair and open society.

When the government does not fully recognize social pluralism and lacks a sufficient understanding of and tolerance toward social organizations, the voice of civil society is silenced and its objectives are left unrealized. Currently, nonprofit legislation has three primary objectives: to protect citizens' right to free association, to control nonprofits' illegal activities and programs, and to ban and eliminate illegal nonprofits. As it stands now, the system has several problems, including overly restrictive control, a low level of legislative development, and ineffective channels for judicial solutions. The right to free association is a basic civil right that defines the relationship between the state and its citizens, as well as the relationship between state power and individual rights. The National People's Congress and its Standing Committee are responsible for producing legislation, which has the potential to guide and control this complicated web of relationships among stakeholders. In this way, legislation serves as a means to directly impose the government's will on the people. The guiding principles behind current legislation are focused on maintaining social stability, limiting the development of nonprofits, and minimizing competition among them. This is owed to authorities placing great importance on their personal interests and convenience. In addition to simply expanding its scope and reach, this legislation will have to explicate civil rights as they pertain to associations. The most important of these are the rights to independently establish nonprofits and independently manage their internal affairs. Currently, these rights do not exist. Strict registration requirements have prevented many non-profits from being established. Those that do obtain registration must deal with burdensome interventions and controlling measures imposed by administrative authorities. For instance, evaluation procedures and complex reporting systems limit the independence and social integration of nonprofits.

The result has been the widespread operation of illegal, unregistered nonprofits, and this has further complicated the legislative process. In its 2000 publication, *Interim Procedures for Unlawful Civil Organizations*, the Ministry of Civil Affairs classified illegal organizations into three cat-egories: registered nonprofits that prepare programs or activities without first obtaining approval, unregistered nonprofits that operate illegally, and nonprofits whose registration has been revoked but continue to imple-ment programs. Regardless of whether the aforementioned, unregistered organizations serve public needs, they are considered illegal. It is unrea-sonable to base the legitimacy of a nonprofit on its identity rather than its impact; certainly, many registered organizations conduct their affairs without scruple. Although the Chinese registration process simplifies the task of monitoring nonprofits, it also creates barriers to starting up an or-ganization. In contrast, other countries have established simple, clear-cut codes to manage illegal organizations and have integrated those codes into criminal law. Government monitoring, to some extent, can also translate to social oversight by identifying violent and criminal organizations. The broad definition of "illegal organization" conflicts with the legitimacy of nonprofits and affects the legitimacy of the government and the public's recognition of government efficacy.

Another gap in legislation pertaining to nonprofits is the lack of legal recourse for the nonprofits themselves. Regulations do not specifically ad-dress any legal recourse for nonprofits in response to rejected applications for registration or sanctions. In the 1989 revision of the national Regula-tions for Registering Civil Associations, applicants may no longer appeal to higher civil affairs departments when their applications are rejected. Perhaps, the promulgation of the "administrative reconsideration" law will alleviate the problem. This law plans to make it possible for applicants and nonprofits to safeguard their rights by applying for administrative reconsideration and participating in administrative proceedings. These opportunities, however, will likely be limited within the current legal environment.

Additionally, current regulations surrounding nonprofit management are too rigidly principled and lack maneuverability. Legislators will need to develop provisions for intrabranch management, membership, performance reporting, and information disclosure, each of which is conducive to the independent management and oversight of nonprofits. To survive in a pluralistic society, nonprofits must demonstrate self-discipline and strong supervision. They must also be subject to regulations and standards. It is also very important to establish an effective performance-evaluation system. In turn, ineffective associations can be weeded out, which can prevent the waste of social resources.

Finally, nonprofits serve as intermediaries between the nation and society. For this reason, it is crucial for them to be governed by a fair and comprehensive set of laws. Currently China does not have a tax code specifically for nonprofits, and legislation relating to finances and government purchasing do not account for the recent development of civil society. In developed countries, the situation is quite different: over 50 percent of nonprofit funding comes from service fees and government support. In China, however, there is a great deal of skepticism surrounding the public services offered by nonprofits. As nonprofits have expanded and developed, there have been a number of public scandals involving abuses of power. For instance, price-fixing in the nonprofit sector is antithetical to the interests of the public and requires government intervention in the form of antitrust law. Continually amending the regulations pertaining to nonprofits is simply a delay tactic; instead, the legal environment must be fundamentally adapted.

Despite the significance of these issues, the core problem facing China's nonprofit legislation is its lack of guiding principles. First, current laws that regulate social management only focus on short-term social stability, rather than long-term peace and security. These regulations lack foresight and generally disregard the recent developments of civil society in this era of pluralism. This has led to misunderstandings about the status and role of nonprofits. Traditionally in China, nonprofits have been regarded as tools used by the government to implement policies and a bridge spanning public opinion and the CPC. It is often forgotten that nonprofits can be government affiliated, market focused, or nongovernmental and that each distinct form is a necessary mechanism for social integration and stable governance. These different types of nonprofits satisfy the range of needs at different levels of society. In most countries, with the exception of totalitarian states, the interplay of these different types of nonprofits is important, despite their distinct roles in social development, diverse cultures, and varying levels of autonomy. The balance among the market, government, and nongovernmental mechanisms is what guarantees prolonged social stability and peace.

Second, China's history of administrative management has been replaced by an unstable political system that features low administrative standards. Long-term social oppression and limited autonomy initially led to the broad failure of social management. Subsequently, the government became diffident about the capacity of civil society to manage itself. In the name of managing and educating nonprofits, the government imposed burdensome, controlling standards of oversight. In the absence of clear distinctions between political responsibility and administrative responsibility, short-term "stability" and financial indicators have become the only criteria for evaluating government programs. It is sometimes assumed that ignoring a problem may produce the desired outcome in the short run but will backfire in the long run. Similarly, based only on financial indicators, both the central and local governments support and foster the development of economic nonprofits, including trade associations, chambers of commerce, and agricultural collectives. This is the result of systemic change—the improvement of government functioning and the implementation of economic considerations. Many nonprofits perform unique functions. For instance, social service associations and fraternal associations, which certainly meet important social needs, also have the potential to act as agents of change for financial organizations, helping to expand their capability and reach.

Alexis de Tocqueville once suggested that civil associations contribute to the development of political associations, which in turn promote further development among civil associations. Given the diversity and interconnectedness of civil associations, their recent challenges will not necessarily lead to greater instability and conflict. The government maintains its monopoly on political mobilization by imposing restrictions on civil organizations and limiting their social integration. On the other hand, the government must face the public and take responsibility for social conflict. This will, in turn, affect the public's conception of the government's legitimacy and social stability. Sociologist Georg Simmel pointed out that significant conflict could lead to the elimination of divisive elements in society and help to reunify the people. Conflicts could also stabilize opposition and thereby act as balancing forces. Loosely structured nonprofit groups are somewhat tolerant of conflict and can actually serve to clarify core values and minimize the risk of a societal schism. Interdependence and challenges among opposing groups help to stabilize society and prevent irreparable divisions. The government must take advantage of the current, stable social environment to learn how to cope with crises and govern civil society effectively. As nonprofits have developed and expanded in recent years, the government's ability to manage and regulate them has likewise expanded; however, the government's concerns about nonprofits are seemingly unwarranted.

As for the legal basis for nonprofits, the civil right of association enables people to meet their own needs through locally established organizations and provides opportunities for political involvement. Without nonprofits acting as protective barriers, individuals would not be able to withstand or confront government abuses or the harshest realities of the market system. The government is responsible for safeguarding the civil right to association and encouraging the development of nonprofits. In recent years, however, the government has made minimal efforts to implement its stated policies. In fact, it has resisted the establishment of nonprofits that serve vulnerable populations, including migrant workers and the unemployed, and has restricted the creation of fraternal associations. These vulnerable populations urgently need nonprofit organizations and associations to intervene on behalf of their rights.

Conclusion

A mature society is one that fosters tolerance and competition rather than oppression and monopoly. There are many ways, ranging in effectiveness, to deal with the existing challenges that face nonprofits in China. Some have adopted a passive attitude, choosing to ignore, deny, or downplay the importance of these issues. Others have suggested measures to wholly eliminate the problems, have attempted to relieve social pressure by overstating the problems and their consequences, have addressed the existing problems by proposing technological solutions, or have deceived themselves and others by pointing to problems that do not exist. In solving these problems, the most important steps will be to squarely face the issues and reasonably assess their gravity. In most cases, fear and hopelessness stem from misunderstanding. For this reason, problems can only be solved through direct confrontation. In a dynamic, pluralistic society, problem solving requires the implementation of both political wisdom and skilled governance.

According to this analysis, nonprofit legislation in China must address a number of important issues. These include political issues, such as the distribution of political power and delegation of authority, and technical issues, such as the establishment of effective mechanisms of governance and supervision. Political and social participation are also involved. Currently, social resources are available only to elites; this has become a serious problem. In such a polarized society and amid mounting conflicts, social crises are more likely than ever before. However, the systematization of social forces may be an effective means to address these conflicts. Systematization makes it possible to promote political reform through transitions in governance, even within an unchanged political system. This approach will also help to stabilize society and the political system over the long term. In other words, society is not only the source of problems but is also the solution to those problems. Regarding outcomes, an expanded civil sector has developed new ways to address social problems. This has set the stage for a multifaceted model of social governance. Nonprofit legislation relates to the civil right of association and to the rational arrangement of various social forces. Given that the Chinese Constitution entitles all people to freedom and to respectful and equal treatment under the law, the problem of governance is essentially a problem of how to govern. This problem can be solved by the rule of law. Although public management cannot take the place of public participation, it can be used as a means to promote pluralism, transparency, and eventually democracy. Public management also emphasizes the importance of public power and individual survival. Currently, the Chinese government does not sufficiently recognize civil society's pluralism, autonomy, and early development or the checks and balances that exist within society. In this regard, the right to association is obstructed by a lack of recognition and institutional barriers. It is, however, possible to resolve the right to association and strong social management through sound practices and institutions. As demonstrated earlier, a basic feature of social management is the coexistence of rigid control and leniency.

Currently, the government does not fully comprehend the level of societal pluralism or its impact on civil society in China. This lack of understanding, magnified by institutional barriers, inherently limits the people's right to association. There are ways to address these problems though. One possibility is to limit the government's role in oversight by requiring organizations to submit detailed strategic plans in lieu of registration. This would increase the number of organizations that are granted permits, which would thereby encourage organizations to form through legal means. Organizations would be held accountable to their initial plans, but the government would play a smaller role in regulation. Through this process, previously rejected organizations would have a second chance to gain legal status. It would also make it easier for the government to monitor nonprofits and would allow nonprofits to operate independently. Local governments are currently piloting this system, and many scholars have proposed using it to expand access to nonprofit registration. Second, the system of dual oversight, which is often criticized, could be reformed. The current system prevents some organizations from registering simply because they cannot locate an appropriate sponsoring department. In cases of nonprofits that are approved, these sponsoring departments interfere with their internal management, which restricts their development. In view of China's relatively poor management capacity, the system of dual oversight should be replaced by a centralized, integrated system. However, neither dual oversight nor a centralized system can fully address the nation's management capacity challenges. For instance, a centralized system would not be able to properly oversee all nonprofits. Because of this, the inevitable path would be toward the systematic management of nonprofits. Obligations to disclose information should be placed on political nonprofits, particularly those nongovernmental organizations that deal with foreign affairs, possess large funding bases, and raise funds publically. Regarding other nongovernmental organizations, the government should grant them some degree of autonomy as a means to promote their development. At the same time, the government should support regulatory organizations or individuals who can provide intermediary oversight. Certainly, the government must establish effective means to report offenses. Such technical approaches will help the country achieve a balance between nonprofit development and government administration and state power and state capacity.

As nonprofits mature, they will inevitably participate in the development of nonprofit legislation. In fact, there are two ways to deal with this: introduce competition or improve the quality of participation by instituting technical and procedural regulations. As civil society becomes more differentiated, the political system is becoming segmented, which obstructs competitive participation in the system. At present, it is important to systemically enhance competition. Political reforms since the 1980s have reflected strong efforts by the government to expand public participation and improve the quality of governance. These goals are reflected in the

Constitution and the party constitution. As nonprofits mature and develop and structural reforms expand, the conditions for further progress are becoming ripe. Differentiation is common among interest groups, and current participation problems can be solved by gradually and systematically introducing new organizations. In addition, appropriate decentralization of authority, along with policy decisions being delegated to lower levels of government, will improve the relationship between the government and the nonprofit sector. It will be more practical to introduce new systems and policies at the provincial level. Other approaches to achieving improved participation include consultation programs and making government affairs more transparent. Social participation is a matter of governance, a realm that has matured with respect to integrating nonprofits into the legislative process. The current priorities should be to craft policies on public funding, diversify social services, and provide the opportunity for nonprofits to participate in policymaking. Expanded participation of nonprofits, along with diversified methods of social governance, will not only improve social management but will also enable the government to focus more on its own affairs. Subsequently, the government can transform from an all-powerful force to a limited force; in time, its traditional, controlling structures will give way to new modes of service provision. Moreover, authoritarian governance will be replaced by good governance.

6

Private Nonprofit Organizations:
Their Characteristics and Value to Society

*Guosheng Deng**

In the 1990s the Johns Hopkins Comparative Nonprofit Sector Project organized a large-scale, systematic study of the nonprofit sector in thirteen countries. Their team included 150 researchers and more than three hundred advisors from around the world. Among the project's major findings were that, on average, jobs created by the nonprofit sector accounted for approximately 4.8 percent of the global job market, and that expenditures by the nonprofit sector constituted approximately 4.6 percent of total global gross domestic product (GDP). In developed countries, the nonprofit sector contributed an even higher percentage (Salamon 1999). In recent years, Chinese scholars have frequently cited these data to illustrate the contributions of the nonprofit sector to economies worldwide.

While we admire the effectiveness of the nonprofit sector abroad, it should be noted that there are many different types of nonprofit organizations (NPOs) within the sector. In China, the most important distinction is between membership and nonmembership NPOs. Membership NPOs are associations of individuals, including academic institutions and trade unions. Nonmembership NPOs are collections of property, including private schools, private hospitals, and social welfare agencies. The collections of property is an organization that has obtained ample, and

* Translated by Juliann H. Vikse, Research Fellow, Huamin Research Center, School of Social Work, Rutgers University.

sustainable, funding, whether by charitable donations or sponsorship. The contributions of nonmembership NPOs to employment and the economy far exceed those of membership NPOs. The contributions of the nonprofit sector in developed nations can often be credited to nonmembership organizations. For example, over 46 percent of nonprofit jobs fall within the health care subsector, followed by the higher education subsector at 21.3 percent. Most NPOs in both of these subsectors are nonmembership.

The Chinese counterparts to nonmembership NPOs are private nonprofits. However, until 1996, private nonprofits were not treated as NPOs and were not registered with the Department of Civil Affairs until 2000, when the DCA instituted a two-year review and registration process. While the public is generally familiar with charitable foundations and associations, many people lack a comprehensive understanding of private nonprofits. In turn, they tend to underestimate the potential of private nonprofits, and undervalue their social and economic contributions.

In 2003 our research team conducted a multistage cluster sampling of associations and private nonprofits throughout China. In the first stage we divided China's provinces into the categories east, middle, and west, and chose a northern and southern province from each category. The six resulting provinces from this sampling procedure were Liaoning, Guangdong, Shanxi, Jiangxi, Gansu, and Yunnan. In the second stage we divided the prefecture-level cities in each province into three categories, developed, median, and poor, according to the conditions of their social and economic development. We then chose a developed, median, and poor city in each province, which resulted in eighteen targeted cities. In the third stage we distributed questionnaires to registered associations and private nonprofits in each targeted city. We also included equal proportions of associations and private nonprofits at the provincial level in the six provinces. We handed out 3,954 questionnaires to private nonprofits, and 1,733 valid questionnaires were returned, resulting in a return rate of 43.8 percent.

Before 2003 the Department of Civil Affairs only recorded the amount of currently operating NPOs in each province and the amount of NPOs that ceased operating. After 2003 the department also counted the number of NPOs by category. According to the 2005 Statistical Yearbook of the Department of Civil Affairs, private education-related nonprofits comprised 51 percent of all NPOs, followed by private health care nonprofits (18 percent), private nonprofits relating to culture and sports (7.2 percent), labor (8.2 percent), civil affairs (7 percent), those serving as intermediaries (1 percent), law (0.45 percent), and other spheres

Table 6.1
Private Nonprofit Categories, as per Valid Questionnaires

Category	%
Culture and entertainment	7.74
Education and research	71.17
Health care	4.71
Social service	7.03
Environment and animal protection	0.49
Development	0.84
Advocacy	0.70
International cooperation and communication	0.35
Charity intermediary	0.63
Trade organizations	1.27
Others	5.06

(3.4 percent). Our research group adopted the classification standards of the Johns Hopkins Comparative Nonprofit Sector Project, which are quite different than the standards used by the Chinese Department of Civil Affairs; still, the sampling structure is representative of the population. Both classification systems are dominated by education. Table 6.1 shows the basic distributions using the Johns Hopkins classifications.

Private Nonprofit Organizations: An Introduction

According to the Interim Regulations for the Registration and Administration of Private Nonprofits, issued by China's State Council in October 1998, private NPOs are social organizations that provide nonprofit social services, which are established by enterprises, public institutions, associations, or individuals, using nonstate-owned assets. In 1999, the Department of Civil Affairs issued a document called Interim Measures for Registration of Private Nonprofits, which established additional regulations. These included requirements that (a) private nonprofits only possess assets that are consistent with their mission and (b) their nonstate-owned assets should comprise at least two-thirds of their total assets.

Statistics from the Department of Civil Affairs demonstrate that 4,508 NPOs had been registered by the end of 1999. After a two-year review and registration process beginning in 2000, there were 82,000 registered private NPOs in China. Thereafter, the number of private NPOs grew steadily each year, but at a decelerated pace. The total reached 146,000 by the end of 2005. In China, NPOs have now reached a crossroads in their development. These organizations are encountering systematic barriers, mainly due to limited funding and government policies that favor public institutions. If the government eventually does recognize the value of NPOs and encourages their development by implementing policies that support them, NPOs could experience another period of rapid growth. However, such growth will be unattainable if the government relaxes its regulations. If NPOs become prone to poor self-regulation, dishonesty, or providing inferior services, they will likewise inhibit their chances of success. Additionally, these behaviors would arouse public discontent and prompt the government to impose harsher regulations, potentially resembling those imposed on less formal nonprofit groups. In certain spheres, such as private education, some local governments have inspected and reorganized NPOs to a limited extent.

Regionally, the distribution of private NPOs and nonprofit groups is very uneven. The private nonprofits in Shandong Province comprise one quarter of the national total, whereas Tibet hosts only four private nonprofits. Figure 6.1 illustrates the relationship between each province's number of private NPOs and nonprofit groups, with a correlation coefficient of .67 ($p < .01$). This indicates that there are many NPOs in locations where there are also many nonprofit groups. This might be explained by the fact that the numbers of nonprofit groups and NPOs are both closely related to levels of social and economic development.

Statistical data (China Statistical Yearbook 2003; NGO Administration website, chinango.gov.cn) show that the correlation coefficient for the relationship between GDP and number of NPOs in each province reaches .74 ($p < .01$), whereas the correlation coefficient for the relationship between GDP and number of nonprofit groups in each province reaches .84 ($p < .01$). This demonstrates that more developed areas have more NPOs and nonprofit groups. The relationship between socioeconomic development and the number of formal NPOs is weaker than the relationship between socioeconomic development and the number of nonprofit groups. A potential explanation for this difference is that the number of registered NPOs in a given area depends largely on the attention that the government pays to them, the discretion that the local Nonprofit Administration Office has in its registration standards, and the extent to which sponsoring authorities (i.e., the government departments that support, guide, and supervise nonprofit business affairs) coordinate their efforts.

Figure 6.1
Distribution of Nonprofit Organizations and Nonprofit Groups in China

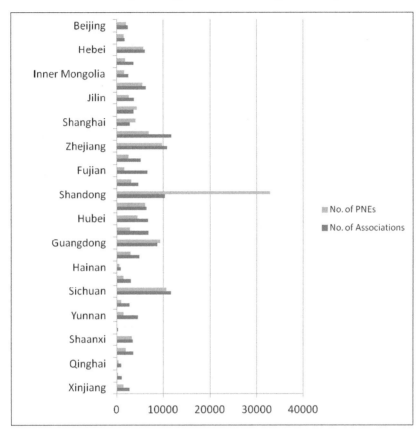

In short, local policies and individual behaviors greatly affect the number of registered nonprofits in each region.

Characteristics of Private Nonprofits in China

Since 1999, private nonprofits have begun to arouse interest within Chinese academic circles and have quickly become a popular research topic. Several practitioners and scholars have identified the roles and functions of private nonprofits from different perspectives. These researchers have pointed out the effects that private nonprofits have had in building a harmonious and civil society (Deng 1997; Zhao 1998; Wang et al. 2001). However, arguing for the necessity of private nonprofits on the basis of their positive effects and social value assumes that private nonprofits are autonomous entities that work for the public interest. When private nonprofits are not autonomous, however, they are effectively no different than the government because they merely act as government agencies. In such cases, private nonprofits cannot play a third-party role. Unless they are working for the public interest, they are essentially indistinct from private enterprises. Moreover, these private nonprofits lack the checks and balances found within the spheres of government and enterprise and cannot promote social fairness and justice.

Private nonprofits can be considered to have two essential characteristics: autonomy and "publicness," or the degree to which the nonprofit's mission serves the public interest. The levels of autonomy and publicness of private nonprofits in China, which are key components of the country's nonprofit sector, determine nonprofits' respective nature and influence on Chinese civil society. The autonomy of private nonprofits refers to organizations' self-governance, which involves organizational control over its personnel and finances, as well as control of its operations. In this chapter, the indices used to measure private nonprofits' level of autonomy are organizations' founders, leadership patterns, revenue structure, and relationship with the government.

The publicness of NPOs fundamentally requires that the mission of these organizations not be aimed at benefitting a specific group of people (i.e., focused on member benefits), that their operations be transparent, and that their outputs contribute to the overall welfare of society (Ku 2000). An organization's level of publicness is determined by its decision-making patterns, financial transparency, property rights, public benefit, and advocacy efforts. Publicness is not always compatible with organizations' private interests.

The Autonomy of Private Nonprofit Organizations

The Founding Context

An organization's founding members, as well as the context of its founding, typically influence its level of autonomy. Therefore, the circumstances of an organization's establishment are an important index for measuring the level of an organization's autonomy. Our survey data indicate that more than half of NPOs are established by nongovernmental actors, 15.4 percent are established by sponsoring authorities (i.e., government departments that support, guide, and supervise NPOs' business affairs), and 15.2 percent lie somewhere in between, meaning that they are founded by public-oriented government leaders in related areas,

Figure 6.2
Founders of NPOs

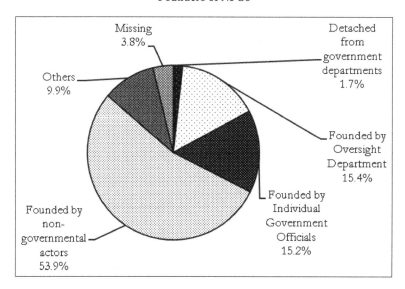

Missing
3.8%

Detached
from
government
departments
1.7%

Others
9.9%

Founded by
Oversight
Department
15.4%

Founded by
non-
governmental
actors
53.9%

Founded by
Individual
Government
Officials
15.2%

not by organizations (Figure 6.2). In other words, NPOs in China come about by people's choice; they are not created by the government. In this respect, private nonprofit organizations and private nonprofit groups differ substantially. In general, their level of autonomy gives NPOs an inherent advantage over associations.

Leadership Patterns

Chinese organizations' leadership is typically comprised of a president, vice president, and secretary general. The election process for these positions reflects the organization's personnel power. Research shows that 58.9 percent of China's NPO leaders are appointed by organization founders, and only 8.7 percent are appointed by government oversight departments. This demonstrates that NPO leaders are mainly controlled by the founders, not by the government; in fact, the government has limited control over NPO personnel in general. This impact is particularly minimal in NPOs founded by nongovernmental actors.

Contextually, although 15.4 percent of NPOs were established by government oversight departments, the leaders of only 8.7 percent of those organizations were determined by the respective oversight department. These NPOs had some degree of control over their personnel decisions. Their leaders were either delegated by a board of directors, nominated

Table 6.2
Revenue Structures of NPOs and Nonprofit Groups

Category	NPO (%)	Nonprofit Group (%)
Public sector	2.5	31.6
Philanthropy and private donations	1.8	13.8
Service charges	95.7	54.6
Total	100.0	100.0

and elected by the organization's members, determined by investors, or appointed in other ways. In cases when boards of directors had delegated leaders, the boards had been fully controlled by their investors.

Revenue Structure

The revenue structure of an NPO directly influences its autonomy. Generally speaking, if an NPO is primarily funded by the government, the organization will be influenced by the government. If funds come mainly from enterprises, the organization's autonomy will be influenced by enterprises. If funds come mainly from international NPOs, the organization's autonomy will be influenced by international NPOs. However, if an NPO's funds come mainly from membership fees or service charges, its autonomy will be preserved. The survey in this study shows that, in 2002, 95.7 percent of the daily gross income of Chinese NPOs came from service charges. Both government support and philanthropic donations added up to less than 5 percent of their gross income (excluding sponsors' investments and bank loans). Because this majority of Chinese NPOs survive on service charges, they are independent from the government, at least in terms of finances.

As shown in Table 6.2, the revenue of both NPOs and nonprofit groups is dominated by service fees. However, because NPOs were much less dependent on government support and private donations than were nonprofit groups, we can assume that the autonomy of NPOs far exceeded that of nonprofit groups.

Relationships with Sponsoring Authorities and Registration Departments

Given China's dual oversight system, every NPO is assigned both a registration department and a sponsoring authority. The registration department is responsible for an NPO's registration, any subsequent changes to that registration status, and annual inspections and evaluations. Additionally, the registration department is responsible for imposing administrative penalties when an NPO breaks any regulations. The sponsoring authority, on the other hand, is responsible for assessing an NPO prior to its establishment, modifying or cancelling its registration, and ensuring the NPO's adherence to the constitution, laws, statutes, and public policies. Additionally, the authority heads the preliminary assessment of the NPO as part of its annual inspection and supports the registration department in investigations into, and penalties for, illegal NPO activity. In some cases, this may lead to the liquidation of an offending organization.

According to our study, among the 1,700 NPOs that responded to the question concerning the status of their relationship with their respective registration department, 12.2 percent reported that they were closely related; 36.9 percent said that they were somewhat related; 43.3 percent said that they were neutral; and 7.5 percent said that the relationship was either weak or there was almost no contact.

Among the leaders from 1,676 NPOs who responded to the question concerning their relationship with their respective sponsoring authorities, 35.6 percent reported that they operated independently, with no intervention from their authorities; 48.6 percent said that they were relatively independent, and that some functions were handled by their authorities; 14.5 percent said that they were completely subordinate to their authorities; and 1.3 percent chose "other."

Regarding development, 55 percent of NPOs responded that during the early development of the organization, the sponsoring authorities had provided the most support; only 16.6 percent responded that the registration department had provided the most support; 11.2 percent responded that media had provided the most support; and less than 20 percent responded that other governmental departments, social organizations, or academic organizations had provided the most support.

According to our collected data, then, sponsoring authorities played the most important role in the development of NPOs. Their influence was, by and large, much greater than that of the registration departments—especially within those NPOs whose establishment required authorities' permission. However, although NPOs were strongly influenced by their authorities, most of them maintained a substantial degree of control over internal management.

Changes in Recent Years

Most Chinese NPOs have been established by the people, as opposed to the government. Furthermore, the personnel choices of NPOs have been

Table 6.3
Changes Experienced by NPOs

	Significantly improved (%)	Slightly improved (%)	No change (%)	Slightly declined (%)	Significantly declined (%)
Control of personnel	30.0	21.6	47.5	0.8	0.1
Control of external affairs	13.9	20.0	64.2	1.4	0.5
Decision-making power	25.4	22.3	50.4	1.7	0.2
Financial conditions	17.1	33.9	33.4	13.2	2.5

minimally influenced by governments and largely influenced by sponsors. Their revenues have depended primarily on member fees and service charges, as opposed to contributions by government or private enterprises, and their relationships with sponsoring authorities have been far more significant than their relationships with registration departments. Generally speaking, NPOs have enjoyed a relatively high level of autonomy.

In the past three years, most NPOs have sensed little change to their level of control over personnel, external collaboration, communication, or decision making. Some NPOs have perceived some expansion of control over personnel, but no change with regard to their control over external affairs. A small proportion of NPOs responded that their control over collaboration and communication had decreased to some extent. In terms of financial resources, approximately half reported an improvement, while 15.7 percent reported that their financial conditions had worsened—perhaps due to rapid development and fierce competition in recent years (see Table 6.3).

In any case, this data indicates that China's NPOs are developing in the right direction. Not only did NPO autonomy become stronger but their financial conditions also improved.

The Publicness of NPOs

Decision-making Patterns
Generally speaking, the more publicness an NPO has, the more democratic it tends to be, the more privacy it enjoys, and the more centralized

Table 6.4
Important Decision-Making Patterns of NPOs and Nonprofit Groups

Decision-making pattern	NPOs (%)	Nonprofit Groups (%)
Decided by formal authorities (i.e., boards of directors)	20.1	69.7
Discussed by all members	17.6	10.5
Decided by two or more leaders	31.1	14.9
Decided by one leader	29.3	2.0
Other	1.9	2.9

its power becomes. Therefore, organizational decision patterns are an important index used to measure an NPO's level of public interest.

Our survey revealed that 20.1 percent of NPOs' decisions were made by formal authorities, such as boards of directors; 17.6 percent were determined collectively by all members; and approximately 60 percent were determined by one or several leaders. The survey also demonstrated that in nearly 70 percent of nonprofit groups, important decisions were made by formal authorities, such as boards of directors, in comparison to 20.1 percent of NPOs. In fewer than 17 percent of nonprofit groups, important decisions were made by one or several leaders. That figure was as high as 60 percent in NPOs (Table 6.4). Clearly, at least superficially, the democratic decision-making regulations of Chinese nonprofit groups are much more robust than those of NPOs.

Financial Transparency

The research showed that 67 percent of NPOs wrote annual financial reports, while 33 percent did not. Among those who wrote reports, 27.4 percent used neither internal auditing nor external auditing; 41.9 percent used internal auditing; 24.8 percent used external auditing; and the remaining 5.8 percent fell into the "other" category.

In terms of the extent of disclosure of these financial reports, 20.3 percent of NPOs disclosed their reports only to directors; 45.3 percent disclosed their reports to employees; 16.1 percent disclosed their reports to their clients; and only 1.9 percent willingly released their reports to the general public through the mass media.

More than one-third of Chinese NPOs did not create annual financial reports, and fewer than 25 percent utilized external auditing. Less than one-fifth disclosed their financial reports to clients or the general public.

From the aforementioned data, we can conclude that China's NPOs lacked financial transparency.

Property Rights

Property rights are one of the indices with which we measure NPOs' level of publicness. If an NPO's property belongs to the organization or to society, the organization has a high level of public interest; if its property belongs to specific individuals, the organization has a low level of publicness.

The topic of property rights is a sensitive one, as far as the development of China's NPOs is concerned. It is also certainly a factor in complicating, even obstructing, NPOs' development. Theoretically, as an independent entity, an NPO would possess the rights to its property, as opposed to sponsors or private individuals. In certain fields, however, it is legally permissible for sponsors to receive some benefits. This serves to encourage private actors to get involved in social undertakings.

Our study revealed that 67.6 percent of NPOs thought their property rights belonged to investors; 9.8 percent thought their property belonged to the co-founders; only 16.4 percent thought the property belonged to the entity itself; and 2.3 percent thought it belonged to society. Most NPO investors regarded the entity's property as their own, which speaks to the NPOs' level of privatization. This is why NPOs have focused on profits, not transparency. Properly dealing with property rights issues not only requires management strategy but also awareness and strong ideas. Adaptation is complex and long term. Case studies have shown that as guidance and regulation by local governments occurs, as NPOs develop to a certain scale, and as NPO leaders' awareness improves, profit-driven concerns give way to reveal more altruistic character.

Public Benefit

Public benefit is a difficult concept to define. In the field of NPO research, public benefit usually corresponds to the concept of mutual benefit. In a broad sense, public benefit defines beneficiaries as a nonspecific majority of people. A more narrow definition identifies beneficiaries as unspecific, vulnerable groups.

Our survey showed that 24.9 percent of NPOs mainly provided services to groups that could not afford market prices, such as health care for migrant workers and skill training schools for female workers; 37.5 percent mainly provided services to those groups who could afford market prices, such as private education; 24.3 percent of NPOs provided services to both of the aforementioned groups; and the remaining 13.3 percent fell into the "other" category.

If we define public benefit in a broad sense, all of these NPOs are providing public benefits regardless of whether their beneficiary groups can afford services. That is because the social services provided in the areas of technology, education, culture, health care, and recreation are beneficial to society as a whole, and they were provided to an unspecific majority of people. Even if the services and products they provided were exclusive and competitive, they also bore notable external benefits. However, if we define public benefit in the narrower sense, less than a quarter of NPOs had high levels of public benefit, two-fifths had low public benefit, and less than a quarter fell in between.

Advocacy

Advocacy is another important index used to measure NPO publicness. David Korten (1990) indicated that NPOs experience four stages of development: NPOs in the first stage devote themselves to helping and supporting the poor; at the second stage they commit to community development; at the third and fourth stages they tend to influence public policies, as well as promote systems and reforms through advocacy. "Advocacy" has become a popular term in the field in recent years, and is a new trend in NPO development in China.

Our survey showed that among those NPOs that answered questions related to this index in 2002, 70.1 percent had not submitted any policy suggestions at any level of government. On average, while each NPO had submitted about 1.6 proposals, only 0.82 of those had been adopted. In this same year, 33.8 percent of NGOs had been invited to policy consulting meetings held by the government, and on average had attended 1.23 such meetings. The nonresponse rate for this question was 44.6 percent. If we assume those nonrespondent organizations had not submitted any policy suggestions, the average number of suggestions would be much lower, and the proportion of NPOs that had not submitted any proposals would be very high; the proportion of NPOs who had been invited to government consulting meetings would be much smaller, and the average times of attending such meetings would also be lower.

Table 6.5 demonstrates that in contrast to nonprofit groups, NPOs much less frequently submitted policy proposals to the government or

Table 6.5
Advocacy by NPOs and Nonprofit Groups

	NPOs	Associations
The proportion of organizations that did not put forward any policy suggestion to governments (%)	70.10	23.40
The average pieces of suggestions to governments (piece)	1.60	4.68
The average pieces of adopted suggestions (pieces)	0.82	2.86
The proportion of organizations that were not invited to government policy consulting meetings (%)	66.20	26.90
The average attendance times to government policy consulting meetings (times)	1.23	2.01

were invited to partake in government consultation. Subsequently, nonprofit groups were more active and played a stronger role in advocacy than had NPOs. On the other hand, this data reminds us that nonprofit groups have benefitted from somewhat better communication channels, which NPOs typically lack. This can be attributed to the fact that most nonprofit groups were established by the government and therefore natural channels of communication exist. Alternatively, most NPOs were established by private actors; therefore, connections with the government were typically weak from the start. If this assumption is true, all levels of governments should pay more attention to the issue, provide NPOs more communication channels, and consider adopting more of their opinions and suggestions.

The Functions and Value of NPOs

Extensive research has focused on the functions and benefits of NPOs. Some scholars approach the topic from the perspective of social innovation, while others focus on the provision of public services or filling gaps left by government and the market. In general, these particular topics are most effectively analyzed through qualitative analyses, rather than measurements or quantitative analysis. This chapter has adopted the method of Lester Salamon, which measures the function and benefits from the perspective of employment and economy. This statistical method has been adopted by the United Nations to analyze trends in many countries in recent years. The United Nations has even tried to incorporate NPOs' contributions to employment and economic development into its national economic accounting system. At this point, more than ninety countries have participated in this program; China, however, has not.

Contribution to Employment

Our survey demonstrates that in 2002 there were, on average, 16.5 full-time employees, 5.6 part-time employees, and 2.9 volunteers in each Chinese NPO. Each volunteer worked approximately 16.9 hours per month. In 2002 there were approximately 1,832,000 full-time employees, 622,000 part-time employees and 322,000 volunteers in China's NPOs, with volunteers devoting 1,876,000 hours of their time every month. According to the Johns Hopkins Comparative Nonprofit Sector Project's calculation (Salamon 1999), the work performed by 5.6 part-time employees in an NPO was equivalent to that of 1.87 full-time employees. Accounting for part-time employees, according to this calculation, each NPO provided 18.4 full-time job opportunities on average, and as a whole they provided 2,039 thousand job opportunities. These comprised 0.97 percent of service industry employment and 19.3 percent of public sector employment. If we account for volunteers, assuming that a full-time employee works eight hours each day, or 160 hours each month, one volunteer is equivalent to 0.106 of a full-time job employee. According to these standards, in 2002 every NPO in China provided 18.7 job opportunities and NPOs as a whole provided 2,076 thousand job opportunities, which comprised 0.98 percent of service industry employment and 19.7 percent of public sector employment. This data reveals that China's NPOs have provided considerable employment opportunities, particularly full-time job opportunities.

Nonprofit groups provided fewer full-time jobs than NPOs. However, the number of volunteers at NPOs was much smaller than at nonprofit groups. Table 6.6 demonstrates that the average number of full-time employees at NPOs was 4.58 times higher than that of nonprofit groups, while the average number of nonprofit groups was 3.62 times that of NPOs. The reason that NPOs had more full-time employees is most likely related to their organization structure. As a non-membership entity, an NPO operates under a specific set of conditions. This is especially clear in private schools, where not only administrative staff is employed, but also a certain number of teachers; therefore numerous full-time employees are needed. Nonprofit groups, on the other hand, are more loosely organized and their daily operations require only a small number of full-time employees. Most activities depend on the participation of their members or volunteers. Therefore, nonprofit groups—particularly those serving the public good—often hire few full-time employees and use numerous volunteers.

Table 6.6
Average Employment of NPOs and Nonprofit Groups

	NPO	Nonprofit Group	Ratio (NPO/ Nonprofit Group)
The number of full-time employees	16.5 (people)	3.6 (people)	4.58
The number of part-time employees	5.6 (people)	5.3 (people)	1.06
The number of volunteers	2.9 (people)	10.5 (people)	0.28
The participation time of every volunteer every month	16.9 (hours)	5.9 (hours)	2.86

A research study of twenty-two countries, including the UK and Japan, conducted by John Hopkins University, demonstrated that when fewer employment opportunities were available in traditional sectors, including the service industry, employment within the nonprofit sector saw rapid surges. In the nonprofit sector, Western European countries saw the fastest job growth in the social services field, while America saw the fastest growth of job opportunities in the area of health care. This implies that NPOs must develop their potential in scaling up employment, particularly in the social service and health care fields.

Contributions to the Economy

This survey demonstrates that on average, each NPO in China spends approximately 482,000 RMB per year. Therefore, in 2002, the total expenditure of China's NPOs was approximately 53.5 billion RMB. Based on this number, it can be inferred that NPOs represented a considerable economic force. On average, the expenditure of an NPO in 2002 was twice that of a nonprofit group's expenditure, with the total expenditure of NPOs coming up to 20.5 billion RMB more than that of nonprofit groups.

In terms of the distribution of NPO expenditures in 2002 (Table 6.7), 73.2 percent of China's NPOs spent between 10,000 and 500,000 RMB. The proportion of NPOs whose expenses were less than 10,000 RMB or above 500,000 RMB was not high. This demonstrates that the amount of money needed to establish an NPO was high, especially for NPOs that required special registration permits. On the other hand, the economic scale of most NPOs in China was relatively small. This is likely due to limited revenue sources available to NPOs, as well as the lack of financial support from government or public donations.

Table 6.7
Expense Distributions of NPOs and Nonprofit Groups in China, 2002

Total Expenses (RMB)	Percentage of NPOs	Percentage of Nonprofit Groups	Comparison (%)
< 10 thousand	11.0	39.8	−28.8
10 ~ 50 thousand	31.6	26.5	5.1
50 ~ 100 thousand	17.2	10.2	7.0
100 ~ 500 thousand	24.4	16.4	8.0
500 thousand ~ 1 million	7.1	2.9	4.2
1 ~ 5 million	7.0	2.2	4.8
5 ~ 10 million	1.0	0.5	0.5
> 10 million	0.7	1.5	−0.8
Total	100.0	100.0	

Discussion

Conclusions and Recommendations

Although NPOs comprise an important segment of China's nonprofit sector, research relating to NPOs has been relatively limited. The following conclusions can be drawn from the above analysis:

In 2002 China's NPOs provided 2.07 million full-time job opportunities. This is far more than the 763,000 job opportunities offered by China's nonprofit groups in the same year. If the former figure were considered nonprofit employment, this would significantly raise the nonprofit sector's contribution to employment in China (at that time, the China Statistical Yearbooks only counted the employment of state organs, political parties, and nonprofit groups, and did not count or release employment data for NPOs). In light of the worldwide trends of declining employment opportunities in traditional industries, nonprofit sector employment, whether in social services, education, or health care, is rapidly increasing. Clearly, then, NPOs have great potential as means to alleviate China's unemployment problems. These enterprises might become one of the main sources of job creation in China. In 2002 the total expenditures of China's NPOs reached about 53.5 billion RMB, which was twice that of nonprofit groups. Although China's NPOs still operate on a relatively small scale, there is tremendous room for future development. They represent an economic force that cannot be ignored. People often compare the employment and economic contributions by the nonprofit sector to the nonprofit sectors of foreign countries; in fact, the gap is largely due to the limited contributions of government-affiliated nonprofit groups.

Generally speaking, NPOs are less politically sensitive, and, as previously stated, contribute significantly to employment and the economy. Additionally, NPOs will be extremely important to the future provision of public services in China. The development of NPOs will better support social undertakings in fields such as technology, education, health care, culture, and recreation. Also, NPOs could potentially serve the important role of encouraging reforms among public service agencies, simply by providing competition. For all of these reasons, NPOs should be embraced as a development priority in China's nonprofit sector.

As our statistical data demonstrate, however, following a period of rapid growth from 1999–2002, China's NPOs have now begun to encounter systematic barriers. Their growth rates have slowed, and in some cases stagnated. It will be important to pay close attention to these growth rates as time moves on. Society and government departments at all levels should develop a better understanding of NPOs and attach more importance to their development. They should also recognize NPOs' provision of public services, contributions to employment and the economy, and their influence on institutional reform in China. Local governments must also support NPOs through policy reforms, and in particular, set up regulations for purchasing NPOs' public services. Given NPOs' nonprofit status, they should receive tax preferences and deductions and be granted equal opportunities to compete with public service units and nonprofit groups.

From a structural point of view, there is very uneven distribution of NPOs in different regions of China. Additionally, while NPOs in the field of education are thriving, those focused on other fields are not doing as well. This will require adjustments in the state strategies toward NPOs. An important step will be prioritizing the development of NPOs in the areas of health care and social welfare: services that are urgently needed, and that fall in step with world development trends. Our research demonstrated that China has utilized very different strategies in its approach toward education and health care. In the area of education, the state has largely focused on supporting private, nonprofit education organizations. With regard to health care, most local governments have supported private, for-profit health organizations. The reforms made in the health care sector have not been particularly effective, and private, proprietary health care organizations are developing at a much slower pace than NPOs.

In this respect, the development experience of private nonprofit education organizations is worth replicating in other fields.

In Japan, following widespread reforms, the government clearly outlined in the law that private education and medical institutions could only be registered as NPOs. Japan did not open its nursing or health care sectors to the market, and did not allow the registration of private, for-profit organizations until 2000. By choosing these private nonprofits, the state allowed vulnerable groups to enjoy basic education and health care service provision, relatively early on in the country's economic transformation. As the choice was made fairly early, the resistance to reform was minimized, the pressure to reform was relieved, and the government was able to smoothly push reforms forward.

The Importance of NPO Development to Chinese Civil Society

The development of NPOs will not only contribute to the provision of public services and social economic growth but also to the formation and evolution of Chinese civil society. The concept of civil society varies widely. For example, David Booth regarded civil society as the social and economic life, separate from the state (Booth 1987). Helmut Anheier said that civil society is the space where people unite to build common interests outside of families, governments, and markets (Anheier 2004). Gordon White pointed out that the most common use of the term civil society refers to a voluntary, organized association of activities (White 2000). That is to say, an independent and autonomous nonprofit sector lays the foundation for civil society. Civil society is not sound if the nonprofit sector in the region lacks autonomy.

Edward Shils went further by emphasizing the concept of civility. The term "civility" is typically interpreted to mean courtesy, moderation, respect for others, self-restraint, refinement, and good manners. Civility is a virtue of civil society, which at all times places the common interest first, and places a limit on individual, parochial, and group goals (Shils 1991). The essential difference between a well-ordered civil society and a disordered civil society is civility. A civil society that embodies civility is certainly one worth pursuing.

In contemporary China, civil organizations within the nonprofit sector are commonly referred to pejoratively as the "second government" or "quasigovernment." However, the research in this chapter indicates that NPOs, representing an important part of China's nonprofit sector, possess a high level of autonomy (Table 6.8). Most NPOs in China were established by private actors, and have experienced limited government intervention and high levels of operational independence.

In the past, NPOs experienced tight control over personnel, external collaboration and communication, and decision making. However, the terms "second government" and "quasigovernment" do not appropriately describe the nonprofit sector in China as they currently operate. The expansion of highly autonomous NPOs will contribute directly to the vitality of future nonprofit sector development. These NPOs hold great conceptual and practical value with regard to the formation of a strong, healthy civil society in China.

Nevertheless, forming a sound and healthy civil society also calls for tremendous civility on the part of individuals and organizations. Publicness is an essential measure of NPOs' civility. If an NPO bills itself as a public service, nonprofit organization, but cannot achieve basic standards of publicness, it can hardly embody the civility and virtue that Shils' concept requires.

Unfortunately, our research demonstrates that the publicness of China's NPOs is very limited (Table 6.8). The democratic decision-making

Table 6.8
Evaluation of NPO Autonomy and Publicness

	Very high	Somewhat high	Neutral	Somewhat low	Very low
1. Indexes of NPO autonomy:					
(1) Nature of its founding		√			
(2) Election of leaders				√	
(3) Revenue structure	√				
(4) Relationships with sponsoring authorities and registration departments		√			
Overall evaluation		√			
2. Indexes for NPO publicness:					
(1) Decision-making patterns				√	
(2) Financial Transparency				√	
(3) Property rights					√
(4) Public benefit			√		
(5) Advocacy				√	
Overall evaluation				√	

mechanisms of China's NPOs are substantially flawed; they suffer from limited financial transparency, weak volunteer participation, and inadequate public benefits. Although the charters of most NPOs clearly define the organizations as nonprofit, they consider property rights as belonging to the organization's founders. China's NPOs clearly have a long way to go before attaining "civility." For China to achieve an ordered and harmonious civil society, NPOs must continue to improve, exercise self-discipline, and adhere to their core principles. These ends also require governments to protect NPOs' legal rights, and at the same time inspire, guide, and supervise NPOs as they carry out their obligations. This will require every citizen to cultivate virtue and good habits, and thereby contribute to a broader civic culture.

7

Trends in Charitable Donations

Zhenyao Wang* and Huajun Gao

Since the 2008 Wenchuan earthquake led to an upsurge in disaster-relief contributions, charitable donations have gradually become the norm in China. In recent years charitable donations have been growing steadily. In-kind donations and volunteer service have become social trends. This chapter specifically discusses recent developments in charitable donations in China.

These data in 2011 indicate that, despite the impact of several negative events, charitable donations have not suffered; rather, they have continued to develop. The basic patterns of annual donations consist of declines in donations from the government and state-owned enterprises and increase in the establishment of university-based foundations, donations from private enterprises, and types of donations made in general.

Increasing Diversity of Donations

While maintaining a steady growth in overall amount, charitable donations in China began to show some new patterns in 2011. First, national donations used to flow to only two entities: local civil affairs offices and government-affiliated foundations (national and local). However, public foundations with no governmental ties began springing up and absorbing a large number of public donations. Wealthy individuals, who

* Translated by Shuang Lu, Research Fellow, Huamin Research Center, School of Social Work, Rutgers University.

were used to relying on the government to manage their charitable funds, started to build their own foundations and manage the donated money by themselves. These changes impacted the patterns of donations in China in 2011. Second, 2011 has been described as troubled times for Chinese charities. Amid a series of crises in official charity agencies, donation amounts fluctuated in certain months, which led to a decrease in total annual donation amounts. Finally, along with the upsurge of donations from major university alumni, often at school anniversary celebrations, college foundations continued to grow in size and receive large amounts of donations, which also influenced the general pattern of charitable donations in 2011.

Trends in Annual Donations and Fund Raising

According to the annual inspection conference held by the Ministry of Civil Affairs NGO Administration in January 2012, by the end of 2011 the total assets of Chinese foundations had reached ¥60.42 billion. Over the past year, Chinese foundations had an annual donation income of ¥33.7 billion and a charity expense of ¥25.6 billion (China Philanthropy Times, 2012). In 2010 Chinese foundations had a donation income of ¥24.48 billion, which accounted for 87.44 percent of their total income of ¥27.98 billion (China Foundation Center). By contrast, the donation income increased by ¥9.6 billion in 2011—a 39 percent growth rate. Among other donations, multiple large contributions, especially the ¥3.55 billion in stocks that Heren Foundation received from Dewang Cao, accounted for a large portion of the growth.

Large donations from individuals, especially people from Hong Kong, Taiwanese, and overseas Chinese, made a great contribution to the growth in donation amounts. For example, in April 2011, Hong Kong Chuanglv Group donated ¥200 million to Tsinghua University to establish the Chuanglv Science Foundation, which would be used in part to construct a 20,000-square-meter modern laboratory building for the school's Department of Physics. In May, Zhongying Tang and Moxi Li, two American alumni of Zhejiang University, donated ¥50 million at a school anniversary celebration to support scientific research. In late 2011, Yongzai Chen, a Filipino Chinese who is President of Philippine Airlines, donated ¥50 million to establish the Huawen Education Center at Huaqiao University. Additionally, many charitable activities, such as donating books and subsidizing children in poor areas, became regular monthly events. The continual inflow of international donations energized donations in 2011.

In addition to the typical donation recipients mentioned above, college foundations that sprung up in 2011 also attracted quite a bit of attention. In January 2012, the China Alumni Association website released the "2012 Chinese Universities Evaluation Report," which included updated rankings for 2012 of donations by university alumni. According to the list, Peking University had received a total of ¥1.2 billion in alumni donations from 1990 to 2011, the highest amount of alumni donations among Chinese universities during that time. Nubo Huang donated ¥900 million alone, which was the highest single donation on record and made a decisive impact on the rankings. As a result, Peking University transcended Zhejing University and ranked number one in alumni donations. Meanwhile, at Tsinghua University's 2011 anniversary celebration, alumni intensified their donations, contributing ¥1.085 billion, which moved Tsinghua University to second place in the donation rankings. Yuan Chen, the President of Runwu Holdings, and Chun Lan, the President of Beijing New Talent Academy Group, contributed ¥100 million each. Zhejiang University ranked third on the list with a total donation amount of ¥553 million. Xiamen University and South China University of Technology also received numerous donations at their respective 2011 anniversary celebrations, which consolidated their places in the top ten of the rankings. Table 7.1 shows the top twenty universities on the alumni donation list.

Data from the China Foundation Center indicated that college foundations flourished in 2011. According to the center, as of December 31, 2011, there were 239 Chinese college foundations. Among the thirty-nine universities in Project 985 (Project 985 was announced in May 1998 and involves both national and local governments allocating large amounts of funding to certain universities to build new research centers, improve facilities, hold international conferences, attract world-renowned faculty and visiting scholars, and help Chinese faculty attend conferences abroad (Department of Education of the People's Republic of China 2004), thirty-six have established their own foundations, and a few have established two to three foundations at the same time. In the last three years, the annual growth rate of college foundations stayed above 20 percent, and this was almost the same rate experienced by private foundations.

In addition to the leading alumni donations mentioned above, many other philanthropists funded colleges or their alma maters in 2011. For example, Yajun Wu, President of Longfor Properties, donated ¥100 million

Table 7.1
2012 Chinese University Alumni's Donation Ranking List
(Cumulative Donations from 1990 to 2011)

Ranking	University	Location	Alumni Donation (millions ¥)
1	Peking University	Beijing	1,240
2	Tsinghua University	Beijing	1,085
3	Zhejiang University	Zhejiang	553
4	Renmin University	Beijing	263
5	Wuhan University	Hubei	206
6	South China University of Technology	Guangdong	134
7	Xiamen University	Fujian	109
8	Central South University	Hunan	107
9	Nanjing University	Jiangsu	105
10	Northwestern Polytechnic University	Shanxi	101
11	Jinan University	Guangdong	61
12	Tianjin University	Tianjin	61
13	Sun Yat-Sen University	Guangdong	58
14	China Agricultural University	Beijing	56
15	Central University of Finance and Economics	Beijing	48
16	Shanghai Jiao Tong University	Shanghai	46
17	Fudan University	Shanghai	46
18	Beijing Normal University	Beijing	41
19	Nankai University	Tianjin	40
20	Shandong University	Shandong	40

to establish the Yajun Wu Reward Fund at his alma mater, Northwestern University. The fund was used to reward outstanding students with scholarships, assist low-income students with financial aid, and subsidize the salaries of young teachers and the pensions of retired alumni. Dongsheng Chen, President of Taikang Life Insurance Company, also donated ¥100 million to construct an art museum at his alma mater, Wuhan University, at its 120th anniversary. It is estimated that more than twenty private entrepreneurs made donation agreements with universities of at least ¥10 million in 2011 alone. With these donations, college foundations are growing rapidly and have become another pillar of donations in the country.

The Emergence of New Forms of Donations

Equity and Trust Donations

Although large donations were common in 2011, it still attracted a great deal of attention when Dewang Cao donated his shares in Fuyao Group (worth ¥3.55 billion) to the Heren Foundation. In addition to the astonishingly large amount of this donation, the foundation itself garnered attention because it was the first Chinese foundation to receive a donation in the form of equity.

In fact, Cao had already expressed his intention to donate 70 percent of his Fuyao Group shares, which are held by his family, to establish the Heren Foundation. After the first meeting of the foundation's executive board and supervisors, the equity donation was in an intense process. However, many difficulties occurred with this sensational donation. For instance, because relevant processes and regulatory guidelines for establishing private foundations with equity donations were lacking in China, in the end Cao donated 300 million shares instead of the 700 million expected to avoid a transfer of Fuyao Group's control rights. In the meantime, although the Department of Finance and the State Administration of Taxation released a special notification that allowed Cao to avoid paying a tax on his equity donation immediately and to make the full payment in five years after establishing his foundation, there were still many holes in taxation details.

Despite many difficulties, Cao's act of generosity had a great influence on policy. Not only did he create a brand new approach to philanthropy but he also challenged the maturity of the philanthropy system. When explaining why he chose an equity donation as the form of this large donation, Cao explained that at first he did not want to impact the capital market, so he chose to invest shares instead of currency to gain the confidence of investors. Second, this type of donation effectively guaranteed that the foundation would maintain or increase its assets, which was the shining point of Heren Foundation's establishment and Cao's donation in the view of Zhenyao Wang, Dean of the China Philanthropy Research Institute at Beijing Normal University. Unlike foundations that only have to make decisions about how to spend money, foundations that receive equity donations must figure out how to maintain or increase assets and how to avoid risks related to the stock market. These tasks require experienced professionals. Therefore, the establishment of the Heren Foundation has far-reaching implications for expanding charity funding sources and enhancing the vitality and development of charity foundations.

After Cao's donation, Gensheng Niu, the President of Mengniu Group, fully transferred his foreign-equity assets to Hengxin Trust as a philanthropic contribution. Foreign-equity assets have become another effective type of equity donations.

With the development of the Chinese economy and financial market, donations of negotiable securities, including stocks, will become important in the future. The current Chinese tax system, however, is not conducive to the development of such donations. Therefore, there is an urgent need for policy keep up with the emergence of these new types of donations. Only by allowing equity donations to be tax-exempt, as is done in Europe and the United States, can charitable donation channels be expanded. If this is done, a great deal of monetary donations could be facilitated.

Declining Effectiveness of Government-Affiliated Donations

In the twenty-first century, donation days (often called Charitable Donation Day or Poverty Relief Day by local governments) have become more popular throughout the country. In 2010, donation amounts hit a high record in various cities. For instance, Qingdao received donations of ¥68.3 million, Taiyuan received ¥54.6 million, Dongguan received ¥180 million, and Wenzhou received ¥53.29 million. Qingpu, which is just one district of Shanghai, received ¥76.87 million on Charitable Donation Day in 2010, an amount equal to 2.4 times the cumulative donation amounts of previous years. In conclusion, Charitable Donation Day becomes the mode of charity activities in many cities.

In 2011, it was still common to see charity days, and many provinces and cities that had never held such activities started joining the trend. On June 6, the cities of Nanning, Jiyuan, Nanchang, and Lu'an initiated their first local Charity Day, which brought in more than ¥1 million each in donations within a short time.

But even more noticeable was that donation amounts on Charitable Donation Day declined in many areas where philanthropy had already been developed. For instance, the fund-raising amounts in cities that had active donations in 2010—Qingdao, Taiyuan, and Zhengzhou—declined in 2011. The fund-raising amounts in the three cities were only ¥58.11 million, ¥33.11 million, and ¥68.47 million, respectively, representing a decrease of more than ¥10 million. Meanwhile, in Guangdong, a province where philanthropy has traditionally flourished, ¥3.22 billion were received on the second Poverty Relief Day. Although this surpassed the previous year's amount by about ¥200 million, Dongguan City, previously a large contributor to the province, only received ¥36.55 million from its residents that year, which was quite a decline. Within national areas, only Chengdu achieved a substantial increase on its second Charity Day in 2011, raising more than ¥30 million.

Although charity days have become more common throughout the country, the donation amounts have declined in quite a few areas. The declines can probably be attributed to two factors. First, magnates, who used to have full confidence in the government's management of their charitable funds, are now inclined to set up their own charitable organizations, control large donations by themselves through private foundations or other agencies, and manage their funds by themselves or hire professionals to use their funds more efficiently. As a result, fewer large donations are being given to the government. Second, because of the influence of a series of philanthropy scandals in the second half of 2011, the public seems to be holding some grudges against charity agencies that are affiliated with the government; some people are even no longer willing to make donations to these agencies. Meanwhile, with the development of online charity activities, the public has more ways to participate in charity, which naturally brings down the appeal of charity days and reduces the source of small donations to the government. As a combined result of these factors, fund-raising totals from charity days have lessened in some areas.

In the long run, the government should gradually exit from the fund-raising market, leave room for social charity organizations to handle relevant functions, and shift attention to the support and regulation of philanthropy. As Zhenyao Wang proposed several years ago, long-term social contributions in China will not be dependent on administrative mobilization or organizational launches; instead, they will move toward independent and voluntary contributions, ultimately making contributions truly a third-party, nonprofit, public philanthropy cause.

Trends in Individual and State-Owned-Enterprise Donations

In other countries, magnates make regular donations over the years, which allow nonprofit organizations and foundations to exist comfortably and create large philanthropy programs that benefit many people and therefore improve the overall philanthropy level in a country. In 2011, donations of more than ¥1 million were common from both state-owned enterprises and private enterprises, and donations of even more than ¥10 million sometimes occurred. In this chapter, the Top 100 Donors in China in 2011 list, which was published by Beijing Normal University's China Philanthropy Research Institute at the beginning of 2012, and the Table of State-Owned Enterprises' Donation Expenditures in the First Three Quarters of 2011, which was published by the State Council's State-Owned Assets Supervision and Administration Commission in November 2011, will be used to analyze the development of large donations in China.

Large Donations from Individuals and Private Enterprises

Over the past few years, private enterprises have always been the main force behind charitable donations in China. In 2010, private enterprises contributed more than ¥11.3 billion in cash and in kind to philanthropic causes (Yang 2011), and this number was expected to continue. The country's top 100 donors as of January 2012 had donated more than ¥12.1 billion, and this figure does not even include many donations below ¥1 million.

As the first list of large individual donations released by an industry-leading professional philanthropy research agency, the Top 100 Donors in China in 2011 list aims to reflect the distribution and typical features of charitable donations in the country and construct a modern charity recognition system through the publicity of individual donors. On the top 100 donors list, the highest single donation amount was ¥3.75 billion, and the lowest amount was ¥14.78 million. Twenty-two donors made a donation of more than ¥100 million. Among others, Cao ranked number one because of his equity donation of 300 million shares to Heren Foundation, which were valued at ¥3.55 billion in the market at the time of the donation. Next, Nubo Huang and Jianlin Wang ranked second and third on the list, respectively, with donations of ¥920 million and ¥817 million. Large donations were very common in 2011. According to incomplete statistics from the China Philanthropy Research Institute, there were more than 250 single donations of more than ¥10 million, and the top 100 donors contributed more than 140 of these donations.

Investment Areas and Donors

An analysis of the top-donors list reveals the following trends in large donations from private enterprises in 2011 (Table 7.2).

Table 7.2
Top 20 Rankings from the 2011 Top 100 Donors in China List

Rank	Donation (millions ¥)	Donor's name	Company	Major donation purpose
1	3,749	Dewang Cao	Fuyao Group	Donated ¥200 million to Xiamen University and 300-million-share equity donation to the Heren Foundation, valued at ¥3.55 billion in the market
2	920	Nubo Huang	Zhongkun Group	Donated ¥900 million to Beijing University's Zhongkun Education Foundation, ¥10 million to the Ningxia Yinchuan Vocational and Technical Center, and ¥10 million to the China Europe International Business School
3	817	Jianlin Wang	Wanda Group	Has agreed to donate ¥600 million to support Chinese football and ¥100 million to the Wanda School of the Chengdu No. 7 Middle School
4	705	Jiayin Xu	Hengda Group	Donated ¥318 million on Guangdong Poverty Relief Day, ¥245 million to support urban poverty relief in Guangdong Province, ¥110 million to the Zhoukou City government in Henan Province, and ¥18 million to Qingyuan City, Guangdong Province
5	614	Yanbao Dang	Ningxia Baofeng Energy Group	Has agreed to donate ¥600 million to Ningxia Yanbao Charity Foundation
6	300	Mengyi Zhu Family	Pearl River Investment	Donated ¥300 million on Guangdong Poverty Relief Day

(*continued*)

Table 7.2 (*continued*)

Rank	Donation (millions ¥)	Donor's name	Company	Major donation purpose
7	220	Xiucheng Lin	Fujian San'an Optoelectronics Ltd.	Donated ¥220 million to the Anxi County Charity Federation, Quanzhou City, Fujian Province
8	200	Jinshi Chen	Zhongnan Group	Has agreed to donate ¥200 million to establish the Jiangsu Zhongnan Charity Foundation, including ¥50 million as registered capital
8	200	Changcai Hou	Yuen Cheong Group	Donated ¥200 million to establish the Nan'an City Charity Federation's Changcai Permanent Fund
8	200	Wenzi Huang	Star River Real Estate	Donated ¥119 million to Shixiang Village, Lvtian Township, Conghua City, Guangdong Province; ¥81 million on Guangdong Poverty Relief Day
11	186	Yingcheng Guo	Kaisa Group	Donated ¥150 million to support the establishment of the Charity Federation at Puning City, Guangdong Province
12	165	Xingtian Ma	Kangmei Pharmaceutical Ltd.	Donated ¥150 million to support the establishment of the Charity Federation at Puning City, Guangdong Province
13	130	Yuankui Shi	Shanxi Luhe Coal Group	Donated ¥30 million to build new high schools in Linfen City, Shanxi Province; has agreed to donate ¥100 million for prolonged support
14	113	Zhuolin Chen	Agile Property	Donated ¥50 million to the Zhongshan City Charity Federation, Guangdong

(*continued*)

Table 7.2 (*continued*)

Rank	Donation (millions ¥)	Donor's name	Company	Major donation purpose
				Province; ¥30 million to support preschool education at Lingshui County, Sanya City, Hainan Province
15	112	Yajun Wu	Longfor Group	Donated ¥100 million to Northwestern Polytechnic University
16	103	Dongsheng Chen	Taikang Life Insurance Ltd.	Donated ¥100 million to Wuhan University
16	103	Fuli Wu	Fujian Zonshine Group	Donated ¥100 million to Xiamen University
18	101	Yuan Chen	Shanghai Runwu Holdings	Donated ¥100 million to Tsinghua University
19	100	Chun Lan	Beijing Talent Real Estate	Donated ¥100 million to Tsinghua University
20	100	Jianhua Li	Yinsai Holdings	Donated ¥100 million to the China–Africa Project Hope run by the China Youth Development Foundation
20	100	Junqing Lu	Tianjiu Group	Donated ¥100 million to the China–Africa Project Hope run by the China Youth Development Foundation
20	100	Xinhong Qin	Huangshan Hongji Group	Donated ¥100 million to support the establishment of the Charity Federation at Puning City, Guangdong Province

Major Donation Areas: Education and Poverty Relief

Unlike 2010, not much donation money was given for disaster relief in 2011 because no natural disasters occurred that year. Accordingly, education and poverty relief became the major contribution areas for large donations in 2011. Among all donations, education donations totaled about ¥3.3 billion, which accounted for 27 percent of all donations.

Donations for poverty relief totaled about ¥1.25 billion and accounted for 11 percent of all donations. Other areas accounted for less than 3 percent on average. In addition, general donations (i.e., donations made without a specific or clear focus) totaled about ¥5.4 billion and accounted for 45 percent of all donations.

Major Funding Recipients: Foundations and Other Philanthropic Organizations

Foundations and the charity system in general received total donations of more than ¥10 billion, accounting for 83 percent of all donations received in 2011. That year, the government received donations of about ¥1.7 billion, accounting for 14 percent of all donations received. Even with the exposure of a series of scandals, magnates did not seem to be swayed from donating to government-affiliated charity organizations. As in 2010, more enterprises preferred to donate to foundations rather than the government. Meanwhile, a number of private entrepreneurs chose to establish private foundations and have trusted professionals manage their charitable donations, which actually facilitated the growth of donation amounts received by foundations.

Major Fund-Raising Events: Poverty Relief Days and College Anniversary Celebrations

As mentioned before, education and poverty relief have become the major areas of charitable donations. As examples of these two areas, Guangdong's Poverty Relief Day and the anniversary celebrations of several elite universities were highlights among the large donations of 2011. At Guangdong's Poverty Relief Day, a total of ¥900 million was raised, accounting for 8 percent of the country's donations that year, and another ¥900 million were raised at university anniversary celebrations, such as the events at Tsinghua and Xiamen University, which together accounted for 40 percent of all college fund-raising efforts. In addition, the establishment of some local charities has generated a number of large donations as well.

Provincial Breakdowns of Donors and Donations Amounts

Donors from the Top 100 Donors in China in 2011 list came from twenty-two provinces, cities, autonomous regions, and metropolitan municipalities across China. In particular, entrepreneurs in western China, the minority areas where charitable donations were not as prominent before, also made great contributions in 2011. Western entrepreneurs such as Yanbao Dang, Yongming Xiao, and Binghua Zhu donated over ¥40 million. The common thinking that charitable donations only come from developed areas has been changed.

In terms of the number of donors in the top 100, however, developed provinces still accounted for a more significant portion. For instance, Guangdong Province, which had thirty-one entrepreneurs in the top 100, ranked first among all administrative areas. With nine listed donors each, Beijing and Fujian tied for second place. Jiangsu Province had eight people on the list, the fourth highest in the country.

Biggest Donors: Real Estate and Appurtenance Industries

Despite the volatility of the real estate market from the second half of 2011, real estate entrepreneurs' enthusiasm for charitable work was not impacted much. Similar to 2010, individuals and corporations in real estate and related industries contributed donations of ¥4.8 billion, which was the highest among all industries. Among all large donations, real estate enterprises contributed over 40 percent. The glassmaking industry ranked second, mostly due to Cao's individual donation of ¥3.75 billion. The coal, chemical, and mineral industries ranked third, with a collective donation total of over ¥1.6 billion. The remaining large donations were dispersed across other industries.

Donation Trends

The list of the top 100 donors indicated two development trends in donations from private enterprises: the professionalization of the donation system and the normalization of donating.

Donations Tend to Be More Professional and Purposive

Since 2011, establishing a specific charitable foundation or fund has become a significant method for individuals and enterprises to make donations. For instance, donations at school anniversary celebrations were rarely contributed simply in the name of supporting the school; rather, many were devoted to specific funds, scholarships, or student subsidies. Moreover, establishing a special fund under charity associations became quite common as well. These phenomena reflected the institutionalization of large donations. According to the top-donors list, funds through charity associations totaled about ¥5.3 billion in 2011, accounting for 50 percent of all donations that year, which meant that donors experienced more control in how their funds were used.

Large Donations Are Becoming More Normal

Among the Top 100 Donors in China in 2011, twenty-four donations were made in amounts over ¥100 million. Among others, Dewang Cao's equity donation of ¥3.55 billion was the largest individual donation in mainland China. Meanwhile, Nubo Huang's ¥900-million donation to Beijing University and Jianlin Wang's ¥600-million donation to China's national sports programs were expected to significantly facilitate the development in relevant fields in the long run. In conclusion, the number of large donations exceeded the number made in previous years; for instance, over 250 donations were made in amounts over ¥10 million, and many long-term donation agreements were signed. All of these developments show that large donations are becoming a norm.

Decreases in Donations from State-Owned Enterprises

In 2010 Chinese state-owned enterprises, especially enterprises with a monopoly in their industry, had donated actively. From January to December 2010, 110 state-owned enterprises made donations totaling about ¥4.2 billion. Clearly, donations from state-owned enterprises still play an important role in Chinese philanthropy.

In November 2011, China's State-Owned Assets Supervision and Administration Commission announced the donations from state-owned enterprises in the first nine months of that year. Ninety-two state-owned enterprises had donated a total of ¥1.69 billion during this period. Compared with the nine-month figure from the previous year (over ¥2.2 billion), the donation amount in 2011 indicated a decline. Meanwhile, a lower number of enterprises donated in 2011 (ninety-two) than in 2010 (one hundred and nine). Therefore, the decline in state-owned enterprises' donations is in stark contrast with the thriving engagement of private enterprises in charitable causes.

Donation Areas and Goals

Charitable donations from Chinese state-owned enterprises in 2011 can be characterized as follows.

Major Donation Areas

In 2011 Chinese state-owned enterprises donated ¥560 million in relief work (accounting for 33.1 percent of their donations), ¥976 million in charity work (57.8 percent), and ¥154 million for other purposes

(9.1 percent). Among all donations for relief work, donations for disaster relief were ¥76 million, and donations for poverty relief and aid in targeted areas totaled ¥484 million. Among all donations for charity work, donations for science, education, culture, health, and sports causes totaled ¥228 million. More than half of state-owned enterprises that made donations had their own programs for poverty relief in areas that the government designated as target areas for donations. Meanwhile, state-owned enterprises were the main force of donations for strategic programs, such as programs supporting minority areas and other countries.

Limited Amounts of Large Donations

Among the ninety-two recorded donors announced by China's State-Owned Assets Supervision and Administration Commission, only sixty-five donated over ¥1 million in the first nine months of 2011, and only twenty-five donated over ¥10 million. Compared to private enterprises, which made over 250 single donations of more than ¥10 million, the gap with donations from state-owned enterprises was quite large.

Major Donors: Monopoly Enterprises

The five largest state-owned-enterprise donors in 2011 were Shenhua Group, China National Petroleum Corporation, China Petrochemical Corporation, China National Offshore Oil Corporation, and China Telecom, all of which were enterprises in industries monopolized by the government. Actually, the top-10 enterprises were from monopoly industries, and eight of them were in energy and electricity industries. Among all donating state-owned enterprises, monopoly enterprises accounted for a more significant portion than in the previous year (in 2010, nine of the top ten were from monopoly industries).

Corporate Social Responsibility and Transparency in Charity Information

For years, because of their own attributes and political strategies, state-owned enterprises have made limited charitable contributions, and the public denounced such limited contributions. Indeed, while many state-owned enterprises made profits in the hundreds of billions, their donation amounts were quite low. For instance, according to the data announced by the China Department of Finance in January 2012, Chinese state-owned enterprises made a total profit of ¥2.26 trillion from January to December 2011, a 12.8 percent increase from the previous year. Meanwhile, state-owned enterprises achieved a net profit of ¥1.69

trillion (People's Daily Online 2012). The total amount of donations from the ninety-two state-owned enterprises that made contributions in the first nine months of the year, however, was just ¥4.2 billion. State-owned enterprises are generally deficient in large donations given their financial ability.

The insufficient donations by state-owned enterprises have aroused a great deal of public criticism. Some people have even denounced state-owned enterprises as "misers" or the "heartless rich." However, state-owned enterprises have their reasons for not being very active donors. First, the leaders of state-owned enterprises are just holders of state-owned assets. If they use state-owned assets to make donations too easily, they may create a public image of inappropriately using these assets. Second, state-owned enterprises have a lot of staff, large-scale industries, and a responsibility to make large annual payments to the State-Owned Assets Supervision and Administration Commission. Therefore, although state-owned enterprises make a lot of profit, their budgets are not as big as they seem to be.

To deal with these two issues, China first has to establish relevant laws to regulate and guide the charitable donations of state-owned enterprises. Currently, China is in the process of establishing national standards of corporate social responsibility. Charitable donations will be specifically addressed in establishing these standards. With concrete evaluation criteria, enterprises will be assigned specific task indicators or charity work and will be urged to fulfill particular social responsibilities. For instance, to encourage corporate donations, indicators such as social reputation can be included in the evaluation of state-owned enterprises. In addition, the standards can include suggestions of major donation areas for each corporation, which will enable corporations in different industries to develop their own charity emphasis. This should lead to a more effective allocation of state-owned enterprises' resources.

In addition, the disclosure of state-owned enterprises' donation information needs to be done in a more timely fashion. The 2011 data on state-owned enterprises' donations were made public quite late. This tardiness impeded the public's recognition of state-owned enterprises' charity behaviors, which resulted in a public image that these enterprises were only concerned about making profit and not about making contributions for the public good. If large enterprises and the State-Owned Assets Supervision and Administration Commission gave a higher priority to communicating enterprises' charitable behaviors to the public, they would receive more recognition from society.

Conclusion

Due to the decrease in disaster-relief needs and the impact of an economic crisis, the amount of charitable donations in China declined significantly from 2008 to 2009. At that time, some people argued that Chinese donations would not last over the long term. In other words, charitable donations were usually made as an act of conformity, which made for unstable donation amounts. Although the country's disaster-relief needs were still low, national donation amounts rose significantly in 2011. This trend demonstrated that the Chinese people had formed a consciousness of charitable donations. Particularly, amid a series of scandals in official charity organizations, the large growth in donations demonstrated that donors from all income levels were maturing in their donation consciousness.

In 2011, charitable donations were no longer focused on disaster relief, but on long-term poverty relief and education. The publication of China's Top 100 Donors in 2011 list indicated that college foundations were on the rise and that large donations to particular funds during school anniversary celebrations strengthened these foundations. Meanwhile, Charitable Donation Days and Poverty Relief Days organized by local governments played an important role in supporting poor areas in various provinces. In 2011, the most interesting news in the field of Chinese philanthropy was the frequency of large donations. For instance, Cao's equity donation of ¥3.55 billion, Nubo Huang's ¥900-million donation to Beijing University, and Jianlin Wang's ¥600-million donation to Chinese football were very impressive to the public. Private enterprises, especially real estate enterprises, maintained a high level of enthusiasm in charity work throughout the year. In contrast, state-owned enterprises reduced their charitable donations. In conclusion, large donations have become a normal event in Chinese philanthropy. Mobilizing state-owned enterprises to make more charitable donations will promote further development of Chinese philanthropy.

8

The Charity Industry Network: A New Driving Force in China's Nonprofit Sector

Huajun Gao[*]

Questions surrounding the charity industry network emerged one after the other in 2011, and the development of charity organizations seemed precarious; still, a careful analysis of the situation revealed some encouraging signs. The main players in and supporters of the industry became increasingly involved. They actively responded to questions from outside the industry and created great potential for the sector's further development. We observed several characteristics of charity organizations in 2011, as discussed below.

First, China's charity industry has emerged, and some key voids in the industry have been filled. In general, the charity industry network can be divided into three parts: the core, through which donations flow; internal support institutions; and external industry support. The major trend in 2011 was that the flow of funds from donors to charity organizations and to beneficiaries was recognized by more and more foundations. Yet a consensus was not reached on this issue within the industry. Internal support institutions with different functions started to emerge at some critical points—and hopefully can help develop into a whole industry itself. All kinds of external industry support have gradually filled the void

* Translated by Cathy Wang, doctoral student at the Bloustein School of Planning and Public Policy, Rutgers University.

in the sector and are working together to build a constructive external environment for the charity system.

Second, the rapid growth of private foundations has facilitated the structural changes of the charity organizations. Since the number of private foundations surpassed that of public foundations at the end of 2010, private foundations continued to grow rapidly in 2011. Each year from 2009 to 2011, the annual growth rate of private foundations was over two times the growth rate of public foundations. About 70 percent of provinces had more newly developed private foundations than public foundations in 2011. The rise of private foundations will pose an important challenge in the structural adjustment and prioritization of resources for public foundations.

The Emergence of the Basic Model of the Charity Industry Network

The concept of the charity industry network was initially put forth in 2006. At that time, China's charity network was still far from being born, the relations between donors and beneficiaries were unclear, and the multiple actors in the industry were still not very influential. Five years later, the relations between donors and beneficiaries in China's charity industry gradually crystalized, the model for how the network would function became more recognizable, increasing numbers of nonprofit organizations (NPOs) joined the network as support institutions, and the external support of charity organizations also surfaced.

Figure 8.1 demonstrates the charity industry network. First, the core of the network is composed of three entities that process donations: donors (e.g., venture capital funds), charity organizations (e.g., social enterprises), and beneficiaries. Second, depending on their functions, internal support institutions can be further divided into fund-raising platforms, charity start-up investments, assessment institutions, and professional service institutions. Third, external industry supports include the government, the media, research organizations, consulting firms, the industry platform, and assessment institutions.

Figure 8.1 presents an ideal model of the interrelationships among all participants in the network based on each participant's function from the perspectives of both internal and external forces that influence the industry. In reality, quite a few participants have multiple functions and can even work both within and outside the industry; other institutions mainly play different roles on different projects at different times. Below, we will take the main functions of specific entities as the core basis of understanding their places within the network.

Figure 8.1
Demonstration Chart for the Charity Network

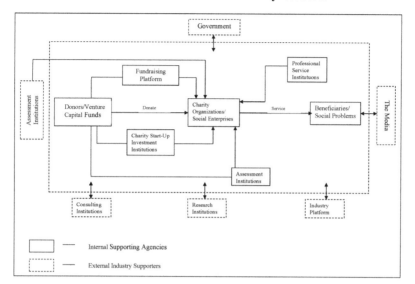

There were three overall trends in 2011: (a) all the major connections in the network achieved a breakthrough in development, (b) some key voids were filled, and (c) the basic model of the network emerged. However, there is no consensus on how donations should be processed. The flow of donations, hereafter referred to as the *donation chain*, is the core of the network. Most emerging internal support institutions and external support participants are new, and it will take two to three years for them to fully develop. For the whole charity network to work effectively, social consensus and policy support are necessary. We believe that with the mutual efforts made both inside and outside the industry, the charity network can develop fully in the next three years. If so, this period would mark the establishment of China's modern charity system.

Core Donation Chain Emerges and a Consensus Awaits

In recent years, mutual exchanges between higher level charity organizations in China and the United States have become more common. The major charity foundations in China's charity industry have been familiarizing themselves with the operational model used by their US counterparts. "Over 90 percent of U.S. private foundations are grant-giving foundations, providing funding support to public charity institutions," and this fact has become known to more and more founders of Chinese foundations. Some foundations started to realize that, to build a constructive charity environment, they would have to transform into grant-giving foundations; that is, foundations would have to become supporters of the network as funding providers, while letting professional charity organizations and social enterprises plan and implement programs.

By the end of 2011, dozens of foundations had begun to finance charity organizations or explicitly expressed their intention to become grant-giving foundations in the future. These foundations include the Narada Foundation, You Change China Social Entrepreneur Foundation, Vantone Foundation, Tencent Foundation, One Foundation, Shanghai United Foundation, Alashan Ecological Foundation, China Foundation for Poverty Alleviation, Chinese Red Cross Foundation, China Environmental Protection Foundation, China Foundation for Disabled Persons, China Population Welfare Foundation, and China Charities Aid Foundation for Children, among others. In addition, more than twenty organizations operate as both grant-giving foundations and service providers. Compared with more than 2,600 private foundations in the country, the number of these grant-giving foundations seems too small. However, all change starts small, and with the rapid growth of private foundations and the leading role of industry pioneers, we are confident that more and more organizations will become grant-giving foundations. In the near future, the core donation chain and the charity network as a whole will work smoothly.

Internal Support Institutions Help Develop the Charity Network

Numerous NPO support institutions with a variety of specific functions emerged in 2011. These organizations all form part of the network, and each has a different role. The major players are charity organizations and social enterprises. These support institutions aim to connect key participants and improve the performance of charity organizations. At present, these support organizations are still in an initial stage of development. It will take time for them to fully integrate into the network. This chapter presents an overview and trends of these support institutions.

A Social Media Fund-Raising Platform and Increased Charity Fund-Raising Channels
Professional fund-raising institutions and fund-raising platforms were neglected by charity organizations for a long time, until a scandal referred

to as the Meimei Guo incident occurred. Since then, the Red Cross Foundation and the World Outstanding Chinese Business Association have begun to enter the public view. In the past, these professionals worked for government charity foundations as fundraisers because private charity organizations did not exist. In May 2009, a "10-cent monthly donation plan" was initiated by the Tencent Foundation, which was the first online fund-raising platform used by charity foundations. In December 2009, the Shanghai United Foundation established fund-raising institutions to serve private charity organizations.

Social media became a new addition to charity fundraising in 2011. Social media quickly filled the void in fund-raising efforts and were fully utilized by charity organizations. The fund-raising network of China's social media as of the end of 2011 is shown in Table 8.1.

Table 8.1
Social Media Charity Platforms

Type	Name of platform and website	Introduction
Online portal platform with small amount of giving	http://love.alipay. com, http://gongyi. weibo.com, http:// gongyi.qq.com/ donate.htm	Charity organizations submit fund-raising program applications to these online portals and establish a special column on them. Donors can click DONATE to make electronic payments.
Online charity stores	http://www.buy42. com	The money made from selling secondhand or charitable goods after deducting the operational costs of the website is donated to charity organizations.
Giving platform within the industry	http://www. chinag360.com	This is an affiliate of the Foundation Center website and is a platform for connecting charity resources. Foundations can release their program information and conduct fund-raising functions.
Fund-raising platform for presale products	http://www.dreamore. cn, http://demohour. com	This type of platform draws on the presale dream of Kickstarter by letting fundraisers initiate program applications. The website assists in producing fund-raising videos and building webpages for each program. Supporters choose certain amounts of presale products and make payments

(*continued*)

Table 8.1 (*continued*)

Type	Name of platform and website	Introduction
		in advance. After the fundraising is complete, the fundraisers produce the products and provide them to the supporters who made payments. For the time being, both websites state that they do not support charity activities; rather, they only support businesses and programs related to design and artistically creative work that are involved in selling and buying activities. Yet in practice, many programs are charity related or have a social-enterprise component.

The emergence of these fund-raising platforms has positively influenced the fund-raising efforts of private charity organizations. It is predictable that, as the public and the media become more passionate about charity activities, these types of platforms will play a bigger role in society. As a newly developing factor in the fund-raising network, social media faces some challenges, such as ensuring the security of internet transactions, performing background checks of fundraisers, monitoring the use of funding, and regulating legal risks. These are all normal challenges to face in the early stages of development. We are confident that all these issues can be addressed with the development of charity organizations, fund-raising institutions, donors, and legal regulations.

Diversification of Assessment Institutions and Methodologies

The assessment of charity projects is a venue for improving the transparency of, public trust in, and professional capacity of charity organizations. The assessment of nonprofit projects in China can be traced back to the early 1990s. At that time, assessments were mainly conducted by foreign experts who were invited to China by international corporate donors. The widely acknowledged method was called the logical model. Later, some research institutions and professors in China began to develop a methodology that was suitable to the local context. In 2007, Guosheng Deng from the School of Public Administration at Tsinghua University created a comprehensive assessment theory called accountability, performance, and capacity. This theory marked a milestone in developing methodology suitable to the Chinese context.

According to the 2011 China Charity Resources Allocation Report, a survey was conducted to assess thirty funded programs. Thirty-seven percent were assessed by those who financed them, only 18.5 percent hired a third party to conduct an assessment, and another 18.5 percent reported that they had conducted no assessment or another type of assessment not listed on the survey. Some respondents reported that it was difficult to determine evaluation criteria and evaluate projects. The respondents hoped that funded charity organizations would be able to set up quantified criteria to conduct self-evaluations. Meanwhile, they hoped that the professional third-party assessment agencies could assist in these efforts. In other words, donors should have certain standards for program evaluation. Given that most respondents were from well-developed international financial institutions or corporate social responsibility (CSR) departments in transnational corporations and that the newly established private foundations are growing rapidly, the future market of program evaluation should be more robust.

Some private think tanks and CSR consulting firms also entered the field of nonprofit program evaluation in 2011 and actively explored advanced international methodologies and developed more practical evaluation methods and criteria. The next section discusses some of the methods that have had large impacts in China.

The Social Resources Institute's SROI Evaluation Method
In July 2011, the Social Resources Institute, a private think tank, introduced a tool to evaluate the social impact of NPOs. The tool measured social return on investment (SROI). The Social Resources Institute released a Chinese version of the tool's user guide (the Guide to Evaluating Return on Social Investment). The institute also promoted the use of SROI through group discussions and seminars.

The SROI method emerged in 2000 from Great Britain and the United States. The assessment method's main functions are to accurately measure—with the input of stakeholders—an organization's social impact and ability to monetize resources. As more and more enterprises have established private foundations or CSR departments, donors have begun to prefer quantified evaluations of the returns on and social impacts of their investments. Because of this, the SROI evaluation method is likely to become increasingly popular.

A Highly Publicized Foundation Evaluation

In November 2011, Recende CSR conducted an evaluation on behalf of Narada Foundation of Gesanghua Education's Aid, an agency that was involved in a scandal at the time. As a third party, Recende evaluated Gesanghua's legitimacy and risk, current status of and mechanisms to ensure information transparency, major administrative expenditures, management structure, and volunteer management. Based on the results of the evaluation, Recende came up with a proposal for Gesanghua's organizational development and further explored the influence and significance of this case for China's charity organizations.

Narada Foundation convened a special seminar at the end of December 2011 to release the evaluation results to the media and all related parties. The results showed that the three problems previously suspected of Gesanghua did not exist at all, which helped Gesanghua to quickly distance itself from its negative image. Recende had already published the three reports that resulted from the evaluation on its website: the Report on Organizational Evaluation on Qinghai Gesanghua Education's Aid, the Proposal for Qinghai Gesanghua Education's Aid Regarding Its Organizational Development and Its Impact and Revelations for China's Charity Organizations, and the Possibility of Excellence: Revelations from Organizations Such as Gesanghua.

This third-party evaluation was meaningful because it clarified some controversial issues. This shows that program evaluation can play a positive role in strengthening the transparency of charity organizations, improving their program planning and management capabilities, leading and building a charity environment, and bolstering the public's trust in these organizations.

Professional Subservices and the Growth of Professional Volunteers

Professional service institutions are an important factor in improving the professional competence of charity organizations and in building a healthy charity network. In the past, the most well-known professional service institutions were mainly capacity-building institutions and incubators for NPOs. In 2007, some well-known companies, including Deloitte, McKinsey, and Ogilvy, formed New Philanthropy Partners, a new public-private partnership, which aimed to build a platform that would provide comprehensive professional services. However, this partnership fizzled out in 2010. In the same year, the Public Interest Law Initiative, a US organization, introduced the concept of pro bono work to China's legal circles. In conjunction with top law firms in Beijing and Shanghai, the initiative held pro bono roundtables and encouraged lawyers to provide free legal services for the public good. At the same time, the initiative tried to build a pro bono clearinghouse as a platform for information exchange for free public-interest legal services. The platform was intended to periodically connect NPOs that need legal advice with business lawyers. Those who volunteered to provide pro bono services were called professional volunteers, skills volunteers, or *Ai ke*.

More and more professionals became interested in the public-interest field in 2011. A few institutions and programs emerged that specifically provided personalized professional services to public-interest organizations. These organizations can be divided into three types based on their characteristics. First, volunteer organizations are mainly made up of young, skilled professionals. These are mostly online organizations. Second, official NPOs and social enterprises are most likely to be initially built by some NPO employees who are familiar with public-interest circles or by senior volunteers. These organizations provide specialized, professional services to nongovernmental organizations (NGOs) at either no cost (through volunteers) or low cost. Third, CSR programs are created by the CSR departments of famous companies by motivating their employees to provide free professional services and donate goods needed for those services, such as computer software and hardware.

These institutions and programs have different service specializations. They can be differentiated by how active their services are: extremely active, active, and inactive. As shown in Table 8.2, there are eight extremely active institutions in China, five of which provide IT services and three of which provide management consulting. There are three active institutions, two of which offer financial services and one of which offers graphic design. To date, there are no active institutions that provide pro bono legal, human resources, and public relations (PR) services. However, we believe that these areas will become active with the rapidly spreading voluntary spirit and the growth of CSR.

The Increasing Development of the External Support Environment

In 2011, three entities—the government, the media, and research organizations—all provided substantial external support to the charity industry. These three entities are discussed in detail in other chapters in this book, and therefore we do not cover them here. Instead, the next section introduces the recent emergence of assessment institutions and provides an overview of the charity industry platform. These external supporters

Table 8.2
Professional Service Institutions That Specifically Serve Charity
Organizations or CSR Programs

Type	Name of organization, type, website/Weibo	Introduction
IT technology	China Eagle, social enterprise, http://www.iyiyun.com/	China Eagle is a social enterprise that is devoted to "promoting charity development and social innovation through the Internet," with a mission to offer internet-based information technology (IT) solutions for charity organizations and social innovation and improve their IT capabilities.
	Itnpp.cn, volunteer organization, http://www.itnpp.cn	A member of Beijing Volunteer Association, this organization serves IT enterprises and professional volunteers. The organization provides charity IT services to support charity organizations and programs.
	Volunteer organization, http://weibo.com/ictygl	This organization's mission lies in assisting in the transparency and professionalization of the charity industry through IT, advancing the sustainability of the charity system, and advancing the formation of civil society and the spread of a culture of charity. The major institution is Ren Ai Charity Foundation.
	Microsoft NPO IT Day, CRS program, http://www.microsoft.com/china/mscorp/citizenship/	The CSR activities held by Microsoft nationwide in China help NPOs to build their capacity for IT and improve efficiency and transparency through IT skills training, donating software and secondhand computers, and volunteering. At present, NPO IT skills training and case studies are held twice annually in China.
	Information and Communication Technology (ICT) Professional Volunteer Federation, CSR program, http://weibo.com/ictvolunteer	Baidu, Intel, and Ericsson and some other companies initiated CSR programs, with a plan of relying on Web 2.0 platforms, building up the strength of the volunteers of the ICT industry, and enhancing the practical capacity of charity organizations in information technology

(*continued*)

Table 8.2 (*continued*)

Type	Name of organization, type, website/Weibo	Introduction
		through capacity-building training, technological support, and organizational development consulting for charity organizations. These CSR activities are still not that active.
Management consulting	A Better Community (ABC), volunteer organization, http://www.theabconline.org/	From an independent perspective of a third party, ABC integrates high-end professional skills of volunteers and offers for free individualized management strategy consulting services for NGOs. These consulting services include but are not limited to strategy study, volunteer management, market expansion, industry study, feasibility study of programs, PR management, and human resources, among others.
	iJoin, volunteer organization, http://ijoin.vjoinunion.org/	iJoin is a social-innovation consulting program managed by volunteers. Its mission is to provide consulting services to charity organizations that need improvement in specific areas by those trained volunteers who have charity experiences.
	Boston Consulting Group (BCG) Social Impact Team, CSR program, http://www.bcg.com/about_bcg/social_impact/default.aspx	This program is BCG's worldwide pro bono program. In China, it mainly provides free management consulting for some international organizations, holds Social Impact Luncheons regularly, and invites communications between charity professionals and consultants at BCG.
Financial management	NGO Friends, NPO, http://www.nfriend.org	This is a charity organization that provides financial services to NGOs, and through its professionals and volunteers, it offers phone consultations and on-site instructions related to accounting and tax issues and trains staff members on financial management. The organization also evaluates and monitors the financial status of NGOs or programs and comes up with proposals on improvement.

(*continued*)

Table 8.2 (*continued*)

Type	Name of organization, type, website/Weibo	Introduction
	Ants Consulting Company, NPO (no website)	This company chose its name because the pronunciation of the Chinese word *ants* is similar to the pronunciation for the Chinese word for *charity*. Charity is composed of people who have experiences and passion in NGOs. Charity efforts provide services, including financial trust, program management, a variety of consulting services, and volunteer training.
Graphic design	Frolac Studio, http://www.frolac.org/	Frolac Studio is the first support service institution in the field of NGOs that provides image design, brand promotion, and marketing and strategy services. It hopes to integrate all professional services and utilize industry platform resources so as to provide professional graphic design, brand promotion, and event plans for NGOs.
Law	None	The China NGO Legal Support Website was built in 2006 but it no longer exists. The previously mentioned Public Interest Law Initiative's pro bono clearinghouse seems to never officially operate. So far, there are some lawyers as individual volunteers who provide legal services for some charity organizations. Also, some international law firms provide free services for international charity organizations.
Human resources	None	There are still no human resources organizations or programs serving charity organizations. Some management consulting organizations partly deal with human resources.
PR	None	There are no PR service institutions or CSR programs serving for charity organizations. Ogilvy and Mather, as a sponsor of New Philanthropy Partners, used to serve international organizations and large-scale foundations in China.

are gradually filling the void in an important field and mutually contribute to the construction of a beneficial environment for the charity industry.

The First Third-Party Charity Assessment Institution in Mainland China

China Charity Navigator (CSZN.org) first began operating on December 14, 2011. It is the first third-party charity assessment institution in mainland China. Its basic mission is to enhance the monitoring system of charity organizations; to promote the regulation, transparency, and development of charity organizations; to facilitate the diversification of charity oversight; to lessen the influence of government ideology; to pay close attention to the needs of all social circles to the charity industry; to foster a culture of donation; to encourage the development of China's service industry; to effectively allocate and utilize social resources within the system; to fill the void left by the primary and secondary sectors; and to help more people in need. At present, China Charity Navigator operates as a private organization, and its staff members are not employed with any charity organizations. As of March 20, 2011, China Charity Navigator had 2,523 members and offered assessment to 1,536 charity organizations. All its members are foundations and social groups, none of which were private or unregistered NPOs. This is mainly because very few private charity organizations in mainland China have published their annual reports online so far.

China Charity Navigator was modeled after the US charity navigator CharityNavigator.org and Hong Kong's theIdonate.com. According to the assessment methods published on its website, China Charity Navigator mainly assesses charity organizations' financial indicators, and at the same time, takes some nonfinancial indicators into account (e.g., the transparency and accountability of organizations). In general, there are four assessment dimensions: efficiency of institutional operations (40 percent), other financial performance (30 percent), transparency and accountability (20 percent), and public opinion (10 percent). The rating scale ranges from zero to five stars. Meanwhile, the assessment offers suggestions and comments to every charity organization assessed. At present, only one charity organization has been assessed as a five-star organization, and fifty-nine charity organizations have been assessed as four-star organizations.

Third-party assessment institutions are important factors in building public trust and creating more transparency in charity organizations. They are also a bridge that connects charity organizations with ordinary people. In a well-developed charity market, usually charity institutions are subject to the following four monitoring systems.

The first system is governmental oversight. In China, this mainly comes from administrative actions from the Ministry of Civil Affairs and the Department of Taxation, such as policy making, organization registrations, audits, taxation, and annual assessments, so as to monitor and regulate charity organizations. The second system is oversight by stakeholders. This can take place through selective donation and the creation of public opinion pressure by donors, the media, and the public. The third system is oversight by the industry's regulating institutions, such as the US organization GuideStar.org, the China Foundation Center (FoundationCenter. org.cn), and the Chinese organization USDO (ChinaUSDO.org). This oversight occurs through making and implementing industry regulations. The fourth system is oversight by third-party assessment institutions, such as the American CharityGuide.com and the China Charity navigator through independent evaluations and public assessments.

The emergence of the China Charity Navigator marked the establishment of China's charity oversight system. We hope that the China Charity Navigator will continue to improve its assessment methods and establish standardized guidelines for private charity organizations to make assessments more effective.

Off-Line and Online Communication Platforms in the Charity Industry

The charity industry's external communication platform is a professional platform where charity organizations reveal information and display and promote themselves to outside industries. In 2011, breakthroughs were made in both off-line and online platforms.

For the off-line platform, in 2011, Nonprofit Incubator collaborated with the Ministry of Civil Affairs in both Shenzhen and Shanghai to hold two large-scale conferences on the display and communications of charity organizations. The event in Shenzhen was the city's first Conference on Charity Programs Display and Communications, and the event in Shanghai was the city's first Charity Partnership Day. For each conference, over 120 private charity organizations, foundations, and enterprises were in attendance. Unlike the World Bank's China Developing Market Program and the Nonprofit Incubator's Beijing Conference on Charity Programs Display and Communications, which were held in 2009, the 2011 conferences had three new characteristics. First, there were more enterprises at the 2011 conferences, with over twenty enterprises setting up booths in Shanghai's conference alone. Second, the number of public visitors increased, with about 10,000 people visiting during the three days of the Shenzhen's conference. Third, discussion groups, seminars, and public interaction activities increased. During the Shenzhen conference, there were five seminars, eight public activities, and fourteen charity discussion groups. In the summer of 2012, the Ministry of Civil Affairs worked with the Shenzhen Municipal Government to hold a national-level display and communications conference for charity programs.

Regarding the online platform, the earliest effort was ChinaCSRmap. org, built by SynTao Sustainability Solutions, which mainly serves enterprises that aim to develop CSR departments and helps enterprises form partnerships within their field, such as with experts, consulting institutions, NPOs, service providers, and the media. In 2010, the China Foundation Center website (FoundationCenter.org.cn) went live. As an information-service platform in the foundation industry, it provides both information and professional services. The Ministry of Civil Affairs designated the website as the official public platform for foundation information in places such as Yunnan and Beijing.

In February 2012, the China Development Brief released its list of NGOs online. This platform has 762 members so far, including almost every private and international charity organization that has been active in recent years. The list is organized clearly, and the search function works well. Users can search by area of concern, geographic location, and alphabetical index. These functions are very convenient to those users who look for specific partnerships. From November 2011, when the website's database was first tested, to when it was officially online three months later, an average of 100,000 visitors per day reached. As of March 2012, the total number of visitors had reached 12,530,000.

These off-line and online foreign exchange platforms complement each other; together, they broaden the channels through which charity organizations can display themselves and exchange ideas with other organizations. Yet, building the platform is only the first step. The next step, which is more important, is how to further enrich the content of the platform, improve the functions of the platform, and strengthen effective communication.

9

The Media and China's Nonprofit Sector

Gaorong Zhang and *Zhenyao Wang*

Prior to 2010, charity was not a mainstream topic in public opinion. At that time, public reports on charity donations were limited to when serious natural disasters occurred. But, in 2011, a series of events occurred that became hot topics and finally brought public service into mainstream media and public discussion. These events included a high-profile shooting that saved trafficked children, the Free Lunch program, the controversial Meimei Guo incident, and the China Charity Federation's Invoice Event. In the present context, in which the public questions the credibility of public service organizations and both traditional and digital media pursue news stories from a critical perspective, it is impossible to ignore acclaim or criticism in the media. The charity industry cannot ignore the power of the media either. Therefore, we cast our eyes over the media outlets that actively reported on the public service industry and charity participation in 2011. We believe that our study reveals that the media not only recorded the transformation and innovation of China's public charity industry but also became an important force in driving the development of China's public service enterprises.

* Translated by Cathy Wang, doctoral student at the Bloustein School of Planning and Public Policy, Rutgers University.

Macrolevel Attention Limited to Hot Topics

The year of 2011 was a difficult year for China's public service enterprises. Public service was increasingly becoming a main topic in people's daily conversations, both in person and online. Therefore, logic would have it that the media, as disseminators of information and respondents to public opinion, would increase its reports on public service enterprises. In reality, however, our observations show that, on the macro level, the frequency of media reports on charity events did not show a notable increase from 2010. The reports on and broadcasts of charity events were mainly due to the frequent occurrence of the hot topics. The following discussion is broken into two parts to illustrate (a) the media reports on the overall atmosphere of the public service industry and (b) widely discussed events that occurred in 2011.

The Media's Limited Attention to Public Service

We conducted preliminary statistics by using the Text Database from China Core Newspaper Databases (CCND) to examine the extent of change in the media's attention to the charity industry. This database has stored academic and informative literature from China's major newspapers since 2000. By the end of 2010, it had collected 795 million pieces of literature from over 500 major newspapers. Therefore, the statistics from this database can ensure not only the credibility of the sources but also the depth and breadth of the information. When we searched the database by typing in key words that we predetermined were related to public service, we obtained the following results.

By and large, the key words *philanthropy* (*gongyi*) and *charity* (*cishan*) were the closest to the meaning of charity enterprises, and their frequency of appearance as a main topic of the reports in the database in 2011 was 9,124 and 1,753, respectively. Compared with the data from 2010, the frequency of appearance for *philanthropy* decreased by 14.7 percent, and the frequency for *charity* increased by 13.2 percent. The frequencies of appearance as a report headline in 2011 were 2,017 and 1,470, respectively, representing a 20.9 percent increase for *philanthropy* and a 15.2 percent increase for *charity* from 2010. As such, the number of reports that were at all related to philanthropy in 2011 was almost the same as or even a little smaller than the number from 2010, yet the number of reports with philanthropy as the focus of the content clearly increased in 2011. The frequency of appearance for other terms whose meanings are closely related to philanthropy, such as *nonprofit, voluntary, donation*, and so on, decreased as both main topics and headlines from 2010 to 2011. These trends were mainly an outcome of the fewer natural disasters in 2011, which resulted in fewer disaster-relief activities and donations and less media coverage. For details, please see Figures 9.1 and 9.2.

The media gave enormous coverage to philanthropy and charity organizations in 2011. Compared with 2010, the terms *nonprofit organization, nongovernmental organization, social organization*, and *civil organization* appeared less frequently as a main article topic but increased in headlines in 2011. This shows that the media is paying increasingly close attention to public charity organizations. In addition, the number of reports that had the term *foundation, charity meeting*, or *grassroots organization* as a main topic increased as well, with a 42 percent increase for *charity meeting*. The media seems to be paying more attention to organizations that have clearer functions. It is undeniable that charity associations have been playing an increasingly important role in local philanthropy activities since 2011. Surprisingly, although a variety of information related to the Red Cross was reported in 2011, the organization was mentioned less

Figure 9.1
Frequency of Main Topic Appearance of Media Reports on
Overall Philanthropy and Charity

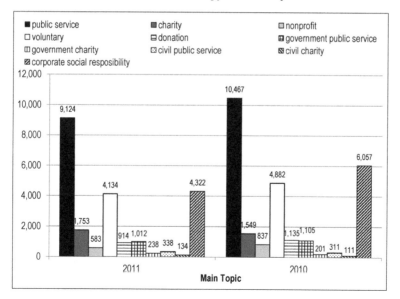

Figure 9.2
Frequency of Headline Appearance of Media Reports on Overall
Public Service and Charity

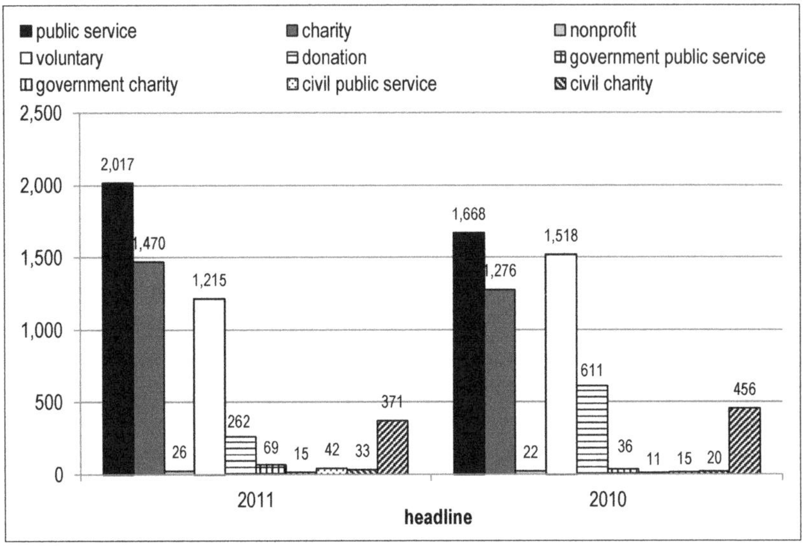

frequently as a main topic but more frequently as a headline. For details, please see Figures 9.3 and 9.4.

Regarding philanthropy activities, since the terms tend to be more conceptual, they usually do not appear in the headline of the news. Therefore, we only selected relevant information related to headlines for our research. In 2011, the form of philanthropy activities diversified and the number of activities increased. But the data show that reports on these activities did not increase appreciably—and even decreased for the majority of terms. Compared with 2010, except for the term *philanthropy programs*, the frequencies of appearance of the terms *philanthropy activities, philanthropy actions, philanthropy poverty relief, philanthropy assistance*, and *philanthropy disaster relief* all reduced to varying degrees. Among these terms, the frequency of appearance for *philanthropy disaster relief* reduced by 113 percent. The sharply reduced number of natural disasters had a large impact on news reports. On the contrary, media reports on charity activities in 2011 increased from last year, including both macrolevel terms (such as *charity activities, charity action*, and *charity programs*) and terms related to particular events (such as *charity donation* and *charity fundraising*). This could be an outcome of the frequent, large donations

Figure 9.3
Frequency of Main Topic Appearance of Media Reports on
Philanthropy and Charity Organizations

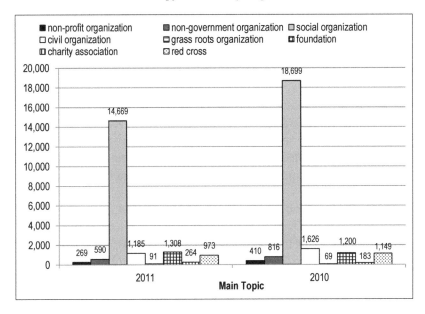

Figure 9.4
Frequency of Headline Appearance of Media Reports on
Philanthropy and Charity Organizations

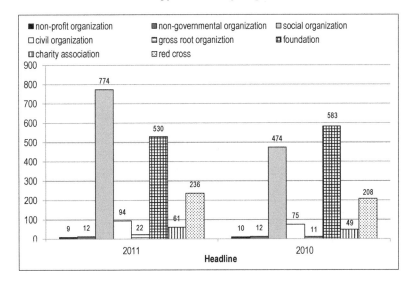

due to local Charity Day events and university celebrations. For detailed information on these trends, please see Figures 9.5 and 9.6.

Regarding negative news reports, we chose the search terms *donation fraud, fake charity*, and *violent charity* as key words because these actions were being criticized by society. Compared with 2010, the media paid increased attention to these three behaviors in 2011. Among these terms, there were more reports on donation fraud, followed by violent charities and then fake charities. Overall, the number of negative media reports on philanthropy is very small. For details, please see Figure 9.7.

In summary, our findings show that government-run media coverage on the public service industry, public service organizations, and public service activities all decreased to different degrees but that the coverage on charity activities and negative charity phenomena increased.

Heavy Media Focus on Hot Topics in Public Service

A few events in the public service industry became hot topics in 2011. The One Foundation's transition from a private fund-raising organization to a public fund-raising organization at the start of the year, the registration

Figure 9.5
Frequency of Main Topic Appearance of Media Reports on
Philanthropy Activities

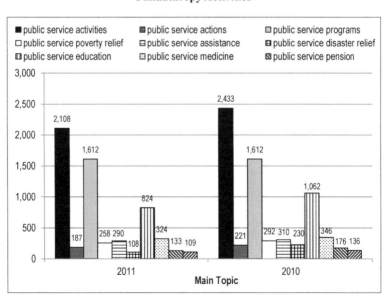

Figure 9.6
Frequency of Headline Appearance of Media Reports on
Public Service Activities

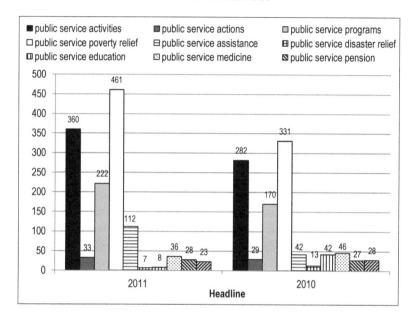

Figure 9.7
Frequency of Appearance of Media Negative Reports on Charity

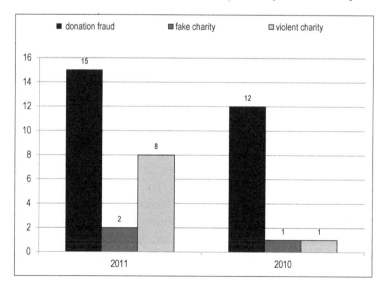

of the Millicharity Service Center in Dongyuan at the end of the year, and the Free Lunch program throughout the year, all illustrated the progress and development of China's public service industry. In the latter part of the year, a negative storyline broke out about a government-run public service organization and exposed the many problems and challenges that China's public service enterprises were facing. Recognizing both the challenges they were facing and the progress they had made, public service enterprises saw an opportunity to use the media as a way to overcome their difficulties and achieve sustainability. Intuitively, we thought that the media would give more coverage to the hot topics in public service than to the state of public service in general. But this was not supported by the data from China's major newspapers' database. In searching two of the common public service key words, *Meimei Guo* and *Free Lunch*, they only appeared as a headline 127 times and 235 times, respectively, far lower than the frequencies for major public service macro words. For the other common public service words, such as *Henan Soong Ching Ling Foundation* and *Heren Charity Foundation*, they appeared fewer than ten times each. So to speak, the government-run media does not pay much attention to philanthropy events, particularly negative events, that are popular among ordinary people; rather, the media tends to cover the overall situation of the philanthropy industry.

Given that most widely discussed events were reported online first and then by newspapers and TV stations, we chose to search Baidu to study the degree of attention on public charity events, coupled with special reports on websites oriented toward public charity. Through searching the frequencies of appearance of widely discussed events within article bodies and headlines in Baidu news, we found eighteen hot terms in the public charity field over the year 2011 as samples. These terms include *Meimei Guo, Red Cross; World Chinese Union General—China-Africa Project Hope; China Charity—Shangde, Wuxi City; Henan Soong Ching Ling Foundation; Free Lunch; Dewang Cao's Heren Foundation; Guangbiao Chen's fraud donation; registration of Guangdong social organizations (one out of one thousand); costly meals of Luwan Red Cross; establishment of the Amway Foundation; kidnapping Red Cross staff; Ge Sanghua Education's Aid Fraud; voluntary service fairs; Shanghai Public Charity Partnership Day; China City Public Charity Index; snapshots of children being trafficked; cars stopping to save dogs on the highway*; and *establishment of the One Foundation*. These eighteen terms cover almost all hot events that occurred in the philanthropy field in 2011.

After searching, we found that the most covered philanthropy event in 2011 was the Meimei Guo incident, which was associated with the China Red Cross. The next most common event was the Free Lunch program. These two philanthropy efforts received far more media coverage than other events. It is worth noting that almost half of the hot terms were negative in some way. This is because 2011 was a year marked by frequent scandals. On the other hand, the data show that the media regards exposing scandals as a job responsibility and is good at squeezing news value out of existing issues. Of course, among the highly ranked hot events, there was positive news. For example, the establishment of the One Foundation was reported on 5,240 times by the media in 2011. Among these instances, 266 of the mentions occurred in headlines or as the focus of the article. As one of the few nongovernmental public charity organizations that was legally independent from the government, the registration of the organization caused a certain degree of attention. Similar events also included the registrations of the Dongyuan MilliCharity and the Amway Foundation, among others. Still, positive events such as these received less attention than did the negative events.

By looking at the content written about specific topics, we can see that the media has, more often than not, determined the direction of the stories. With the media's efforts, these events became hot news topics from beginning to end, which allowed readers to have a better understanding of how the news reports dissected a variety of issues and questions. Without the media's reports, it would be difficult for people to know what goes on behind the scenes in philanthropy organizations, to understand their programs or actively participate in them, and to advocate for reform. The key role that the media played in philanthropy events in 2011 cannot be ignored.

The Media's Involvement in Philanthropy

The role that the media plays in China's public charity industry has not just been that of a bystander. In many cases, the media also serves as a practitioner, advocate, and even leader for a variety of philanthropy activities. There are numerous examples from the past few years of active media coverage of philanthropy activities, including special editions of newspapers, charity magazines, TV programs, and websites dedicated to philanthropy topics. In addition, the media has begun to collaborate with charity organizations and has established several kinds of special funds for the purpose of developing the philanthropy industry. As far as we can see, the media's involvement in the philanthropy industry extends beyond its traditional role of reporting news and now includes direct participation in activities and programs. This has made the media's role in philanthropy increasingly diverse. The following discussion gives an overview of the media's involvement in the philanthropy industry in 2011.

Media Reports of Philanthropy Events

Reporting news about current events is the media's mission and reason for existence. The media now regards philanthropy as one of its main areas of reporting. In 2011, the media was actively involved in philanthropy, and its involvement became increasingly institutionalized. Throughout the year, the total number of columns and publications initiated by the media exceeded the sum from all previous years. All major media outlets and news websites opened channels for philanthropy. In essence, the framework for media reporting on philanthropy began to take shape in 2011.

In 2011, the mainstream newspapers began to create a wide range of special editions on philanthropy, which helped gradually introduce the industry into the mainstream discourse. In collaboration with the Guangzhou City Charity Organization and China Mobil in Guangdong Province, the newspaper *New Express* worked to start a philanthropy project called the Public Service Alliance: A Friendly and New Guangzhou. It created the first *Philanthropy Daily* special edition, reporting the difficulties facing the disadvantaged and their stories, and at the same time organizing all kinds of activities to help make their dreams come true. The edition ran successfully all year, directly or indirectly helping the disadvantaged to solve many real-life problems.

In mid-2011, there was an impressive run during which three philanthropy newspapers were created in forty days. On May 17, the influential *Jing Newspaper*, which was created about ten years ago, published *ShenZhen Philanthropy Weekly* for the first time. Since then, Shenzhen City, which ranked number one in donations per capita, has had its own professional philanthropy newspaper. On June 7, *Eastern Philanthropy Weekly* was created. The publication was sponsored by Zhengzhou City's *Eastern Today* and is published every Monday. *Eastern Philanthropy Weekly* is the first urban philanthropy weekly newspaper in Henan Province and the entire middle region of China. On June 27, *South Capital Philanthropy Weekly* was another stunning success. The publication was created by the Nanfang Media Group, which puts the publication out every Monday and aims to make it a philanthropy guide for the people throughout the Pearl River Delta.

In early July, the Southern Metropolis Daily Group, in collaboration with China's Poverty Alleviation Foundation and the Citizen's Charity Research Center at Beijing University, came together to create a magazine titled *China Wealth*. The focus of this magazine is on issues related to people's livelihood, and the primary issue is the redistribution of wealth. In October, Chengdu Daily Group and Chengdu Charity Association published the *Voice of Charity*, which marked the existence of the first philanthropy magazine in the western part of China. The magazine reports on the city's charity activities and helps to encourage social interest and involvement in Chengdu's charity enterprises. In November, *Charity and Philanthropy*, another new philanthropy newspaper, claimed its fame as China's first professional newspaper on charity and philanthropy. The newspaper was originally *Today's Information*, which was affiliated with China Publishing Group. After the newspaper restructured its company, the publication was administered by the Ministry of Civil Affairs and sponsored by China Charity. The newspaper reports on charity and philanthropy information and policy, promotes charity and traditional culture, and focuses on popular charity and philanthropy events. It is published in China and abroad.

In addition to print media, TV media is also a primary force for reporting philanthropy news. *Helping the Vulnerable* was one of the prize efforts of Hunan Satellite TV in 2011 and was also the country's first live program on philanthropy. This program aims to help people who are in need by broadcasting philanthropy programs and promoting the "Five Dollar Donation Plan" to bring together all levels of charitable contributions, large or small. This program is also part of the new model for Happy Charity developed by Hunan Satellite TV Station. The activities promote the concept of small charities and support the establishment of the Mongo V Foundation. The Qinghai Satellite TV program *Flowers Everywhere* was part of the Spring Buds Plan initiated by the Qinghai Satellite TV Station and the China Children and Teenagers' Fund. The plan's philanthropy purpose is to assist poor, female dropouts to resume their education and to seek their "most beautiful flower." At the end of 2011, China Central Television Station opened a new program, *Dream Choir*, which invited famous singers to return to their hometown and select about twenty local residents to form a dream choir group. After training, the residents took part in competitions. The TV station promoted their stage performances, and they received varying amounts of funds to help them achieve their philanthropy dream for their hometown. Compared with Gansu Satellite TV's *Charity*

China Trip and Yunnan Satellite TV's *Becoming Eco-Citizens*, the philanthropy TV programs in 2011 reached new heights, in terms of both recreation and diversification. The programs attracted more attention from the audience, which has undoubtedly been beneficial to enlarging the impact of the programs and promoting philanthropy enterprises.

Compared with the attention given to newspapers and TV stations, online media activities were less prominent. In 2011, the only mainstream websites to enter the philanthropy arena were Xinhua.org and Nandu.com. They began to publish online material about the philanthropy industry beginning December 5 and December 17, respectively, adding two platforms for the promotion of philanthropy concepts and organizing philanthropy activities. Xinhua.org continues to operate even today.

Media-Driven Charity Institutions and Funding

Compared with opening philanthropy columns, editions, periodicals, and websites, the media has made slower progress in establishing charity institutions. After all, not all mass media have access to the resources and venues to participate throughout the entire process, from fundraising to establishing the programs to implementing the programs. Nevertheless, the media was still somewhat active in building charity organizations in 2011. Still, we believe that the media can play an important role in promoting the development of the philanthropy industry as a whole. Tables 9.1 and 9.2 illustrate the charity organizations and special funds initiated by media organizations and professionals in 2011.

Table 9.1
Charity Organizations and Special Funds Initiated by Media
Organizations in 2011

Organization or fund	Media participation	Location
Xiaoxiang Morning News Charity Foundation	Xiaoxiang Morning News	Changsha
Beijing Youth Innovation Fund	Beijing Youth News	Beijing
Information Times Love and Charity Fund	Information Times	Guangzhou
Zhude Fund	Tencent Charity	Shenzhen

Table 9.2
Charity Organizations and Special Funds Initiated by
Professionals in 2011

Organization	Professionals	Location
Microfund Charity	Shuxin Liang	Guiyang
It Fund	Jing Li	Beijing
Wardrobe Care Fund	Kai Wang and Hongtao Ma	Beijing

In 2011, the first media organization to start charity organizations is the Xiaoxiang Morning News Charity Foundation, which was created in Hunan Province on March 10. As one of the major media outlets in Hunan, this newspaper has been putting philanthropy into practice since its inception. Now the newspaper is the first print media company to create a philanthropy foundation. The foundation's start-up funding consisted of ¥10 million, including ¥7 million from *Xiaoxiang Morning Post*, ¥2 million from the Hunan Publishing Investment Holding Group, and the rest from the Hunan Yongtong Automobile Group and the Hunan Yunda Industrial Group. The foundation is devoted to addressing issues that occurred in China's transitional period, promoting the positive growth of Chinese youth, advocating citizens' responsibilities, defending the public interest, and facilitating harmonious societal progress.

On July 3, 2011, the Beijing Youth Innovation Fund was established. The fund was sponsored by the Communist Youth League Beijing Committee and was created by *Beijing Youth Daily* and the Beijing Youth Development Foundation. The fund is supposed to help foster the talent to build an innovative country and facilitate youth development in philanthropy enterprises. The fund is affiliated with the Beijing Youth Development Foundation. Its steering committee is composed of *Beijing Youth Daily* and the Beijing Youth Development Foundation. On August 14, *Lingnan Information Times* declared its intention to establish the Information Times Love and Charity Fund in cooperation with Guangzhou City's Charity Organization. The program's goal is to fund news reports on special cases and offers ¥200 for each family in difficulty that it has on file. On October 27, the Tencent Foundation declared that it would contribute ¥5 million to establish the "Zhude Fund," whose mission would be to "advocate social civilization, guide society toward goodness and other ideals, foster healthy social trends, and build a love-and-good-deeds force." This special fund is used to compensate those who volunteered in a philanthropy activity but were in accident or suffered a financial loss and to help and encourage philanthropy activities that have positive impacts on society.

Compared with the government-run media, media professionals are not that powerful in promoting philanthropy. But this did not prevent some of them, particularly the most influential, from helping to create foundations and charity organizations. On April 5, Shuxin Liang, the well-known philanthropy advocate, signed a strategic pact with the Guizhou Youth Development Foundation to establish the Microfund Charity. The Microfund Charity is the first grassroots public fund to try to make an impact on large societal issues by making small contributions a little at a time. The fund planned to raise ¥10 million online from Chinese individuals living abroad. The fund is used to improve the situation of rural schools in the western part of China, particularly by providing schools with dining tables and beds.

On May 29, a philanthropy gala was held at the China Millennium Monument in Beijing. The gala's theme was Voice of the Earth: Loving All Living Creatures. At the event, the Global Green Media Alliance and "It fund," the first Animal Protection Foundation in mainland China, were officially established. The chairman of the foundation was Jing Li, a TV anchor. Jing Li, Yongyuan Cui, and some other founders and members declared that we should love all living creatures, small or large, strong or weak. The goal is to fight against cruelty to animals, improve the living situations of animals, and facilitate the harmonious development of nature and human beings. The animals that the foundation seeks to protect include domesticated pets, wild animals, farm animals, lab animals, and working animals, among others.

On June 9, the Wardrobe Care Fund was established by the China Youth Development Foundation along with Kai Wang and Hongtao Ma, anchors at the China Central Television Station. The fund urges celebrities and anchors to donate memorable actors' clothes to offline auctions. The funds raised from the auctions are used to make windproof, waterproof, and warm clothes for children in poor areas and to nurture their artistic and aesthetic education. The China Youth Development Foundation, Sina.com.cn, Taobao.com.cn, Artrade.com, Analysys.com.cn, and China Central Television Station's program the *First Class When School Opens* are all involved in this activity. On July 22, the fund was officially initiated.

Large-Scale, Media-Led Philanthropy Efforts

In 2011, China's official philanthropy enterprises suffered a reputation crisis. Despite this difficult situation, philanthropy activities are rapidly developing. Among them are some large-scale programs that have wide-ranging impacts on society. Regardless of whether an event is run by the government or a private organization, media outlets and professionals always have a presence. The most important philanthropy activity conducted in the beginning of 2011 was the Love and Future Beijing Charity Night, which was held at the National Convention Center on January 25. Many media organizations were present at this event, including Souhu.com.cn, Beijing Media Group, and Daily Media Group, among others. The purpose of the event was to thank celebrities and people from all circles for their contributions to philanthropy and charity and, at the same time, call for more organizations and individuals to care about the health and development of women and children. On the same night, more than ¥10 million were raised for the Beijing Women and Children's Development Foundation. On March 27, one of the sponsors for the charity gala was Eastern Popular Media, which, along with the China Foundation for Poverty Alleviation and Sequoia Capital, made another charity party in Beijing (with the theme Having You Along the Way) possible. The party raised ¥11.01 million via auctions and received another ¥1.37 million in donations, for a fundraising total of ¥12.38 million.

The most influential philanthropy program in 2011 was the Free Lunch program. This program was started by more than 500 journalists, including Fei Deng, the China Social Welfare Education Foundation, and dozens of Chinese media groups. The initiators asked people to donate ¥3 every day to provide free lunch for students in poor areas. This program aims to help students who cannot afford their lunch and calls on more companies and individuals to donate so that the shabby kitchens in some poor mountainous areas can be renovated. The Free Lunch program officially began operating on April 2, 2011. In just half a year, the program had made nationwide impacts. In direct response to the program's success, on October 26, the Chinese government decided to implement a nutrition improvement plan for rural students of compulsory education; this action set another vivid example of making public charity a national activity.

In addition, the media is a frequent guest for all types of large philanthropy forums. On May 7, the 2011 Chinese Women Philanthropy Forum, which was held in Huaiyin District in Huai'an City, Jiangsu Province, was sponsored by the China Charity and Donation Information Center, the Chinese Women Development Foundation, and *Philanthropy Times*. During the forum, the 2010 Chinese Women Philanthropy Development Report was issued. It was edited and published by the China Charity and Donation Information Center and the Chinese Women Development Foundation.

Environmental-protection projects are an important part of the media's philanthropic activities. On July 1, the environmental-protection program of Sina.com.cn, along with the China Green Foundation, initiated the Green China philanthropy activities. When online users log into Sina Weibo to make a donation, they can immediately make a contribution to a program that plants trees. China Green Foundation allocated the donated money to poor families located in the Dingxi District in Gansu Province. Specifically, the program helps poor families by providing them with some income to plant the trees, which in turn improves the local climate of the arid region of the west.

The first Zhujiang Charity Festival (with the theme "love people") was held on August 10, 2011. The festival received a great deal of media attention. Nanfang Media Group played a big role in this event. The festival's mission was to "promote charity ideals, develop philanthropic enterprises, and foster the growth of nonprofit organizations." The festival was jointly organized by the Youth League Provincial Committee of Guangdong Province, the Ministry of Civil Affairs in Guangdong Province, and Nanfang Media Group. The matching of charity programs with philanthropic resources was the highlight of the festival. That night, more than fifty companies were matched with charity programs and organizations. In total, ¥61.09 million in matched funds were pledged to the charity organizations, and in-kind donations worth ¥42.70 million were pledged as well. This was truly an amazing outcome.

In conclusion, the media has played an active role in the development of the nonprofit sector in China in recent years. Newspapers, magazines, TV, and the Internet have provided platforms to raise awareness about social issues. Additionally, the media is a conduit for the public's oversight of nonprofit organizations and foundations. The media has even taken its role a step further by actively organizing, hosting, and sponsoring charity events. As Chapter 11 will show, the media's and the public's awareness of and participation in charity work have intensified even more in recent years with the advent of a new outlet in the field—social media.

10

The Transformation of Public Foundations in China

*Yongguang Xu**

Foundations are considered public when their donations come from the public, and they are considered private when they do not receive public donations (rather, they receive money from corporations or utilize their family wealth). The year 2011 was the thirtieth anniversary of the birth of China's first public charity—the China Children and Teenagers Fund. Public welfare foundations in China are a product of the country's Reform Era policies. Before the reform, the government monopolized all social resources and controlled all public affairs, but this changed when nongovernmental charitable foundations began to mobilize their own resources. These foundations give the public the opportunity to participate in social welfare. People can donate money and volunteer, and this has become the beginning of society's participation in public affairs.

In thirty years, Chinese public welfare has gradually grown out of nothing through a difficult, exploratory process. Public funds have played an important role in this development process. Many influential programs have been created, such as Project Hope, the Spring Bud Plan, Mother Water Cellar, the Happiness Project, Project Angel, Health Express, the Loving Parcel, the Overseas Chinese Heart Project, Qiming Action, and 592 Legal Aid. These projects have a positive impact on and play a positive

---

* Translated by Yuqing Zhu, graduate student, College of Chinese Languages Studies, Beijing Language and Culture University.

role in promoting public welfare culture, advocating a volunteer spirit, promoting social innovation, solving social problems, and promoting social harmony.

The year 2011 was an eventful year for China's charity industry. A series of charity scandals and incidents leaded to a crisis of public confidence in several famous charities. The public's questions point to the charity system in which the roles of governmental and private sectors were mingled. Indeed, over the past thirty years, both the government and the market have gone through continuous reform and innovation, but reform of the charity system remains on the back burner. With the power and policy and resource advantages from the government, nearly 10,000 government-affiliated charity organizations, including public foundations, grow increasingly, but the public's enthusiasm for, trust in, and support of these organizations is decreasing. Reform of the charity system is urgent and necessary.

China's public foundations have good traditions and a knack for innovation. To comply with the requirements of the times and take the development challenge head on, these organizations strive to explore the approach of innovation and reform, a wise choice if they are to rejuvenate their vitality and make a breakthrough in development. Donations from the public have been an important part of charity reform in China; meanwhile, a small number of highly competitive nongovernmental public foundations have stood out, which are quickly becoming the new direction of charitable donations in the country.

Crisis of Governmental Public Foundations

The Meimei Guo Incident

On June 21, 2011, a blogger with the screen name Meimei Guo Baby attracted a great deal of public concern. The blogger was a twenty-year-old woman who posted a video in which she claimed that she was a business manager for the Red Cross and "lived in a big villa and drove a Maserati." The video raised questions about the Red Cross' corporate operations and handling of its donations. The incident triggered a crisis of confidence in the nonprofit organizations in general and the Red Cross of China in particular.

On December 31, 2011, the China Red Cross website issued a report of the findings from a report by an independent investigation group. In particular, the report said that Meimei Guo was part of a different organization with a similar name (the Red Cross Business Association) and that the woman and her display of wealth had nothing to do with the Red Cross of China or the Red Cross' donations or finances. However, it is unclear whether the Red Cross Business Association exists.

Through the Meimei Guo incident, people became aware of the relationship between the Chinese business system and a company called China Red Cross Fraternity Asset Management. The company's president was Meimei Guo's boyfriend, who later resigned when questions began to surface after the Meimei Guo incident. The company's goal was to work together with the Red Cross organization to help it fulfill its humanitarian mission through market means. The idea was to build 30,000 fraternity stations to benefit 120 million people without using a penny from donations. This project would have only required a business investment of ¥3 billion. But there were some "innovation dilemmas" with the project design, and the original estimate did not consider policy risks and operational costs; that is, it would have cost more than ¥3 billion just to obtain the support of all the relevant government departments. As a result, the project began to fall apart.

China–Africa Project Hope

In August 2011, because the city of Beijing closed a number of schools for children of migrant workers, netizens began to question why Project Hope was providing aid to children of Africa when Chinese children are not able to learn. Thus, the executive chairperson of China–Africa Project Hope, a twenty-four-year-old woman named Xingyu Lu, became the focus of public attention, and netizens began to call her "Meimei Lu."

China–Africa Project Hope is a joint effort with the World Eminence Chinese Business Association (WECBA), the Global Chinese Business Leaders Club, and China Youth Development Foundation. The main donors will be the global Chinese businessmen's children. China–Africa Project Hope plans to build 1,000 Hope primary schools for Africa in ten years, which will cost about ¥1.5 billion. The WECBA is responsible for fundraising, and China Youth Development Foundation is responsible for implementing the project and for covering 10 percent of the project's operational costs. The netizens' inquiry had to do with the China Youth Development Foundation's operational costs.

The chairman of the WECBA is Junqing Lu, father of Xingyu Lu. There are no questions about China–Africa Project Hope's program design and management; rather, the dispute is whether the business practices of the WECBA are unethical and whether a twenty-four-year-old is equipped to be the organization's executive chairperson. Although the China Youth Development Foundation's managerial practices are not perfect, international service projects such as China–Africa Project Hope are very valuable for enhancing China's soft power. Still, the project has suffered immensely from the public questions surrounding its ethics and operations.

In a public service awards ceremony on December 16, 2011, China–Africa Project Hope was given two awards for its work in Africa: the Jinghua Award of Innovative Projects and the Jinghua Special Award for philanthropy. But China–Africa Project Hope has been scarred so deeply that it seems difficult that these awards alone can revive the public's faith in the organization.

Henan Soong Ching Ling Foundation

The newspaper *Southern Weekly* reported in September 2011 that, according to rankings created from data from the Foundation Center, the assets of the Henan Soong Ching Ling Foundation (SCLF) totaled nearly ¥3 billion at the end of 2010, which ranks first among more than 2,000 charitable foundations in the country. Henan SCLF has ranked first three years in a row, and the rapid climb in its asset size is very surprising. In 2008 the foundation had 1.5 billion in assets, and in 2009 the figure was 2.1 billion. Not only that, as a provincial charity organization, Henan SCLF's donations that it obtains from the province's residents are equally staggering. Its provincial donation income in 2010 was more than ¥1 billion, which was first in the country. However, in strong contrast to its fund-raising ability, the foundation was nowhere to be found on official lists of charitable donors.

A further investigation discovered that Henan SCLF's funds mainly came from individual medical insurance reimbursements. The foundation collaborated with local insurance companies to offer people a health insurance plan that, in addition to offering some medical benefits, also allowed people to get their money back after one year at an interest rate higher than the rates offered by banks. Instead of using the money toward social welfare projects, the foundation was using the money for other purposes, and on top of that, it was counting its interest payments as donations to obtain a tax break. It wasn't long before questions began to surface about the foundation's operations and use of funds.

The charity credibility crisis in 2011 had two common themes. One was that the institutions whose practices were in question were well-established, government-affiliated organizations, and the other was that all of these organizations work closely with commercial companies. It is not possible to avoid collaboration with commercial enterprises; if charitable organizations do not cooperate with enterprises, they will lose almost all opportunities for development. To avoid the controversies against charity–enterprise cooperation, the Narada Foundation and the Tencent Foundation, in cooperation with the Peking University Nonprofit Law Research Center, and with the industrial discussion which was co-ordinated by China Foundation Center, proposed nine codes of conduct for corporate–charitable collaboration.

On December 17, 2011, at the Charitable and Commercial Cooperation Seminar, twenty-four domestic foundations claimed their willingness of accepting the nine codes of conduct. These foundations pledged to follow these regulations when conducting commercial activities. These foundations also promised that, in any commercial activity undertaken for the public welfare, the organizations will ensure the public welfare nature of the organization and maintain dignity. After the guidelines were issued, more charitable funds expressed interest in joining. The institutions that are part of the commitment are willing to listen to the opinions of others inside and outside the industry, which is what makes the guidelines a true check of the cooperation between charities and enterprises, and form of professional self-discipline.

An Analysis of the Flow of Public Charity Funds

At the end of 2011, Secretary Xiangjun Gao of the Yilong County Rural Development Association came to Beijing to report that the Qinba Mountain Welfare organizations had experienced a drop in foreign donations, and the public resources couldn't fill the gap. Some of the long-time village service organizations were in danger of closing. Meanwhile, according to an investigation by Xiaoyan Liang, secretary general for the Beijing Western Sunshine Foundation, sixty-three of the 150 educational institutions that had joined the 2011 Annual Meeting of Educational Charity had accepted international funding, but that funding ended before 2011 or will end soon for thirty of them. The lack of local resources to support is a roadblock in the development of education NGOs.

Almost at the same time, the China Charity and Donation Information Center published its "2011 China Philanthropy Donation Report." The report indicated that, in 2010, 58.3 percent of Chinese donations were flowing to the government or government-affiliated organizations, broken down as follows: 20.6 percent of donations went directly to the civil affairs offices at all levels, 9 percent went to other government departments, 6.7 percent went to the Red Cross, and 22 percent went to official charity institutions. Only 1.3 percent of donations went to non-profit groups, private nonprofit organizations, and welfare institutions other than government-affiliated charities.

According to the *Annual Report on China's Philanthropy Development* (2011), the charitable donations nationwide totaled ¥70 billion in 2010. Therefore, the 1.3 percent that entered nongovernment-affiliated charitable organizations amounted to ¥910 million, and this relatively small amount also has to cover government-run nursing homes and shelters. It seems quite likely that very few donations are given to non-profit organizations.

Data from the Foundation Center provide a preliminary understanding of the contributions from public funds in support of nonprofit organizations. By the end of 2011, there were 2,558 foundations in total, and 1,200 of these were public foundations. By the end of 2010, there were 2,178 foundations throughout the country, with 1,080 being public and 1,098 being private. The major financial data from 2010 are shown in Table 10.1.

The information in Table 10.1 indicates that the donation income of public foundations in 2010 was ¥15.2 billion, and their public welfare expenditures were ¥12.7 billion. Even if 10 percent (1.27 billion) of the welfare expenditures from public foundations went to grassroots organizations to fund their public service projects, that would be a

Table 10.1
Major Financial Data for Public and Private Charitable
Foundations in 2010

Index	Public foundations	Private foundations
Total assets	32,458,057,389	22,485,078,032
Net assets	30,987,643,720	20,198,390,357
Total income	17,854,639,290	10,234,261,914
Donation income	15,171,778,585	9,467,364,244
Total expenditures	13,546,503,032	5,217,320,226
Public welfare expenditures	12,745,629,492	4,913,897,251

Note: Values in Yuan.

considerable amount. However, public foundations gave only 1 percent or less of their welfare expenditures to grassroots organizations.

The funding of public foundations is a problem that deserves attention. In developed countries, public participation in charitable activities is very common, and most contributions come from individuals rather than institutions. Annually, US charitable contributions total around $300 billion, of which more than 80 percent comes from individuals, only about 5 percent comes from companies, and the rest is mainly from foundations. In contrast, corporations are the main source of public foundations in China. Below are nine national public foundations as an example (Table 10.2).

The China Social Welfare Foundation (CSWF) and the China Charity Aid Foundation for Children (CCAFC) received the highest percentage of donations from individuals. A closer look at these two organizations

Table 10.2
Individual Donations as Percentage of Total Donations among Nine
National Public Foundations in 2010–2011

Organizations	Year established	Donations from individuals, as percent of organization's total donations (year)
China Children and Teenagers Fund	1981	20 (2010)
China Foundation for Disabled Persons	1984	2 (2010)
China Population Welfare Foundation	1987	18 (2011)
China Women's Development Foundation	1988	24 (2011)
China Youth Development Foundation	1989	10 (2011)
China Foundation for Poverty Alleviation	1989	21 (2011)
The Red Cross of China Foundation	1994	12 (2011)
China Social Welfare Foundation	2005	54 (2011)
China Charity Aid Foundation for Children	2009	54 (2011)

reveals that they do more creative grassroots work that is closely tied to the people's interests, so it is not surprising that they receive more contributions from the public. According to a survey of citizens' donations, in 2011 the China Foundation for Poverty Alleviation (CFPA) was at the top of the league, reaching 13.4 million individual donors, while the other foundations rarely reached more than 100,000 donors. The CFPA collaborated with a bank to create a bank card and a monthly donation debit. The pledge from each donor is not large, but by only asking for small donations and asking for feedback from donors about the effectiveness of donations' use, the foundation is earning the trust of more and more people. Trust is the foundation for the sustainable development of public foundations.

Reforming Public Foundations: Breaking the Path Dependence

Path-dependence theory explains the evolution of technology or institutional change in society as being similar to inertia in physics; that is, once someone enters down a path, societal forces will make it difficult for the person to stray from that path. The theory of path dependence can be a good explanation for the dilemma of public foundations' reform.

Government affiliation and systematic effects are the important conditions in guaranteeing funding sources of public foundations. When public foundations first appeared, China had no pure sense of nongovernmental organizations. Almost all public foundations were established through government departments. Government affiliation not only gave organizations legitimacy in their public fund-raising activities but also allowed these organizations to use the status to gain public support. Many of these foundations' projects and the government's public service projects are intertwined; this allows the government to use the public's donations to foundations to pay for its public services, which it was not investing in enough on its own. At the beginning of the Reform Era, with the lack of government financial resources and public utilities in many cases, this kind of social resource mobilization model was reasonable. Thirty years later, the rationale for this method of obtaining and using public resource has been lost.

Through this system, public foundations can obtain government support in funding and human resources. The supervision of public charitable foundations is handled by the government's local oversight department. For instance, Project Hope's programs have been organized by the Communist Youth League for the past two decades, and the Hope Project uses its funds to pay the league's personnel, who run its projects; this system is not only convenient but also saves money. According to regulations, such top-down administration of public welfare donation projects needs matching capital from the local government. Thus, a donation of ¥1 could become ¥2 or ¥3. Organizations that receive contributions have to accept supervision and evaluation—more often than the government's own public projects—to ensure better quality and efficiency. That no one died in Project Hope's primary schools during the Wenchuan earthquake is the best example of the effectiveness of this system of operating charity projects.

Government affiliation and in-kind donation in these projects greatly attracted corporate donors. Public foundations gradually found a "shortcut" in project facilitation: among public donations, the average donation from a person is small but the management cost is high, whereas the average donation amount from a corporation is high and the management cost is low, so public foundations tend to implement a "big customer" strategy. Coincidentally, corporate donors tend to prefer projects that are government affiliated and provide in-kind donations. By donating to government-affiliated projects, corporations develop a stronger relationship with the government. Additionally, the government makes in-kind donations in the name of the corporations that donated the funds, which is great publicity for the corporations and improves their reputation in society. Government-affiliated projects, corporations' preferences, and public foundations have formed a triangle of interest that continuously strengthens these types of donations; at the same time, fewer donations are going to public organizations that are not affiliated with the government.

In China, grassroots organizations are local, independent organizations with an altruistic mission; they can be loosely organized (and thus, following the terminology in other chapters, would be considered nonprofit groups) or more formally organized (and thus would be classified as nonprofit organizations). The costs and risk of cooperating with grassroots organizations are high, and often it is a thankless task. As grassroots organizations and the government's frontline, public foundations are not inherently connected, so why should public foundations support some "outsiders?" In addition to a lack of trust, grassroots organizations are few in number and do not have many staff to carry out projects. Whether one looks at the issue in terms of efficiency or risk, it is not in the best interest for public foundations to cooperate with grassroots organizations. Narada Foundation spent ¥10 million after Wenchuan earthquake to fund more than seventy grassroots organizations involved in disaster relief and reconstruction. A third-party evaluation concluded that the efforts of these grassroots organizations were a near failure because, despite their high level of enthusiasm, grassroots organizations are not necessarily qualified for professional project or finance management. The standardization and professional development of grassroots organizations is a slow process, during which time public foundations cannot afford to risk investing in them.

The goal of reforming China's charity system is "to eliminate monopoly and bureaucracy," and many people agree on this goal. The biggest issue in eliminating monopoly is to determine who will have control over funds and resources—the government or public organizations. The problem of eliminating bureaucracy has already been targeted in the government's reform efforts, namely to cancel the charity organizations' status as government institutions. The end result, however, is that foundations have to sit back and wait for the government's notice, as they neither have the power nor motivation to eliminate government bureaucracy.

Reforming the charity system is challenging, not only because it is difficult to break the force of path dependence but also because reform runs counter to the interests of the government and public foundations. Indeed, much of the resistance to reform has stemmed from government departments and government-affiliated foundations. If the government and public foundations cannot realize that the current charity system is deviating from the purpose of charity or that their misuse of the public's donations is stifling the development of the public charity system, Meimei Guos will continue to surface, and the public will eventually give up on government-affiliated charitable organizations altogether.

The Reform of Public Foundations Has Begun

Reform Goal: Grant-Giving Foundations

The CFPA went through its own de-administration process ten years ago, during which it gave up its status as a government department. After the Wenchuan earthquake in 2008, CFPA began to explore ways to change its mission from operating projects to grant giving, began to support NGOs doing disaster relief, and collaborated with the Narada Foundation and the Red Cross of China Foundation in Closed Circuit Television's Charity Navigation program. In 2011 CFPA arranged for ¥5 million to be awarded to NGO projects as merit-based grants, to promote the social development of Wenchuan disaster area. In the end CFPA selected twenty-three outstanding projects, which focused on community public service, community development, poverty, environmental issues, and NGO capacity building. During the process of community project bidding, CFPA timely dealt with problems that showed up, constantly refined the screening and evaluation system, and finally formulated a management mode of "open evaluation, participatory training, project follow-up, and summarize experience." Through this mode, CFPA also facilitated NGO capacity building.

CFPAs have also met some institutional obstacles during its transition to a grant-giving foundation. One example is the Fund Ordinance, which stipulates that a foundation's administrative expenses shall not exceed 10 percent of all expenditures. This is problematic for grassroots organizations, as the figure is not realistic to meet its labor costs. A metaphor that is sometimes used in the field is that this is like having to drink salt water to survive—that is, funds can be accepted but ultimately the funds are not sufficient to maintain the organization's existence. In addition to the reform of related policies, it is important to inform the public that charity organizations do not just process and route donations; most offer services and run projects that require a continual flow of volunteers.

With the same value of CFPA supporting grassroots organizations, the Narada Foundation also supports grassroots charity works; the Narada Foundation has offered some assistance when CFPA has difficulties providing for its labor costs.

In contrast, the CCAFC, which was founded in 2009, has been running smoothly and has already made substantial impacts after its transition to a grant-giving foundation. Jiuming Wei, the foundation's president, is an experienced cadre of the Communist Party of China. He finally succeeded in registering the CCAFC after ten years of trying. He gave the foundation a few guiding principles: nongovernmental, grant giving, cooperative, and transparent. After its establishment, CCAFC first received a donation of ¥50 million from the Zhejiang New Lake Group, which laid the foundation of its transition. In July 2011, CCAFC launched a collaborative project named "Tongyuan," with ¥20 million, funding nearly 150 child charity organizations to carry out aid and services. This effort formed a cooperation alliance in children charity area. Some famous child-focused grassroots organizations, such as Angel Mom, became close partners with the foundation.

Public foundations' transition to grant-giving foundations not only benefits supported grassroots organizations, but also enables the foundations' own sustainable development. If we view public foundations as a tree, only those with deep roots can grow well. The roots should be anchored in the fertile soil of the people and civil society, rather than depending on the government. CCAFC is a very young organization and cannot be expected to develop fully overnight. By collaborating with competent organizations to implement projects, the CCAFC gains access to staff support and resources to help move the projects forward with more momentum. Providing grants and collaborating with other organizations have greatly improved the CCAFC's reputation and impact within the industry. The fact that, out of about ¥80 million in charitable donations in 2011, 54 percent came from individual citizens attests to the public's trust in the work of the organization.

A Shortcut to Reform: Special Funds

A highlight of public fund-raising efforts to develop grassroots organizations has been public foundations' use of "special funds." The CSWF and the China-Dolls Association (which was not formally registered in 2009) jointly established the China-Dolls Fund for Rare Disorders in 2009. In the same year, CSWF established a "1 kg" public welfare fund together with Ilie Advisory Company. Since then, CSWF has cooperated with some famous public welfare projects and made setting up of special funds an innovative way of supporting grassroots organizations' development. In 2010, the head of the Ministry of Civil Affairs, Liguo Li, inspected the China-Dolls Fund for Rare Disorders and encouraged it to register in Beijing city as a private nonprofit organization. CSWF has created a special fund development mode that is similar to charity incubator. These special funds help grassroots organizations to overcome two big roadblocks—gaining legitimacy and qualification of public fund-raising, and ultimately register their organization as an independent NGO through capacity building.

In 2011, Fei Deng and more than 500 reporters and many mainstream media, in collaboration with CSWF, launched a public charitable fund, encouraging everyone to donate ¥3 per day to provide free lunches to impoverished students. Since the fund was formally established on April 2, 2011, it has raised more than ¥20 million and distributed the donations to more than hundred schools. CSWF and the Beijing Golden Wings Art Rehabilitation Service Center for Disabled Children came together to establish the Golden Wings Disabled Children Art Development Fund in 2011, which is designed to use art (including painting, music, dance, and handcrafts) to help disabled children increase their self-worth, improve their quality of life, and realize the dream of the art. The Golden Wings Service Center has registered as a private nonprofit organization, and the special fund enables it to receive public donations that are exempt from taxes.

Currently, China's tax code provides pretax deductions for charitable, corporate, and individual donations, but as the lone exception, private nonprofit organizations are excluded from this benefit in the policy. As a component of charitable organizations, only foundations can enjoy tax deduction, whereas private nonprofit organizations must pay 5.5 percent sales tax for receiving donation income, and a "business income tax" for annual budget balance.

Given that private nonprofit organizations follow the same tax code as enterprises, why are the registration procedures so difficult for them? This question can only be answered by the Ministry of Civil Affairs. Now that private nonprofit organizations belong to charitable organizations, why can they not enjoy a tax deduction? This question can only be answered by the Finance and Taxation Department. The Finance and Taxation Department claims that it is difficult to determine which organizations are truly "nonprofit" because, of about 400,000 private nonprofit organizations, more than half are private educational institutions, including private schools and universities and all kinds of education and training institutions. These organizations often receive investments or market resources that can be used to generate profits. Are they nonprofit organizations? Certainly not. Because of this situation, the Finance and Taxation Department prohibited tax deductions for all private nonprofit organizations. To solve this problem, the simplest solution is to place market-invested private schools and training institutions under the supervision of the Department of Industry and Commerce. This will prevent all private nonprofit organizations from being blamed of earning profits and will remove a barrier for those "true" nonprofit organizations to obtain public donations.

Before a breakthrough can be made in reforming the tax deduction system, creating special funds within public foundations can be a shortcut for grassroots organizations to accept more public donations and develop their organizations. In terms of supporting or cultivating NGO sector, setting up special funds with grassroots organizations is also a shortcut for public foundations to reform and take more social responsibility.

In 2011, many more actions surfaced to support the development of grassroots organizations. The China Youth Development Foundation gave ¥6 million from its own funds (which it earned through investments), to establish an incubator that would foster the growth of grassroots organizations. The Amity Foundation accepted a ¥10-million donation from the Zhejiang New Lake Group to set up the New Lake venture philanthropy fund to support the nonprofit innovation projects and the development of social entrepreneurs. In addition, the New Lake Group plans to continuously support social innovations in philanthropic industry in a long term.

Nongovernmental Public Foundations: The Advantage of Being a Late Bloomer

One Foundation

After myriad twists and turns and substantial media hype, Jet Li's charitable foundation (the One Foundation) was incorporated in Shenzhen on December 3, 2010. On July 15, 2011, the One Foundation announced its completion of a new strategic planning effort ("one platform + three areas"), which emphasized establishing a transparent charitable platform and focused on three areas (disaster relief, child welfare, and personnel training for charity cause). For instance, in November 2011 the foundation started its "Ocean Heaven Plan," through which it will provide ¥2.4 million in grants to twenty-six autism agencies in southern China for more than 1,000 children with autism. As a landmark for establishing a nongovernmental public foundation, society will now look forward to the foundation's strategic development, governance, and role in promoting public charity.

Shanghai United Foundation

The Shanghai United Foundation is a grant-giving public foundation that committed to supporting civil charitable organizations. The foundation was established in 2009, and its main initiator is National Pollutant Inventory. The foundation aims to train organizations and national- and city-level public service personnel to promote the development of charity cause. The foundation adheres to the "united fund-raising" philosophy of being a dedicated fund-raising organization, effectively building up social resources, allocating resources to charitable organizations in need in a professional and accountable way, and closely monitoring the use of donations. In April 2011, the foundation launched a project called "The Journey of an Egg," which asked people to donate ¥100 so that children in poor areas would be able to eat an egg every day before going to school (an egg costs about eight Chinese cents). The project became an example for others to follow.

Shaanxi Western Development Foundation

The Shaanxi Western Development Foundation was formerly known as the Shaanxi Open and Reform Foundation, and changed names after the Foundation Management Ordinance was enacted. The organization is a nongovernmental public foundation that is active in China's western region. The foundation promotes the development of volunteers and is committed to mobilizing human resources and material resources to facilitate public welfare projects. In December 2010, the foundation helped to create the Aileyi Volunteer Center, which is committed to promoting the development of volunteer service in China. The center provides extensive volunteer work and offers various forms of training for volunteers. Also, the center publicizes advanced domestic and international volunteer management systems and project management systems to strengthen the capacity-building component of its volunteer management.

Beijing United Charity Foundation

Following the One Foundation's establishment in Shenzhen, the Beijing United Charity Foundation successfully registered in Beijing as a nongovernmental public foundation. The foundation's mission is to support individuals and organizations that have philanthropic goals; collaboratively achieve transparent, feasible, and effective public service. The foundation was born from the public and serves it by advocating participation, scientific management, collaboration, and a highly efficient and sustainable mode of public welfare. The foundation is committed to disseminating philanthropic culture, enhancing the efficiency of philanthropic work, abiding by transparency regulations, and continually benefitting society. The foundation is committed to collaborating actively with other charitable organizations and enterprises to integrate their resources to promote charitable causes. In 2011, the foundation launched a publicly funded project to support the philanthropic efforts of college students and looks forward to growing alongside other nonprofit agencies.

Public foundations have had an eventful couple of years in China. In particular, recent scandals have caused great public concern and have forced the government, the people, and public organizations themselves to reexamine the meaning and operation of their work. In China, the government and corporations are still the main contributors to public foundations. Because of this, the services provided by public foundations often cater to the interests of these large donors rather than the interests of the public. One of the next big challenges for public foundations in China will be to break away from this dependence on big donors to achieve more freedom in their service provision.

11

Microphilanthropy Transforming China

Li Feng* and Xiaoguang Kang

In 2011, the director of journalists at *Phoenix Weekly*, Fei Deng, along with some intellectual elites, used new media approaches to launch a charity program to provide free lunch for students in poor areas. The program aimed to use social donations to improve the diets and nutrition of children in poor areas. With the help of Web 2.0 media (particularly microblogs), traditional media, and television media, the program raised over ¥25 million in its first eight months and attracted over one million donors, of whom 80 percent were individuals from across the country. The program benefited 30,000 children from 110 schools in mountainous areas in thirteen provinces. Additionally, the program directly facilitated government actions. On October 26, 2011, the China State Council decided to initiate a nutrition improvement plan for rural students who were receiving compulsory education. In accordance with a standard contribution of ¥3 per person per day, the Chinese central government would grant ¥16 billion annually to provide nutrition subsidies for these students. The benefit was designed to cover twenty-six million schoolchildren in 680 administrative areas. Professionals commented that the Free Lunch program successfully raised a large amount of donations, harnessed the power of the public, and made an unprecedented achievement. Some netizens also

* Translated by Shuang Lu, Research Fellow, Huamin Research Center, School of Social Work, Rutgers University. This chapter is an excerpt from the Chinese version of the 2013 Observation Report on the Third Sector of China, edited by Drs. Li Feng and Xiaoguang Kang. For complete information, please see the Chinese version of the report.

considered the program to be an example of reform for Chinese charities. The story that circulated online of Ruoqing Lu, a girl with leukemia, impressed many netizens and attracted a great deal of attention for leukemia patients. For instance, Manzi Xue, a famous contributor among a group of people referred to as the angel investors and founder of the Microblog Anti-Human Trafficking program, started the Leukemia Youth Assistance Action together with Ligang Zhang, president and CEO of iKang Group. Through social fund-raising activities, they gathered a team of medical specialists and volunteers for program implementation.

Meanwhile, Jianrong Yu, a professor at the Rural Development Research Institute of the Chinese Academy of Social Sciences, started a microblog titled Anti-Human Trafficking: Take a Picture to Rescue Street Children, and this was referred to as a noteworthy event at the 2011 Spring Festival. In this program, netizens' sporadic and somewhat disorganized actions were united with the efforts of the Public Security Department, the media, the members of the People's Congress, and the members of the Chinese People's Political Consultative Conference. As a result, the program soon became a public focus and facilitated national rescue efforts. In addition, several notable events occurred within the philanthropy industry in 2011. The entire industry was transformed due to an accountability crisis. The Red Cross established an online donation platform, which afterwards was incorporated in the reform plan of charity system. The Ministry of Civil Affairs drafted its Charitable Donation Information Disclosure Guidelines and announced that it was establishing the Chinese Philanthropy Information Submission Platform. The administrative structure of Shenzhen charity society was reformed. Efforts by netizens pushed the government to be more open with its information. Public actions were organized around environmental protection. Various rights advocacy activities took place. All of these events had a great impact on society and brought attention to philanthropy-related issues. Along with elite individuals such as Fei Deng, Manzi Xue, and Jianrong Yu, the general public also started launching different philanthropy activities through new media approaches. For example, a netizen with the screen name SanbingLa proposed a program on his microblog called Giving a Book, Realizing a Dream to collect donated books for primary schools in rural areas. Meanwhile, on the microblog platform Microphilanthropy, countless suggestions were posted by the general public. Therefore, it demonstrated that the new wave of Web 2.0 media, due in big part to microblogs, has changed the ways in which the public communicates about and participates in philanthropy. In particular, the platform allows for an unstructured method of organizing people to engage in philanthropy efforts, without the limitations of time or location. Meanwhile, the phenomenon also brought to light many social problems and big areas of social need in China.

In 2011, two extremes appeared in Chinese philanthropy work. In contrast to the rise and thriving of public philanthropy work, many philanthropy organizations were losing credibility because of scandals such as the "Meimei Guo Incident." In addition, several government-run charitable fund-raising activities were perceived by the public as "mandatory donations" because of the government's power. Soon after, public philanthropy work began to be referred to as *microphilanthropy*. Today, microphilanthropy has quickly become a hot word in society and a part of life for many people. *People's Daily* stated that once the power of the individual was injected into the philanthropy field, online philanthropy went from a spark to a prairie fire. Danqing Chen, director of the Marketing and Communication Department for Lenovo Group, believes that a small step from everyone can together result in a big step for public philanthropy. Indeed, the changes brought about by microphilanthropy have even extended beyond the philanthropy sector.

Looking at the patterns in China's philanthropy sector, since the Reform Era began, it is evident that increasing numbers of people are seeing microphilanthropy as a legitimate philanthropy option. With its rapid development, microphilanthropy, a manifestation of the power of civic philanthropy, has been influencing public philanthropy concepts and quietly transforming the patterns of Chinese philanthropy, politics, the economy, and various aspects of everyday life. Until the twenty-first century, philanthropy work in China was primarily controlled by the government or organizations that were run in whole or in part by the government. Meanwhile, the influence of philanthropy efforts by the public was very weak. Beginning in the 1980s, the government conducted a series of reforms in urban social welfare institutions and brought back a series of social welfare agencies, such as nursing homes and rehabilitation centers. During this time, some official or semiofficial foundations appeared, such as the China Children and Teenagers Foundation, the Soong Ching Ling Foundation, and the China Foundation for Disabled Persons, among others. Over a ten-year period, the government was the leader in the Chinese philanthropy sector, while the public was more passively engaged and lacked initiative. Philanthropy activities focused on just a few fields, such as social welfare, poverty relief, and education, and activities were relatively limited in certain geographic areas. In addition, the activities lacked diversity, with most being cash or in-kind donations.

Beneficiaries were also limited to focusing on poor, disabled, and elderly individuals without families.

As China continued to move toward a more open market economy and people's living standards improved, the main force of philanthropy work was the Chinese government and official or semiofficial charitable and philanthropic organizations from the 1990s to the early 2000s, whereas philanthropy activities of civic organizations or individuals were few in number and had relatively little impact. Since the early 1990s, a large number of local, government-affiliated or semi-affiliated charity organizations sprang up, such as local charities, charity associations, and charity federations. Until 2000, charities, charity associations, and charity federations, which had become members of the China Charity Federation, were established throughout twenty-six administrative areas in China. Although a large number of local charity organizations developed during that time, because of their affiliation with the government, the government was still a dominant force in the philanthropy sector. The power of public participation in philanthropy was still relatively weak, and the public's engagement in philanthropy was still in a passive phase. In addition to traditional efforts in social welfare, poverty relief, disaster relief, and education, new philanthropy areas appeared, such as environmental protection. Philanthropy was not limited to direct in-kind or cash donations, but began to focus on empowerment. The main beneficiaries were still the poor, disabled, elderly without families, and disaster victims. Since the beginning of the twenty-first century, the pattern of Chinese philanthropy has entered a new era of public philanthropy. In this period, individualism and the private market took stronger hold in China. With these trends, the people became less interested in donating to government-run or government-affiliated philanthropy efforts. Additionally, the government's influence on the philanthropy sector weakened, which stimulated the growth of private philanthropy organizations and microphilanthropy efforts. The end result was that philanthropy efforts were brought more in line with the public's wishes.

Individualism and Genuine Altruism

Nongovernmentalism and Individualism

Many microphilanthropy activities have attracted public attention and encouraged people to start or engage in philanthropy work. Examples of such activities include the Anti-Human Trafficking microblog, the Free Lunch program, Take a Picture, Love Save Pneumoconiosis, Exchange a Pencil for a Schoolhouse, the Food Safety website (created by Heng Wu, a college student), a series of public philanthropy accountability activities, public monitoring of PM2.5 pollution, and street activities to advocate environmental protection. To date, there is no universal definition of microphilanthropy. However, microphilanthropy efforts tend to have some common traits: they are nongovernmental, rely on the contributions of individuals, and are based on similar values. Currently, there are two main definitions of microphilanthropy. One definition describes microphilanthropy as a bottom-up philanthropic model in which philanthropic activities begin with small efforts initiated by the public. This concept emphasizes the trends toward the privatization of and people's control over philanthropy. Another concept defines microphilanthropy as philanthropic actions that are launched through Web2.0 media, such as microblogs. This concept emphasizes the role of new media and the strength of public communication. This article defines microphilanthropy as philanthropy efforts that are started and run by individuals (of any socioeconomic status) who are not affiliated with the government. Philanthropy efforts by the government or officially registered nongovernmental organizations are not considered microphilanthropy here.

Microphilanthropy is diverse. For instance, the time, funding, and methods put into microphilanthropy efforts vary greatly. Microphilanthropy activities may have a gigantic influence or next to none at all. Participation can be difficult or easy. Activities may be organized or unorganized. Programs may be long term or short term. Beneficiaries vary from vulnerable groups and marginal communities to developed areas and from the middle to lower classes. Although microphilanthropy takes various forms, all such efforts have two things in common: they are individual efforts separate from the government.

Microphilanthropy has made it clear that anyone can be engaged in philanthropy. People have a long history of contributing to the public good. Since Andrew Carnegie published his book, *The Gospel of Wealth*, people seem to view nonprofit organizations and associations as the major approach to doing charity work and redistributing wealth. With the development of information technology, however, everyone is able to use the Internet to start philanthropic activities at any time, especially in the era of Web 2.0. No longer is philanthropy limited to elites, and the people have gone from passive bystanders or participants to leaders in the industry. People from any profession or social status can initiate, organize, or participate in a wide variety of public services across the country. The full swing caused by microphilanthropy highlights a philanthropic ideology that pervades the people. Some activities are initiated by individual elites, such as media representatives. For instance, the Free Lunch program was launched by Fei Deng, the director of journalists at *Phoenix Weekly*, along with 500 other journalists; Love Save Pneumoconiosis was initiated by Keqin Wang, the director of the Investigation Department of the *Economic Observer*; and Returning Veterans program was launched by Chunlong Sun, the associate editor of *Oriental Outlook Weekly*. Meanwhile, other activities are initiated by people of lower socioeconomic status. For instance, the program, Giving a Book, Realizing a Dream, was launched by a netizen with the screen name SanbingLa. In addition, microphilanthropy has included a large number of ordinary people. For instance, in addition to donating blood, a man named Mingyi Guo organized volunteer blood drives. In Beijing, a taxi driver waved the fare and gave his passenger ¥500 after he found out that the passenger had gone into debt obtaining health services and medications for his son. Another example of a spontaneous public good deed occurred when a rock climber got lost in the mountains, and when he radioed for help, hundreds of listeners from far away immediately began a search, eventually rescuing him. The examples of people helping people are numerous. Some are widely known, such as the participants in the annual television awards show *Moving China*, but many others go unnoticed. The people who do good deeds are diverse, but all of them have one thing in common: they promote the spirit of altruism.

For a long time, a truly civic and individual public service has been scarce in China. Whereas philanthropy has been defined by nongovernmental efforts in many parts of the world; in China, philanthropy efforts were run by the government. Today, with the emergence and development of grassroots organizations and microphilanthropy, philanthropy is being redefined as a nongovernmental activity. Microphilanthropy also exists in the West, but the path to microphilanthropy was more natural there because, in Western countries, philanthropy has always been led by the people and therefore has truly reflected their spontaneity, independence, voluntary spirit, autonomy, and altruism.

The emergence and widespread success of microphilanthropy is changing how philanthropy works in China. In modern society, although the government's major responsibilities are to deal with legislated issues and provide public services, some other issues, such as philanthropy, should be handled autonomously by the people. Meanwhile, autonomy from the government is the essence of civil society. As a self-organized system, the construction, organization, and functioning of a civil society are all based on nongovernment approaches. To emphasize the limits of the government's functions, Taiwanese scholars have translated the term *civil society* as *minjian shehui* (民间社会). According to Alexis de Tocqueville, civil society is a social force and a way in which people can convey their opinions to the government. In the context of a market economy and modern democracy, both society and the government are charged with the mission of fostering individual freedom and civil rights. Democracy means guaranteeing the right to life and the right to own property, among other civil and human rights; therefore, public autonomy should be considered the principal attribute of civil society. Philanthropy is a response to individual needs to protect fundamental personal rights and is a conduit for communicating public wishes to the government. Philanthropy in China, however, has always been perceived as being affiliated with government. Nongovernmental philanthropic activities, especially those at the organizational level, have been controlled and supervised by the government. For a long time, the government controlled nongovernmental philanthropic organizations through a dual-oversight system and by limiting the areas that they can work in. In addition to this control, a series of scandals exposed corruption in government-run and officially registered philanthropy organizations, which severely impacted public trust. In the context of inadequate support for nongovernmental philanthropy and problematic development in governmental philanthropy, the wave of microphilanthropy brought badly needed fresh air and vitality to the field of philanthropy. To some extent, the power of the people that was manifested through microphilanthropy efforts can be considered a reaction against governmental and official philanthropic organizations. The efforts also demonstrated a strong demand and support for individualized and nongovernmental philanthropy. Microphilanthropy has safeguarded the people's civic rights and has given them a way to contribute to the public good. Finally, microphilanthropy is a powerful force that has redefined approaches to philanthropy, influenced public thinking on the industry, and brought public concerns to light.

Pure Altruism

Essentially, philanthropy refers to an altruistic cause or action that puts the interests of others and the benefit of society over the interests of oneself. The altruism of philanthropy should be honest, pure, and not accompanied by any personal interests. In reality, however, the purity of philanthropy has been tainted because some government departments, companies, charities, or individuals have used philanthropy as a tool to serve their own interests. For instance, a series of scandals exposed overly extravagant philanthropy activities that were more organized for profit or to gain favor with the government. Some large philanthropic agencies focus more on their marketing, reputation, and own interests than on doing actual work. However, microphilanthropy, which harnesses grassroots power and advocates for small causes, pursues and performs a spirit of purity, positivity, and practicality. Without any need for extravagance, microphilanthropy attracts a large amount of people. Without any effort to become famous or to reach out to large donors, microphilanthropy has raised public attention, has become a hot topic in society, and has raised millions of yuan from the public. Without much help from local governments or media outlets, microphilanthropy has cultivated a culture in society of contributing to philanthropy work. Simply put, microphilanthropy influences people at all levels of society through its special attraction—its genuine altruistic intentions. Microphilanthropic practitioners are safeguarding this purity with their modest and pragmatic work.

Microphilanthropy has awoken a spirit of philanthropy in society and has bolstered the purity of philanthropy. When we hesitate to help fallen old people for fear of being blackmailed or when we eagerly search for more information about scandals on charitable donations, philanthropy is reduced to a word without meaning. Fortunately, many people insist on doing the right thing, and through microphilanthropy efforts, have inspired others to do the same. The success of such efforts shows that microphilanthropy is a powerful way in which individuals can come together at the grassroots level to address social issues. Microphilanthropy emphasizes transparency, accountability, self-monitoring, and societal supervision, which is in sharp contrast to the covertness and dishonesty of some formal philanthropic agencies.

When explaining how an ordinary person can start a successful microphilanthropy effort, Jianrong Yu, who has begun several such activities ("Take a Picture to Rescue Street Children," "Aid for the Homeless," and "Love for Teachers in Rural Areas"), stated that he

> was trying to encourage everyone to engage within their capacity. For example, in the activity "Love for Teachers in Rural Areas," participants can either donate money or forward a microblog post. The point is to understand what you can do and do it. If you have money, donate some; if you have clothes, donate some; or if you have time, simply forward some microblog posts about philanthropic activities so that more people see them. Do what you want to do, rather than being forced to. Every philanthropic action should come from the heart.

Many people do philanthropic works for superficial reasons or just to boost their reputation. But I believe that philanthropy must "get back to basics," which means working with transparency and openness and that every participant is actually doing something. These are also the reasons why people trust microphilanthropy efforts, whereas the accountability of many other philanthropic activities is often questioned.

According to a traditional Chinese virtue, "don't hesitate to do anything good no matter how insignificant it seems." Philanthropy should not be forced in the name of morality; instead, only genuine philanthropy can last over the long term and truly represent the best of humanity.

Three Forms of Microphilanthropy

Microphilanthropy can be classified by the level of familiarity among participants (acquaintance or nonacquaintance microphilanthropy), work pattern (advocacy or service microphilanthropy), medium (online or offline), level of organization (ranging from unorganized to highly organized), and focus (singular or multiple). Mixed types of microphilanthropy are excluded in this article, such as online-offline microphilanthropy and advocacy-service microphilanthropy. Table 11.1 shows the specific categories of microphilanthropy.

Instead of using the level of organization or type of focus to describe microphilanthropy efforts, the characteristics, influence, and origin of a microphilanthropy effort can be described more clearly with the categorizations of individual-action, collective-action, and social-movement microphilanthropy.

Individual-Action Microphilanthropy

Individual-action microphilanthropy refers to philanthropic actions that are initiated and completed by one individual, without participation by others, and are unorganized and singular in focus. Regardless of social

Table 11.1
Three Forms of Microphilanthropy

Level of organization	Focus	Form of microphilanthropy
Unorganized	Singular	Individual-action
Low level of organization	Singular	Collective-action
High level of organization	Multiple	Social-movement

status, financial status, occupation, age, race, or ethnicity, anyone can start an individual-action microphilanthropy effort. This type of philanthropy can differ in size and amount of resources. Each initiator works separately and has his or her own focus. Individuals work voluntarily at any time or place of their choosing.

Various kinds of individual-action microphilanthropy efforts exist in everyday life. Two types are acquaintance and nonacquaintance microphilanthropy. Additionally, there are advocacy-based and service-based activities. Moreover, any microphilanthropy effort can be conducted online or offline. Countless examples reflect the type of individual-action microphilanthropy, such as a person by the nickname of Jiangma, from Jingzhou City, who has been caring for her disabled neighbor for twenty years, and the story of Lili Zhang, commonly referred to as the "most beautiful teacher in China."

Thanks to a developed social infrastructure, such as modern transportation and information technology, people have greater access to public and private resources. As a result, individual-action microphilanthropy can go beyond traditional offline activities to online or joint online-offline activities. Also, this form of microphilanthropy can expand in amount, scale, and area of involvement. The characteristics of individual-action microphilanthropy are described below.

An Opportunity for Everyone

Individual characteristics do not necessarily determine whether a person can participate in microphilanthropy. Rich or poor, affiliated with the government or not, any individual has the opportunity to do something good as long as he or she cares about others. This universal opportunity is one of the most distinguishing characteristics of individual-action microphilanthropy, which includes making a cash donation of any amount, volunteering for any philanthropy project, or advocating for equality and justice.

All Facets of Life

Modern society is highly complex. Philanthropic needs vary throughout the world. Consequently, individual-action microphilanthropy extends to all facets of life, such as tutoring homeless children and taking care of aging neighbors.

Everyone Can Benefit

With the widespread nature of individual-action microphilanthropy, everyone is a potential beneficiary. Everyone will have problems at some point in their life. Some problems can be solved alone, but others cannot. If someone has ever helped you, you were a beneficiary of microphilanthropy, even if someone gave you directions, held an umbrella for you in the rain, or handed you some water when you were thirsty.

It seems that the goals of individual-action microphilanthropy are not lofty at all. This type of philanthropy, however, is very practical, flexible, and effective. It helps people in need, brings satisfaction to the initiator, builds trust between people, reduces social cost, releases people's stress, and develops a positive culture in society.

Collective-Action Microphilanthropy

Collective-action microphilanthropy refers to philanthropic actions that are initiated by an individual, involve the participation of other individuals, have a low level of organization, and are multiple in focus. Collective-action microphilanthropy usually originates as a response to a certain societal event. The goals often relate to specific material interests or low-level abstract interests. Collective-action efforts call for change but usually not large-scale reform. In collective-action efforts, initiators identify a main issue, and participants take action to address this issue. Compared to individual-action microphilanthropy, collective-action microphilanthropy puts greater emphasis on action goals; therefore, such efforts can be more powerful and influential within a relatively short time. Because individual power is scattered and limited, it is more effective to gather these powers together—even if the result is a small group of volunteers with limited communication. For example, the Free Lunch program attracted thousands of people to help poor children to improve their nutrition, and the Returning Veterans project, which helped seven veterans from the China-Japan War finally return home after seventy years, resulted from the persistent efforts and microblog posts of thousands of participants. These projects identified a focal issue, attracted public and media attention, located various resources, and ultimately succeeded through the efforts of a large number of volunteers. Also, many other projects reflect this type of microphilanthropy, including a microblog to combat human trafficking, a webpage to help people quit smoking, a celebrity program to sell their costumes to raise money to buy clothes for poor children, and a project called Smile to Encourage a Girl with Cancer in Yangzhou City. These microphilanthropic actions have received wide public participation and orderly procedure. Sometimes these projects even enjoy more participation than actions launched by formal philanthropic organizations. The participants may not have intense communication, but they must have a common goal. Generally, collective-action microphilanthropy has four main characteristics.

First, collective-action microphilanthropy must have a key initiator who is an academic or economic elite with some level of social responsibility and ability to rally support. In the beginning, the action relies highly on the key initiator, who must identify and analyze the social problem, think of solutions, and have great insight. The initiator must also devote a great amount of time and energy to the project, which usually means sacrificing some individual interests. As the project develops, it will have a broader support base and therefore will be less dependent on the initiator.

Second, collective-action microphilanthropy breaks the limitations of geography and work area. Collective-action microphilanthropy aims to solve various kinds of problems. With the availability of information, the high mobility of population, and increasing globalization, people have become aware of more social causes and issues, such as environment protection, low-carbon lifestyle, education equality, agricultural development, health care, urban crime, universal scientific education, poverty relief, abandoned children, migrant workers, governmental oversight, and care for the aging. Meanwhile, modern information technology makes it possible to take immediate action in multiple regions. For instance, the Wish Relay program, which was started by a college student in Nanjing City, quickly expanded to a national philanthropy activity; Fei Deng's Free Lunch program helped thousands of children from over a hundred schools across ten provinces; and Keqin Wang's Love Save Pneumoconiosis program aided migrant workers with pneumoconiosis in different provinces. Today, convenient transportation systems and real-time, online communication make it easy for people to come together and contribute their time, resources, energy, and intelligence to a common goal.

Third, advocacy and service exist side by side in collective-action microphilanthropy efforts. With a focal issue and a clear goal, collective-action microphilanthropy challenges participants to devise various approaches to achieve that goal. Because direct service has limited scope and influence, collective-action microphilanthropy usually includes a public-advocacy component to supplement its service provision. For example, the Free Lunch program not only asks people to donate ¥3 for a child's lunch but also raises awareness about the nutrition issues faced by children in marginal or poor areas and has encouraged the government to propose policies to solve the problem.

Finally, collective-action microphilanthropy can benefit more people than individual-action microphilanthropy because the beneficiary tends to be a group rather than an individual. For example, on May 28, 2012, Manzi Xue and Ligang Zhang started an online charity for Ruoqing Lu, a leukemia patient. The action progressed and ultimately developed into a special assistance project that aims to help low-income leukemia patients from birth to eighteen years old. Meanwhile, the project raised public awareness about ways to help people with a serious illness. As a result, netizens actively engaged in other online actions to help seriously ill individuals. Just a month later, the government proposed legislation on health insurance for people with serious illnesses. In September, the China Insurance Regulatory Commission formulated concrete enforcement regulations. As a result, the coverage of health insurance for serious illnesses expanded greatly. The beneficiaries included miners with pneumoconiosis and people with a disability (including deafness and blindness), cancer, congenital heart disease, and epilepsy. Collective-action microphilanthropy is often related to hot social topics, such as concern about quality of life and poor children's right to education.

Social-Movement Microphilanthropy

Social-movement microphilanthropy refers to philanthropic actions that are initiated by multiple individuals, receive wide participation from the public, are highly organized, have multiple goals, and aim for long-term impacts. This type of microphilanthropy is not a single event or even a series of independent events. Instead, it is an ongoing collective action participated in by many people with clear pursuits. Multiple root causes are usually behind a social movement, so participants are still able to continuously engage in collective actions around a common interest even without central leadership. By intentionally changing or reconstructing the established social order, the participants aim to facilitate or resist social change. Social movements always come with unique beliefs, ideals, and encouraging spirits, all of which enable participants to maintain high morale and loyalty despite the influence of the status quo. The main difference between social-movement and collective-action microphilanthropy is that the former tends to have more than one focus. To some extent, having multiple focuses is the same as having no focus. Therefore, social-movement microphilanthropy can also be characterized as decentralized. For instance, in a renaissance of the national culture, some people might focus on theoretical research, some might focus on traditional cultural education, and some might focus on advocacy through art exhibition. Although these activities are fundamentally related, the participants may not have much communication, but eventually the outcome of numerous individuals and their related efforts converge to create the social movement.

Individual-action microphilanthropy and collective-action microphilanthropy, as mentioned above, are responses to a very specific stimulus. Social-movement microphilanthropy, however, usually is a response to macro factors. Some examples of this type of microphilanthropy include increased public concern about the accountability of philanthropic organizations, public environmental-protection activities, public advocacy for an environmentally friendly lifestyle, public advocacy for government integrity, microblog actions that call for transparency of governmental information, social activities for the protection of migrant workers' legal rights, and free philanthropic lectures for the public. Social-movement microphilanthropy consists of a series of actions, including individual-action microphilanthropy and collective-action microphilanthropy, and although social-movement microphilanthropy can easily be confused with the other two, it is distinct. In social-movement microphilanthropy, all activities are connected to underlying political or social issues. Additionally, the time span differs with the three types of microphilanthropy: individual-action microphilanthropy is characterized by promptness, collective-action microphilanthropy can achieve its mission within a certain time period, and social-movement microphilanthropy is the most challenging and lasts for the longest time. In addition, social-movement microphilanthropy is highly organized. Although the events in certain movements may not be strongly related, these events are conducted to work toward a core mission. In today's information society, people are highly connected by the Internet. Once social events and advocacy unite a group of people around a common goal, people are on standby and can be called upon to take action toward that goal through various approaches.

An initiator of social-movement microphilanthropy must be a leader and be prepared to both start and participate in actions. As long as a person recognizes the importance of the movement's central issue, agrees with the initiator's ideology, and is willing to put it into practice, he or she can be a member of the social movement. With respect to geographic location, social-movement microphilanthropy has no boundaries because it contains both individual-action and collective-action microphilanthropy. In terms of focal area, social-movement microphilanthropy usually focuses on urgent but long-term issues, such as reviving cultural traditions and promoting democracy. Additionally, social-movement microphilanthropy involves both service-based and advocacy-based activities. Some characteristics of social-movement microphilanthropy are introduced below.

First, social-movement microphilanthropy can benefit more people than the other two types alone—sometimes almost the whole population. Currently, social-movement microphilanthropy activities in China concentrate on environmental protection, food safety, pharmaceutical safety, revival of cultural traditions, transparency in government and charitable organizations, policy formation, animal rights, and legal aid. Because microphilanthropic activities in these areas emphasize the public interest, the beneficiaries of social-movement microphilanthropy are the general population.

Second, social-movement microphilanthropy must spread over time and throughout various regions. Therefore, social-movement microphilanthropy is more powerful and influential to the public, social opinion, the government, and philanthropic organizations. It not only facilitates the development of government, the market, and the integrity of social resources, but it also plays an important role in rebuilding the relationships among the government, market, and society.

Microphilanthropy Transforming China

Microphilanthropy is a manifestation of kindness among the people. With its appeal to private individuals, its separation from the government, and its trustworthiness, microphilanthropy has shown great strength and power in China.

Many microlevel philanthropic actions take place in daily life. They look small but actually are powerful, influential, and have reformed China in various ways. For example, a famous actress from Hong Kong proposed a donation on her microblog on her birthday; she pledged to donate to charity based on how many times the message was forwarded. The message was forwarded 75,000 times online by her fans within three days, and in response, she donated ¥80,000 to a charitable agency as she promised. Another example is that through an online charity marketplace, a seller successfully raised ¥200,000 for the medical treatment of Shanshan, a girl with leukemia. In Zhengzhou University, 290 students volunteered to collect recycled waste on campus in exchange for money, which they donated to the Dream Fund—the program has lasted for two years, has raised ¥21,000, and has attracted the participation of

1,500 college students in microphilanthropic activities, such as campus recycling, charitable sales or auctions, and volunteer teaching. The Dream Fund has contributed to the care of five low-income, severely ill students and to disaster-relief efforts after the Yushu earthquake. Other examples include college students' ongoing advocacy for transparency in the government, protection of the environment, and the revival of traditional Chinese culture. One famous activity was the effort by Yanfeng Liu, a college student, to advocate for the transparency of government information.

The Benefits of Microphilanthropy

Microphilanthropy Consolidates Power

Microphilanthropy has grown with the development of new technology, such as microblogs. As a new form of public philanthropic participation, microphilanthropy reflects a spirit of building large benefits upon small things. Through creative approaches, such as bloggers donating ¥1 for every time a message or webpage is forwarded, microphilanthropy consolidates the power of individuals. Meanwhile, microphilanthropy has enhanced the diversity of people who begin philanthropic efforts. Anyone can start a philanthropy action, and the idea that philanthropy work is only for elites or organizations has now changed. In addition, the development of information technology and social demands has facilitated the growth of new grassroots organizations' and individual philanthropy efforts. As one example, the Ping An Insurance Company of China offered to donate a bottle of water for every time a message was forwarded, which resulted in a donation of 230,000 bottles of water; although the donation was made by a company, the effort was driven by individual netizens. In another case, an owner of a small restaurant in Xi'an City initiated the "1-Yuan Care" project. The idea started in his restaurant, where he pledged to provide meals to older individuals for ¥1. His proposal was that other businesses make the same pledge for their services, and just two weeks after the proposal was publicized by the media, 150 business owners had signed a pledge to provide people who were over eighty years old and living alone with medicine, meals, laundry, haircuts, and taxi services for only ¥1. This project showed that the kindness of one ordinary individual could influence and facilitate the participation of a city, or even a whole country. The success of projects like these requires that everyone take a new look at microphilanthropy—no effort is too small, and people can come together to have a big influence on society. According to the international edition of *People's Daily*, microphilanthropy is reflected in every small aspect of daily life. Microphilanthropy demonstrates the cumulative power of small individual efforts—simply by connecting to the Internet, anyone can put their passion for helping others into action.

Microphilanthropy Amplifies Kindness

Benevolent ideas already exist in society, and microphilanthropy inspires people to take action on those ideas by providing an accessible platform for participation. The idea is attractive because people do not have to contribute much. In China, philanthropy has traditionally been viewed as the responsibility of wealthy individuals and elites. The microphilanthropy perspective, however, is that the majority of people should contribute to the public good. In addition to accumulating individual power and benefiting the public, the more important meaning of microphilanthropy is to establish a paradigm that everyone can participate, which will then influence all of society through a butterfly effect. For instance, on July 21, 2012, a heavy rainstorm caused the cancellation of 500 flights in Beijing Capital International Airport and the closure of the airport subway, which stranded a large number of passengers in the airport. It wasn't long before messages for help were posted on microblogs. Through discussions on Wangjing website, about thirty netizens worked until 5:00 a.m. the next day taking passengers home, while other netizens posted contact information online and stood by to offer help and businesses volunteered to take passengers in for free. Many similar examples have demonstrated that the small light of microphilanthropy has illuminated the whole world and has awakened the kindness in every human being.

Microphilanthropy Extends to Every Aspect of Life

Unlike traditional philanthropy, microphilanthropy advocates that people do some small thing in their daily life rather than devoting time and energy over the long term. As a result, microphilanthropy has extended, directly or indirectly, to almost every aspect of everyday life, such as helping others in their daily activities, protecting the environment, advocating an environmentally friendly lifestyle, working for educational equality, promoting rural development, working for better health care, fighting urban crime, promoting science education, participating in poverty-relief efforts, supporting abandoned children, addressing migrant worker issues, advocating for governmental oversight, and providing care to the aging.

Microphilanthropy Can Solve Large Social Problems

Due to its cumulative power and influence, microphilanthropy is able to contribute to solutions for some big social issues. Two examples are the Free Lunch program and the project Take a Picture to Rescue Street Children, both of which have facilitated government action to deal with child nutrition and abandonment. Microphilanthropy has leveraged various groups in society and improved their participation through tactful approaches and enormous power. It has even facilitated changes in certain public policies, which helps to solve underlying social problems. Of course, different types of microphilanthropy have different influences. The following sections describe the influences of individual-action, collective-action, and social-movement microphilanthropy.

Limitations of Microphilanthropy

The impact of microphilanthropy cannot be neglected. It changes public philanthropic values and behaviors, facilitates changes in the direction of Chinese philanthropy, demonstrates the nature of nongovernment, individuality, and purity in philanthropy, and reforms the government and philanthropic organizations. The country's economic development and changes in public philanthropic values has caused an upsurge in the public's passion for philanthropy. More and more people are beginning or participating in microphilanthropy. At the same time, inquiries into the legitimacy, professionalism, transparency, and consistency have already begun.

The Challenge of Legitimacy

Questions surrounding the legitimacy of microphilanthropy have focused on qualifications for public fundraising. According to Chinese law, only public charities are qualified to conduct public fundraising, whereas individuals or general organizations are not. Because public fundraising through microphilanthropy is not allowed under Chinese law, the only way to do it is to collaborate with organizations that are qualified to run fundraisers. If not, the effort could lack legitimacy before it even begins. Currently, many online fund-raising activities do not have a sponsoring agency and therefore are not technically legal.

The Challenge of Professionalism

Because microphilanthropic activities are initiated or organized by ordinary people who tend to have little experience in or professional knowledge of philanthropy work, professionalism is a big challenge for microphilanthropy. In January 2011, Xinhua.net quoted Fei Deng as saying that the biggest disadvantage of Free Lunch is the lack of professionals and full-time employees: "Ultimately, philanthropy needs to be regulated and specified, which is a deficiency in our program. . . . We spent eight months locating schools, starting meal programs, and overseeing school implementation. Avoiding corruption and waste was the biggest challenge from the very beginning." For this reason, problems such as a lack of rigorous operational standards and professionalism are common in these activities. For instance, the Department of Public Security recently published last year's outcomes of the Take a Picture to Rescue Street Children program on its microblog, claiming that the phrase *take a picture* should be used cautiously. In particular, the department explained that "a recent picture of a 'street child' is actually misleading information. Actually, of all the pictures that were taken last year for this program, almost none were being trafficked." Also, some critics have emphasized that microphilanthropy efforts should describe their efforts more accurately. Some people have suggested that the assumption that a considerable portion of street children are trafficked might be wrong. Although philanthropic activities begin with good intentions, they may produce totally unexpected outcomes if they are built upon a misunderstanding of the social reality. Therefore, it requires philanthropic initiators to conduct basic social research prior to taking any actions. Simply using common sense does not amount to being responsible in philanthropy work. With the dissemination of information on the Internet, influential public figures can easily stir up emotion among the public; inappropriate use of the Internet, however, may lead to abuse of their influence.

The Challenge of Transparency

Most people who start or organize a microphilanthropic effort will disclose the donation amounts, expenses, and other detailed information on the Internet so as to guarantee program transparency and more public support. However, because many individuals lack management experience and many organizations lack a strict governance system, problems such as auditing mistakes eventually appear, which impacts the public's confidence in philanthropy causes. According to an online survey, 29.58 percent of netizens were willing to donate money to microphilanthropy because "a little money can help many people." Nearly half of the netizens, however, claimed that they would not donate because they "won't know where the money goes." Others were relatively neutral and claimed that "it depends on who you are donating to." When answering "which area of microphilanthropy are you concerned about," over 40 percent of people chose "whether or not to disclose their financial situation online and to make donations transparent." The second most common response was "whether or not to clarify the purpose of donations," and the third was "how to oversee [the efforts] and whether or not the money was actually used for philanthropy." For the Free Lunch program, its microfundraising efforts were questioned quite a bit in the beginning, and even now, after the program has operated successfully for a long time, some people still doubt whether their donations or the lunches they sponsor are actually being sent to schools.

The Challenge of Continuity

More and more microphilanthropy organizers have realized the difficulties in running efforts online, such as trying to find volunteers and not having a regulatory management structure. Current microphilanthropy efforts depend highly on the internet platform, netizens' passion, and the individual power of participants and volunteers. As a result, it is difficult to count on consistent volunteers in the long run. Additionally, individual problems can easily impact or even damage the whole activity. Without a professional agency or operational structure, microphilanthropy efforts cannot last very long. After a successful activity, microphilanthropy programs should either establish an institution, hire professionals to manage their operations, or collaborate with official philanthropic organizations to facilitate the sustainable development of their effort. Meng Tu, the secretary general of the China Youth Development Foundation, expressed his concern about the longevity of the Free Lunch program. Tu believes that "the four elements of philanthropy should be rationalization, professionalization, systematization, and practice. Without the support of these elements, a microphilanthropic activity can hardly have longevity." All of these questions about microphilanthropy and its current problems stem from its noninstitutional nature and inexperienced volunteer base.

The Future of Microphilanthropy

Changes in Microphilanthropic Participants and External Factors

Relaxed Political Environment
When the People's Republic of China was established, the country created a traditional collectivist system, which is characterized by the

government controlling both society and the economy. After having gone through hundreds of years of wars, China was in a social and economic depression at that time. In that context, collectivism was helpful for mobilizing people, effectively centralizing resources, and advancing national industrialization. However, the drawbacks of collectivism showed up increasingly through time. Toward the end of the 1970s, China launched a sweeping reform of its economic system, which freed the economy from government control and opened it up to market-oriented principles. In the years that followed, the market economy established itself, and to date we can say that the market-oriented reform has had some measure of success. Chinese society, however, is still not completely free from the collectivist system; even if the part that was released along with the economic reform is not developing based on intrinsic social ideology, but on the orientation of "market society." The frequent social conflicts and thriving microphilanthropy are like lava, which has been flowing underneath for a long time, looking for a breach to break out and release a gigantic burst of energy.

Around 2005, the Chinese government started to talk more about society, using language such as "harmonious society," "social construction," "social management," "societal well-being," "community development," and "social organization," which have frequently appeared on media and government documents. Just as the economy was freed and reorganized based on market principles thirty years ago, some people infer that social movement and development in China has entered a new stage—the stage of society. That is, the government gradually releases its control of society and reorganizes it based on its own ideology and will, which we can call self-organization. In February 2011, President Jintao Hu stressed the importance of the three "maximizations" in social management innovation: maximally stimulating social energy, maximally increasing factors for social harmony, and maximally decreasing discordant factors.

Specifically, the government has to and necessarily will give sufficient power to society. Today, it is not realistic to regulate the social order by fully controlling individuals and suppressing social resistance. Instead, modern society needs to operate on consensus and rules of conduct. People are able to coordinate their activities for mutual benefit and behave according to basic rules. As a result, each individual enjoys adequate rights and responsibility for his or her own behaviors in a society that is operated stably. Only such a society can be orderly, energetic, productive, and creative. The government should lower the threshold for the registration and operation of nonprofit organizations, allow organizations to work in more service areas, create and develop effective measures to support or cultivate social forces, and curtail its own functions.

Rights and Responsibilities of Microphilanthropic Participants

As Marx stated, society is a union of free people. On the one hand, restricted individual values, suppressed humanity, and deprived rights must be returned to the public in an era of civilization. The legislation and execution of civic rights, such as political rights, economic rights, and social rights, becomes the basic index for examining the legitimacy of a political regime. On the other hand, overemphasizing the justification of individual rights may lead to the neglect of traditional culture and the sustainable development of future generations. The highlight of "individual" and "rights" may produce an extreme situation, wherein society becomes secularized, materialistic, and immoral and lacks history and an ecological conscience, all of which will severely impede human development. In this case, individual responsibility should also be emphasized, with a focus on individual freedom and independence. Individual awareness of responsibilities—for family, society, history, and future generations—must be established in society.

Self-Regulation and Accountability of Organizational Philanthropy

According to the United Nations, Economic and Social Commission for Asia and the Pacific, eight features demonstrate the "good governance" of nonprofit organizations: the nature of participation, public trust, active response, equity and acceptance, transparency, effectiveness and efficiency, governance by law, and a common goal. Achieving these goals requires professional self-regulation, external oversight for accountability, and organizational governance. Furthermore, people with more social responsibility should work as directors in nonprofit organizations so that they can play key roles in decision-making processes and facilitate staff members' professional development through training and education. Nonprofit organizations establish a system of self-regulation; create a professional code of conduct; build common values and culture within the profession; and accept oversight and inquiries by the government, corporations, the public, and the media so as to build a normalized participation system. It is also necessary that the self-regulation and accountability of nonprofit organizations become hot topics in society in addition to being required by the government.

Positive Public Opinion

As a method of socialization, media is especially important in modern society. Because the media greatly influences societal values, the media has a unique social responsibility. A positive media system undertakes two major tasks. First, negative information must be disclosed and criticized—media outlets shouldn't advocate negative values, such as discrimination and materialism, and it shouldn't ignore social inequality and moral deficiency. Second, good values should be publicized. The media is made up of its workers, and they are responsible for disseminating information with a conscience and building a positive atmosphere for public opinion rather than just trying to attract public attention with media sensationalism. Instead, the media should use its advantage to foster social responsibility and a philanthropic spirit.

A Calmer Future for Microphilanthropy

Because both microphilanthropy and organizational philanthropy have their strengths and weaknesses, neither can be replaced. Currently, some specific external factors have made microphilanthropy explode in China, but this is an abnormal phenomenon. The energy will gradually cool down with an increasing balance between microphilanthropy and organizational philanthropy. As demonstrated in our analysis, China's political structure is the core force that influences philanthropic patterns in the country. Therefore, philanthropic patterns will achieve an ideal situation only through the de-administration of the philanthropy sector and the government releasing its control over public space. Some people believe that the development of civil society is necessary to achieve a balanced social structure and harmonious society in the next thirty years, wherein the fundamental approach would be philanthropic de-administration. We conclude that the government will not give up its control over the philanthropy system in the short term but will not take back or arbitrarily invade public spaces that have already been given back to society, which creates an ideal situation for the growth of philanthropy in the country moving forward.

From Microphilanthropy to Organizational Philanthropy

The legitimacy of microphilanthropic activities that involve fundraising is a big issue. With insufficient legislation and regulation, microphilanthropic activities that need a large amount of resources are limited because individuals and certain organizations are not qualified to conduct public fund-raising activities. In this case, microphilanthropic participants (usually those who initiate efforts) begin to explore other ways to run fundraisers; for example, they might look for a related nonprofit organization that is allowed to run fundraisers and set up a special fund under that organization. In this way, they can indirectly obtain the right to raise funds from the public. This process usually occurs in collective-action microphilanthropy because individual-action microphilanthropy only needs small and scattered recourses.

This method is helpful for reducing legislative barriers and maximizing social mobilization. Combining microphilanthropy with organizational philanthropy solves the legal issue of fundraising by individuals. Meanwhile, some microphilanthropic fund-raising activities are initiated by nonprofit organizations, such as Care Package, which was launched by the China Foundation for Poverty Alleviation, and the Journey of an Egg, launched by Shanghai United Foundation. Some fund-raising activities are initiated by corporations or jointly initiated by corporations and nonprofit organizations. For instance, in June 2011 Ping An Insurance Company of China and the China Youth Development Foundation initiated a project to donate a bottle of water to a primary school in an arid region each time their message was forwarded on the Love Commune Microblog. Other examples of fundraisers based on microblog forwarding focused on low-income college students, work-study students, and orphans and were hosted by the Love Relay Alliance, the volunteer association of China Mobile's Henan branch. Also, the Tencent Company initiated a large microphilanthropy project, Cloth Plus Cloth, to collect donated clothes for people in poor areas. Additionally, some microphilanthropic activities are started by individuals and organizations, such as Love Save Pneumoconiosis, which was launched by Keqin Wang, a journalist, together with the China Relief Fund. Compared with pure microphilanthropic efforts, involving nonprofit organizations has improved the efficiency, strength, and internal and external governance of these microphilanthropic activities. In addition, some other microphilanthropic founders include community organizations, such as the Donate One Book project by Hua Guoshan Community in Anhui Province, and social entrepreneurs, such as Cha-gang.com. By all accounts, the individuality of microphilanthropy initiators and participants should always be stressed due to the definition and direction of these efforts. Therefore, this kind of transformed microphilanthropy should be distinguished from traditional microphilanthropy.

Microphilanthropy, Organizational Philanthropy, and Government Action

An ideal nation should have three pillars that complement one another: society, the government, and the market. Government and society should have a nonthreatening relationship and synergistically stimulate each other. These two forces should be independent, mutually balanced, collaborative, and supportive and should work toward common interests. An ideal situation requires that self-organized actions among society, mainly referring to microphilanthropy and organizational philanthropy, interact optimally with the government. As the subjects of public management, government and society share a common goal; that is, to establish an equitable and just society. Therefore, they will improve efficiency and effectiveness only through their mutual oversight, cooperation, and counterbalance.

In addition to maintaining the political regime, the most important function of modern government is to serve the public. However, developing countries, especially countries in transition, usually cannot provide all necessary services to their citizens. As civic awareness increases, the public can improve its situation through two approaches—individual efforts and facilitating governmental actions. The two approaches are indivisible. Citizens' own efforts continue to raise civic awareness and change public thought; on the other hand, public appeals or actions will inevitably influence governmental action.

These two approaches are particularly distinct in microphilanthropy. For instance, the Free Lunch and Health Insurance for Serious Illness projects were transformed through the approaches mentioned above. Through the efforts of individual elites, participation from the public, and the utilization of information technology, the two projects raised public awareness of children's rights of health issues, as well as the need for aid to people with serious illnesses. Step by step, the awareness is reflected in public actions, which in turn creates increasing passive and active pressure on the government to reform its policies.

It is possible that microphilanthropic work will be taken over by either the government or nonprofit organizations. The government will inevitably become involved in issues that are profoundly influential and significantly related to the political regime, such as social security, health care, and educational equality. When China's Reform Era began, these issues were not supposed to be addressed by microphilanthropy, but due to a lack of government resources (or initiative even when resources were available), individuals have had to step in to meet public needs. Jin Qian, a college student who initiated a program that asked people to take pictures to raise awareness about bicycle issues, told the media that he "wished to make 'taking pictures and posting on microblogs' into a communication platform between the government and citizens within one year." Meanwhile, many other microphilanthropic volunteers have expressed their desire to collaborate with government and nonprofit organizations, and it is also in the government's interest to deal with these issues expediently. Regarding issues that are not large in scale but are urgent to address, a more open government will encourage individuals and organizations to participate in efforts to help. Relaxed government regulations will also allow more nonprofit organizations to register and thrive, which will allow them to take over many public services, and with good internal governance and collaboration, these organizations should be very successful. In that case, microphilanthropy in related areas will fade out, although that will take time because the government and organizations require a combination of many factors. After all, the underlying ideology and root cause is China's specific political structure, which is being reformed step by step.

In addition, the government has to form some plans to counter the development of microphilanthropy, especially the outburst of various individual-action, collective-action, and social-movement microphilanthropic activities. Given microphilanthropy's own vitality, openness, transparency, and spontaneity, the government should establish rules and regulations for microphilanthropy to guide it and avoid any potential negative social impacts. At the same time, microphilanthropy should learn from traditional nonprofit organizations and operate with transparency and professionalism so that they can achieve their goals.

Microphilanthropy will not cease to exist, as society will never achieve a perfect utopia. New needs and issues will continue to arise, and society will always face certain basic problems. Individual-action microphilanthropy is especially resilient, whereas collective-action and social-movement microphilanthropy might gradually fade away or will exist more in collaboration with government or nonprofit organizations. The best way to move forward is through positive and frequent information exchange between microphilanthropy, government, and nonprofit organizations—this will achieve a motivating, mutually beneficial, balanced environment for all three.

12

Charting the Development of the Nonprofit Sector in Mainland China: Case Studies of Six Organizations

Kam-tong Chan

In Search of the Nonprofit Sector in Mainland China

The formation and development of the nonprofit sector in mainland China (hereafter China) have been given a high profile in intellectual and public debates since the 1990s, when the sweeping sociopolitical transformations in Eastern Europe were responsible for a surging interest in the democratic possibilities of remaining socialist countries in particular and non-Western cultures in general (for more on China's civil society and nonprofit sector, see Wakeman 1993; Brook and Frolic 1997; Ma 2006; for more on non-Western civil societies, see Dunn and Hann 1996; Hefner 1998; Sajoo 2002; Weller 2005). The extent to which the Western notion of the nonprofit sector, which has been associated with the more controversial concepts of civil society and democratization, can be convincingly and usefully applied to the case of China, remains largely unsettled. The oxymoron "state-led civil society" (Frolic 1997) has been proposed to pinpoint the elusive position of a burgeoning nonprofit sector that is positioned between the market and the state and that assumes a level of relative autonomy that is nevertheless subjected to the directives, if not initiatives, of the government. Although the proliferation of civil-society organizations (CSOs) in China in recent years testifies to the growing importance of the nonprofit sector vis-à-vis the centralized party state, more extensive discussion and elaborate analyses are necessary before definite answers to the above questions can be provided.

This paper attempts to contribute to a better understanding of the evolving nonprofit sector in China before the 2008 Sichuen earthquake disaster by problematizing the sector's idiosyncratic mode of development, which is exemplified above all in its ambiguous relationship with the state. According to the prevalent, structural-operational definition of the nonprofit sector developed by the Johns Hopkins Centre for Civil Society Studies, the nonprofit organizations that constitute the nonprofit sector can be defined as organized entities that exhibit a certain degree of internal organizational structure. These entities are institutions that are separate from the government in that they are self-governed, are run by volunteers, and do not generate profit (Salamon and Anheier 1997).

These defining entities are, however, inadequate in characterizing the nonprofit sector in China, where CSOs are neither structurally independent from the government nor autonomous in governance. Under the legal requirement for a CSO to "articulate with" (read *be subsumed under*) a government registration and oversight department, its internal operations are to a certain extent monitored by the government. The legal environment of China, together with its unique social and cultural background, thus paves a distinct pathway for the development of its nonprofit sector.

Closely related to this is the classification system of CSOs in China, which covers the various types of organizations. *Social organizations*, or *nonprofit groups*, refer to voluntary groups that are formed by Chinese citizens in accordance with a shared objective, a corresponding set of rules, and nonprofit activities. *Private nonenterprise units*, or *nonprofit organizations*, on the other hand, are nonprofit social service organizations run by corporations, institutions, more formal and organized social groups, or individual citizens using nonstate assets. Private hospitals, schools, and research institutes belong to this category. A *foundation* refers to a nonprofit legal entity established in accordance with the regulations that assets donated by individuals, legal entities, or other organizations are employed for the purpose of engaging in activities for the public benefit. *Public charities* are one type of foundation; they can be national or local in scope and *operating or sponsoring* in nature. The former generate funds through project-based fund-raising activities of their own, whereas the latter sponsor projects that are implemented by other organizations.

These preliminary considerations are already symptomatic of the general tendency on the part of the Chinese government to exert a certain level of control and regulation over CSOs. Insofar as a CSO attempts to secure a regular source of financial support, it is necessary to affiliate and articulate with a government unit. While some organizations may remain outside government control while waiting for their registration approval and searching for affiliated units, nonregistered organizations will encounter enormous difficulties in fundraising and risk being banned by the government. As will be shown, however, CSO dependence on the government does not imply a total lack of autonomy. To grasp this somewhat curious position, one has to probe further into the historical pattern of the institutionalization of the nonprofit sector in China.

Historical Development of the Nonprofit Sector in China

The chronology of the nonprofit sector's development in China can be divided into four phases.

The First Phase: Before 1949

CSOs of different scales emerged before the establishment of the People's Republic of China in 1949. According to the figures of the Former Shanghai Social Affairs Bureau, there were 1,320 CSOs in Shanghai in December 1948. Ranging from peasant associations to religious groups to provincial organizations to business federations, these CSOs had a huge membership base of over one million individual members and 884 agency members. During the War of Resistance with Japan (1937–1945), youth-based, patriotic organizations grew rapidly with the Communist Party's encouragement. These organizations later become the core members of the All-China Youth Federation.

The Second Phase: 1949–1978

Numerous national and large-scale CSOs were founded subsequent to the establishment of the People's Republic of China. The All-China Youth Federation, the All-China Women's Federation, and the China Federation of Literary and Art Circles were some examples. Based in Beijing and Shanghai, with branches in provincial cities such as Tianjian and Chongqing, these CSOs formed a network and hence a prototypical nonprofit sector that encompassed the whole country. To facilitate the control and regulation of economic and social affairs, these CSOs were as a rule closely connected with the government. This semigovernmental, semiprivate nature was a major characteristic of Chinese CSOs during this period.

The Third Phase: 1978–1998

The end of the Cultural Revolution (ca. 1966–1976) signaled a general reversal of governmental policy toward market and economic development. In this context CSOs began to flourish, albeit plagued by the problems of poor governance and management. In facing these challenges, some cities and municipalities began to introduce measures and policies aimed at facilitating the development of the nonprofit sector. For instance, Beijing formulated two regulations: Some Provisions for the Regulation of Nonprofit Groups in Beijing and the Measures of Registration of Nonprofit Groups in Beijing in November 1985. These were intended to enhance the role of Beijing's Civil Affairs Bureau as the designated executive arm to approve the registration of civil organizations, while laying the foundation for a more systematic and institutionalized governance of the nonprofit sector.

In 1988, the Chinese government established a Societies Management Unit, which was responsible for formulating and investigation policies concerning the nonprofit sector. A year later, the State Council announced that it would enforce the Regulations for the Registration and Management of Nonprofit Groups, which was a step further toward institutionalized supervision of the nonprofit sector. In response, Beijing, Shanghai, and some provinces and municipalities founded the Office for Nonprofit Groups Management at the subbureau level.

In the meantime, the rise of new types of CSOs—nonprofit organizations and foundations—led to new regulations, such as the Provisional Regulations for the Registration and Management of Popular Nonprofit Organizations and the Regulations on the Administration of Foundations. From that point on the provincial offices of the Office of Administration for Nonprofit Groups and the Ministry of Civil Affairs began to oversee the registration and supervision of CSOs and the implementation of related measures.

This important period of development represented the normalization and legalization of regulations for nonprofit groups. The civic nature of CSOs was prominent during this stage. The underlying reason for this change was a progressive shift from a state-oriented approach to a decentralized approach in the provision of social services. Accordingly, CSOs were expected to bear a greater responsibility in welfare projects.

The Fourth Phase: After 1998

The nonprofit sector in China entered a new, much more vibrant phase in the late 1990s, which involved tripartite interaction, improved corporate governance, and increased transparency and accountability among CSOs. Above all, the original Nonprofit Group Management Unit was renamed the Civil Society Organizations Bureau to achieve a more explicit and better system of governmental oversight of CSOs. The nonprofit sector experienced steady growth due to the government impetus, and by the end of 2003, the number of nonprofit groups and nonprofit organizations had reached 142,000 and 124,000, respectively—about a hundred times the numbers in 1948.

In summary, the status of CSOs in China has changed from disorganized to semigovernmental and from semicivil to civil and finally to state regulated. Three major factors led to this transformation. First, thanks to its enhanced economic power and administrative capacity, the Chinese government developed a growing interest in advancing social service provision by means of formulating policy and normalizing the operations and activities of CSOs. Accompanying this trend, CSOs have made deliberate efforts to forge relationships with international nongovernmental organizations, which have greatly facilitated the exchange of innovative ideas and funding sources and thereby contributed to their capacity building.

Finally, the government wished to shift the financial burden of social services to CSOs, which were pressured into improving service quality. Service users and the public in general also demanded improved services. Within this context of historical and institutional factors, some distinctive structural features of CSOs were consolidated, particularly their autonomous albeit subordinate status vis-à-vis the government.

Emerging Characteristics of the Nonprofit Sector in China

As a result of the historical developments discussed above, several features of the nonprofit sector in China have become more interconnected. First, most CSOs in China are national in scale and aim to serve the whole Chinese community. A political factor responsible for this dates back to the early establishment of the government of the People's Republic of China, when CSOs constituted an important arena for political inclusion and mobilization. Accordingly, an organization usually locates its headquarters in core cities such as Beijing or Shanghai and then establishes a network of regional locations spanning the whole nation. These core cities are often the focus of political and economic reform. Therefore, CSOs play a role in facilitating socioeconomic development.

Second, some of the CSOs in China are closely connected with international organizations and foundations, especially those located in Beijing and Shanghai. More than anywhere else in China, the CSOs in these two cities tend to receive or solicit financial and human resources from foreign foundations. In return, they constitute significant contact points for international foundations wishing to establish a base in China. These CSOs also serve as important bridges between international organizations and resources and their Chinese counterparts.

Despite government control and regulation, CSOs in China, particularly those in Beijing and Shanghai, are able to exert a certain level of influence on governmental policies and measures concerning the nonprofit sector. The government usually gives more weight to the positions and opinions of these CSOs owing to their substantial membership base and considerable social influence. For instance, various women's associations in Beijing have played an important role in formulating the Marriage Law and other regulations concerning women's rights. The All-China Women's Federation conducted investigations to collect opinions from women and provided concrete recommendations on women's behalf for the government's consideration in drafting its recent versions of the Marriage Law.

Still, the relative autonomy of CSOs should not blind us to the fourth and final feature of the Chinese nonprofit sector—the problem of its civic nature. While CSOs have retained some discretionary power and the ability to develop policy initiatives, in the end they are subject to the control of a centralized government that has never lost sight of the potential threat that social powers have for the established political order.

Thanks to a scarcity of resources and unfavorable sociocultural conditions, such as a weak awareness of the freedom of association, the government has generally been successful in making CSOs dependent on the public sector, thereby limiting the nonprofit sector's civic freedom.

Owing to the specific historic background described above, some CSOs, such as the All-China Women's Federation and All-China Youth Federation, have forged an intimate connection with the government. Important posts in these organizations are often occupied by retired or redeployed government officials. For other CSOs, it is also a common practice to invite existing government officials to be consultants and members of the board of directors to enhance communication and relationship (*guanxi*) with the government. This is common among organizations that are waiting for the government to approve their registration in an attempt to establish communication and trust with the government. In addition, the relationship between the nonprofit sector and the private sector is detached at best. With the exceptions of some traditional organizations and large foundations, CSOs in China are rarely supported by local corporations, which may be a result of an underdeveloped sense of corporate social responsibility. The situation has been worsened by the fact that the government does not offer incentives (such as tax benefits) to encourage donations and collaboration across sectors.

But apart from the involvement of governmental officials in CSOs, direct government intervention on the decision making and daily operations of these organizations is not apparent. In general, CSOs enjoy a high degree of autonomy, so long as their activities stay within proper and reasonable limits, which are unspecified as a rule but are tacitly understood. This stands in sharp contrast to the model of civil society and the nonprofit sector in the West, which presupposes a clear demarcation and legally defined boundary between the state and the society. The dichotomy between repression and freedom is not quite applicable to the Chinese case, where a certain level of unarticulated consensus is shared between the centralized state and a burgeoning society regarding its supplementary roles and unclear differentiation.

Case Studies of Civil-Society Organizations in China

To further substantiate the patterns and features delineated thus far, in the following sections we analyze and discuss several cases of CSOs in China.

Background and Case Descriptions

For our analysis we selected a total of six CSOs with different legal statuses—three each in Shanghai and Beijing. The Shanghai CSOs are all regional organizations that aim to serve citizens in Shanghai city and its communities, whereas the Beijing cases are national-level organizations with the mission of helping particular social groups, such as women and youth. For the CSOs located in Shanghai, the Shanghai Luoshan Citizens' Community Center and the Shanghai Cancer Recovery School were registered as "nonprofit groups" before they achieved the legal status of nonprofit organizations. As its name implies, the Shanghai Helping Hands Foundation is an example of a foundation. For the Beijing CSOs, the Maple Women's Psychological Counseling Center was registered as a nonprofit organization under the State Administration for Industry and Commerce and was awaiting approval of registration as a nonprofit organization at the time of our research. The Center for Women's Law and Legal Services of Beijing University, which is affiliated with the Department of Law at the university, was also a nonregistered CSO at the time of our research. Finally, the China Children and Teenagers Fund was registered as a foundation.

The Shanghai Luoshan Citizens' Community Center, a nonprofit organization affiliated with the Shanghai Young Men's Christian Association (YMCA), serves the elderly, youth, and people in need in the Pudong area. The community center became legally registered following the enforcement of the Provisional Regulations for the Registration and Management of Popular Nonprofit Organizations.

The Shanghai Cancer Recovery School is a nonprofit organization affiliated with the Education Bureau of Zhabei District. Like the Shanghai Luoshan Citizens' Community Center, the recovery school obtained legal status under the Provisional Regulations for the Registration and Management of Popular Nonprofit Organizations.

The Shanghai Helping Hands Foundation is a regional fund-raising organization serving youths in a local community. It was first affiliated with the Shanghai Bureau of Prison Administration and then with the Shanghai Bureau of Justice in 2001. This change in affiliation has had a significant impact on the operations of the foundation; in particular, the foundation has adjusted its service targets and mission. It should also be noted that the legal status of the foundation was unclear before the enforcement of the Regulations on Administration of Foundations.

With its research focus on women's issues, the Maple Women's Psychological Counseling Center was affiliated with the China Management Science Research Institute before 1996, after which time the center broke off from the Research Institute and reoriented its services toward the provision of psychological counseling hotlines. At the time of our research the center had not found a government department to affiliate with.

The Center for Women's Law and Legal Services of Beijing University has a good relationship with its affiliated organization, the Department of Law at Beijing University. The department has final veto power on the operations and future development of the center.

Finally, and unlike the Maple Women's Psychological Counseling Center and the Center for Women's Law and Legal Services at Beijing University, the China Children and Teenagers' Fund obtained legal status. Yet because no regulations were designated for foundations before

June 2004, this posed a great challenge for the foundation's public fund-raising activities.

Case Analysis from the Competing Values Framework

The analytic framework for this research was based on the competing values framework formulated by Robert Quinn and his colleagues (Quinn 1988; Quinn et al. 2002). This framework delineates four competing but equally indispensable criteria of effectiveness for any organization, including CSOs. Accordingly, I will analyze the six selected cases from the following four perspectives: (a) the open system perspective analyzes the relationship between an organization and its external stakeholders, such as the government and the private sector; (b) the rational goal perspective examines the impact of legislation and public policies on the development of an organization; (c) the natural system perspective investigates the internal operations of the organization; and finally, (d) the internal process perspective probes into an organization's system of self-regulation.

Open System Perspective

All nonprofit groups, nonprofit organizations, and foundations in China are required by law to operate under the supervision of a dual-oversight system, which consists of the government's registration and oversight departments. CSOs outside these three categories must be affiliated with a government department or recognized organization, or else they risk being banned by the government.

Four of the CSOs described here are under the supervision of a governmental department (such as the Education Bureau and the Bureau of Justice) or a large-scale organization (such as the YMCA). For the nonregistered CSOs, the Center for Women's Law and Legal Services is affiliated with the Department of Law of Beijing University. The affiliated unit should have a legal entity status and be recognized by the government. The CSO may change its affiliated unit without government approval, provided that it has obtained consent from the new affiliated unit.

The Maple Women's Psychological Counseling Center, which has no affiliation with any organization, is registered as a nonprofit organization under the State Administration for Industry and Commerce and, accordingly, is required to renew its license annually. Without official CSO status, the center faces an ever-present risk of being banned from providing social services.

The government exerts supervisory control over CSOs in two ways. First, CSOs are required to submit annual and financial reports to a government registration and oversight office and oversight department. The government also conducts annual inspections. Second, the government monitors CSOs by sending officials to participate in each organization's board of directors. Organizations without affiliated or supervisory units are required to report work progress at the time of license renewal.

Therefore, a CSO's relationship with the government greatly affects its operations and development, especially for an organization that is not registered. As an example, the Maple Women's Psychological Counseling Center is relatively detached from the government. Once a year the organization is supposed to reregister with the Bureau for Industry and Commerce, but in general it has little contact with the government. The government thus has more reservations toward the operation and registration matters of the center. On the other hand, the Center of Women's Law and Legal Services, though not yet registered as a nonprofit organization, has a close relationship with Beijing University's Department of Law and the government, and through this relationship it has won the government's confidence. The organization proactively communicates with the government and invites officials to be consultants and professional members. Of all the CSOs discussed in this chapter, the China Children and Teenagers' Fund has the closest relationship with the government. The organization helps the government allocate resources effectively to the needy, and in return, it receives ample support from the public sector.

Our study also shows that CSOs are competing with other organizations and private companies that provide similar services. Thanks to government recognition and support, CSOs generally exhibit a certain level of competitiveness. The Center of Women's Law and Legal Services, for example, holds a greater competitive advantage than other private law firms because of the greater confidence that the public has in the organization. The Maple Women's Psychological Counseling Center, as the first organization to offer a counseling hotline, also receives a high degree of recognition despite competition with other women's organizations.

Among the three general types of CSOs in China, foundations have the closest relationship with the corporate sector. The Shanghai Helping Hands Foundation and the China Children and Teenagers' Fund often raise money or obtain project sponsors from the private sector. Despite the potential commercial returns of sponsorship, this cooperation is also a result of the good relationship between the Operational Management Unit and the corporate sector (the All-China Women's Federation serves as the oversight department of the China Children and Teenagers' Fund). This positive relationship is undoubtedly beneficial for foundations in their efforts to raise funds in the community. Still, few nonprofit organizations have this kind of connection with the corporate sector.

Generally speaking, the corporate sector emphasizes and exploits the commercial values derived from its cooperative relationship with the nonprofit sector. The opposite is true for CSOs: their major concern remains the possible impacts that such cooperation can have on their image. The Center of Women's Law and Legal Services has refused three offers of sponsorship from the corporate sector because of the companies' requests to rebrand the hotlines with their names. The center believes that these requests reveal the companies' hidden agenda of taking advantage of its brand name for commercial purposes. It can also be noted that the corporate sector tends to cooperate with CSOs that have more public recognition. This consideration obstructs the fund-raising activities of smaller CSOs and organizations without legal status, such as the Maple Women's Psychological Counseling Center.

The majority of CSOs in China are not subsidized by public funding. The Shanghai Helping Hands Foundation and the China Children and Teenagers' Fund are subsidized by the government. But nonprofit organizations that are prohibited by law from using national assets seldom receive financial assistance from the government. The Shanghai Luoshan Citizens' Community Center is an exceptional case in that it occasionally receives project-based subsidies from the government. The Maple Women's Psychological Counseling Center mainly relies on funding from abroad (one of its donors is the Ford Foundation), because its nonregistered status makes it difficult to obtain public resources. On the other hand, the China Children and Teenagers' Fund has no desire for funding from abroad because it has a connection with the corporate sector.

Among the CSOs described here, the Shanghai Luoshan Citizens' Community Center, the Shanghai Cancer Recovery School, and the Maple Women's Psychological Counseling Center have collaborative relationships with and receive financial support from organizations abroad. These CSOs also cooperate with local and international organizations offering similar services. The Maple Women's Psychological Counseling Center organizes seminars and exchange activities with international women's associations to expand its international network. The Shanghai Helping Hands Foundation also cooperates with local youth associations and schools.

All of the CSOs described in this chapter face the issue of low public awareness of the importance of social welfare. This is an especially great challenge for organizations that are heavily reliant on local fund-raising activities. Regulations and policies also constitute external obstacles for nonprofit sector development. The Shanghai Cancer Recovery School is a good example: the school is ineligible for a tax benefit because its clients are not disabled. Leaders from all of the CSOs discussed in this study believe that media coverage and government incentives, such as tax benefits, can facilitate their development.

Rational Goal Perspective

As mentioned above, two of the organizations are nonregistered CSOs, meaning that they cannot legally operate as nonprofit organizations. The Maple Women's Psychological Counseling Center was affiliated with the China Management Science Research Institute early in its existence but subsequently broke ties with the Institute. But because the center failed to obtain certification from the Ministry of Civil Affairs, it is ineligible to register as a nonprofit organization. The center has devoted considerable effort and resources to persuade the Bureau of Industry and Commerce to renew its license as a nonprofit organization. However, because the government regularly changes the managerial level of the bureau to avoid corruption, the center must continually spend time becoming familiar with new staff. In addition to the government's poor understanding of the work of self-initiated women's CSOs, it does not even recognize the center as a nonprofit organization. The center finds this illegitimate status a great hindrance to its fund-raising activities because it can only receive funding assistance from international foundations and has been unable to obtain support from other funding sources.

Another case in point is the Center of Women's Law and Legal Services. The Center was previously affiliated with the Department of Law as a nonprofit organization; however, it can no longer be affiliated with the department. This change in affiliation has had both positive and negative impacts on the organization: on the one hand, the status and influence of Beijing University helps the center to obtain resources and gain public recognition; on the other hand, the veto power of the department ultimately restricts the operations and independence of the center.

Foundations in China have had to respond to changes in law and regulations as well. Before 2004, there were no regulations on the administration of foundations. The government basically adopted the Measures on Administration of Foundations and supplemented those regulations with others, such as the Regulations for the Registration and Management of Social Organizations. On June 1, 2004, the State Council began to enforce the Regulations on the Administration of Foundations, which required established foundations to apply for a certificate within six months. While the China Children and Teenagers' Fund recognizes the positive impact of the new regulations in facilitating the growth of foundations, leaders from the organization have suggested that there is a need to set a buffer period that provides less stringent measures at the initial stage of enforcement but allows flexibility for revisions thereafter.

The impact of the Provisional Regulations for the Registration and Management of Popular Nonprofit Organizations varies for two of the nonprofit organizations in our study. For the Shanghai Luoshan Citizens' Community Center, its illegal status had been a serious problem before the enforcement of the regulations. For a long time the organization could not obtain registration from the Ministry of Civil Affairs or from the Bureau of Industry and Commerce. Owing to its lack of legal status, the center could not participate in activities organized by the government or receive public support. The enforcement of the regulations helps to resolve this problem. However, the Shanghai Cancer Recovery School finds that, while taking into consideration their uniqueness in service targets and nature of services (in particular rehabilitation), some requirements of the Regulations restrict its operation and development.

The above cases illustrate the influence of policies and legislation on the operations and development of CSOs. The scope of the impact, however, depends on the background and operational modes of the organizations.

Natural System Perspective

Board of Directors and Management. In general, CSOs in China are governed at two levels: a board of directors holds ultimate decision-making power, and managers are responsible for implementing initiatives.

The CSOs discussed in this study have different types of boards in terms of their composition and scale and the backgrounds of their members. The directorial board of the Maple Women's Psychological Counseling Center was composed of just two members at the time of this research. The Center of Women's Law and Legal Services faces more restrictions from its board because it is affiliated with Beijing University's Department of Law. There are nine directors from various backgrounds, including legal experts, governmental officials, social service practitioners, and women's service practitioners. Among these individuals, a managerial staff member of the Department of Law and the operational head of the center are represented as ex officio members. Board directors are appointed by the former directorial board, and appointments are often determined by the recommendations of external experts. The board of directors of the China Children and Teenagers' Fund consists of a president, a vice president, and a secretary. A maximum of twenty-five directors may be recommended by fourteen departments of the organization. A president and vice presidents are elected among the directors. In contrast to the Maple Women's Psychological Counseling Center and the Center of Women's Law and Legal Services, the China Children and Teenagers' Fund invites prestigious figures in society to serve as nonexecutive directors. These nonexecutive directors, who now number over 220, are often donors to the organizations. However, they have no actual decision-making or voting power. For the CSOs in Shanghai, the directorial board of the Shanghai Luoshan Citizen's Community Center is composed of five to seven representatives from the government, local citizens, and other community groups.

The division of labor between the board of directors and management is unclear. In some cases, some managerial staff members of CSOs act as ex officio members of the board, as with the Center of Women's Law and Legal Services and the China Children and Teenagers' Fund. The directorial board is responsible for the organization's overall planning and major decisions. Although these issues are usually proposed by the operational head of the center beforehand, the board of directors is highly involved in the process of decision making. They also have the power to veto important issues. From this perspective, the managerial staff members of the organization do not enjoy a high degree of autonomy. While there are channels for the employees to reflect their views, the decision-making model of CSOs is usually top-down.

Staff. CSOs in China usually recruit staff by open recruitment and internal referrals. The operational management units in some cases also assist in recruitment. In Shanghai, as a rule the operational management units or the affiliated organizations take care of recruitment; for instance, the Bureau of Justice handles recruitment for the Shanghai Helping Hands Foundation, and the Cancer Recovery Club recruits for the Shanghai Cancer Recovery School. In Beijing, with the exception of the Maple Women's Psychological Counseling Center, all CSOs recruit staff openly. Some employees of the Center of Women's Law and Legal Services are recruited through internal referrals. Appointments of directors or chief managerial staff in the Shanghai CSOs are usually done by the operational management unit or the affiliated organizations, whereas top-level staff in Beijing are mostly appointed by the president of the board of directors.

All employees of the organizations must undergo an examination and interview before being formally offered employment. The probation period for Beijing CSOs is usually three months, but a six-month "learning period" is required by the China Children and Teenagers' Fund. All CSOs have a clear and objective method of evaluating staff. The Shanghai Luoshan Citizens' Community Center and the Shanghai Cancer Recovery School have a set of evaluation indicators, and the Shanghai Helping Hands Foundation has a year-end self-evaluation system to assess staff performance. Employees of the three Beijing CSOs are assessed regularly. Bonuses are awarded and promotion opportunities offered to employees who demonstrate good performance, whereas those who perform poorly may be demoted or even dismissed.

Accounting and Auditing. The Shanghai Luoshan Citizen's Community Center and the Shanghai Cancer Recovery School commission their auditing tasks to firms appointed by the tax department. Nonregistered CSOs, including the Maple Women's Psychological Counseling Center and the Center of Women's Law and Legal Services, have their own internal accounting and auditing system. The Maple Women's Psychological Counseling Center basically follows the systems required by international funding sources. All audited financial information must be submitted to the funding sources for approval. The Center of Women's Law and Legal Services submits financial information to the internal auditing unit of the Beijing University each year. Foundations can select their own auditing firms, but in the case of a government inspection, they would be audited by firms selected by the government. All annual reports and auditing reports must be openly accessible to the public.

Internal Process Perspective

Decision Making and Staff Involvement. The decision-making power of the nonprofit sector in China is largely concentrated at the senior level, that is, the board of directors and the operational head of the center. Although the views of employees are sometimes solicited, the decision-making process is dominated by senior-level managers. The board of directors has the power to veto major decisions, but the directors rarely exercise this right, as the managerial staff is also involved in the planning process. This is particularly evident in the cases of the Maple Women's Psychological Counseling Center and the China Children and Teenagers' Fund.

There is no institutionalized channel to collect the views of staff in all Shanghai CSOs, but the organizations use their own means to solicit opinions. The Shanghai Luoshan Citizens' Community Center holds monthly staff meetings to collect staff views. Their views are directly channeled to the operational management units and are responded to quickly. Both of the women's organizations also hold regular meetings, which give staff the opportunity to discuss their problems and opinions for new projects. Important issues, such as the financial situation of the organizations, are also open for discussion.

Control of Service Quality. None of the Shanghai CSOs have a well-designed quality control system, although they monitor the provision of services in their own ways. To equip employees with professional knowledge, the Shanghai Luoshan Citizens' Community Center sends staff to international programs and invites professional experts from abroad to deliver training courses. For the Beijing CSOs, the Maple Women's Psychological Counseling Center keeps a record of all incoming hotline calls, evaluates the content of those conversations, and provides advice to its employees. The Center of Women's Law and Legal Services assesses service performance based on client feedback, media reports, and government evaluations. The China Children and Teenagers' Fund invites other organizations to assess its projects. The Shanghai Luoshan Citizens' Community Center has also invited the Social Policy Research Center of the Chinese Academy of Social Sciences, some government departments, and overseas experts to evaluate the performance of its projects.

Among the nonregistered CSOs in this study, the Maple Women's Psychological Counseling Center receives professional assessment from external organizations or overseas organizations, such as the nonprofit organization Information Center, which is based in Beijing. Such assessments might have impacts on decisions to continue an organization's funding. For collaborative projects with international foundations, projects are also evaluated by the assessors sent by the funding organizations. The Center of Women's Law and Legal Services also receives feedback from the Ford Foundation and other organizations. In general, the assessment covers the organizations' strategic planning, leadership, capacity building, financial performance, and operational efficiency.

With respect to client feedback, the China Children and Teenagers' Fund collects views through a working network that is composed of all provincial centers of the All-China Women's Federation (the fund's affiliate organization) and other related organizations. The fund also conducts annual group inspections as a part of its service control system. This inspection allows clients to express their opinions. Compared with the China Children and Teenagers' Fund, the feedback systems of the Maple Women's Psychological Counseling Center and the Center of Women's Law and Legal Services are relatively limited and unsystematic. Both centers collect views mainly through incoming phone calls and correspondence. All of the CSOs we studied follow up on clients' feedback and respond promptly. However, channels to collect clients' views are still generally limited.

In summary, the decision-making process of CSOs is mostly concentrated at the upper levels, with relatively limited participation from the lower levels. With the exception of the Maple Women's Psychological Counseling Center and the Center of Women's Law and Legal Services, which are regularly assessed by overseas organizations, none of the CSOs in this study have a professional assessment system of organizational performance. Regarding feedback systems, CSOs in Beijing have channels for staff and service users to express their views, but this system has not yet been adopted by CSOs in Shanghai.

Conclusion

This chapter has attempted to describe and analyze the nonprofit sector in China. It was found that the conventional Western definitions and characterizations of CSOs are not entirely applicable to the Chinese context. In particular, unlike CSOs in the West, CSOs in China are not self-regulated and do not have a high degree of autonomy.

The development of the nonprofit sector in China is to a large extent oriented and guided by the public sector. By tracing the history of the nonprofit sector's development, this paper showed that the role of the CSOs is largely shaped by the government. The nonprofit sector served as an arena for political inclusion and mobilization in its early stages, eventually developing into the government's partner in social service delivery. In this stage of development, the government attempted to institutionalize and routinize the activities of CSOs by implementing various regulations and measures. Although these policies have successfully legitimized and established the nonprofit sector as a normative arena (which justifies our referring to it as the "nonprofit sector"), the activities of CSOs are subject to government monitoring and legal control. Under the government's dual system of oversight and affiliation, any given CSO is monitored by two government departments. This system is based on the principle of two levels of inspection and supervision and forms a tightly integrated system of registration and operation management.

Six CSO cases were selected in this study to investigate the development and present state of CSOs in China. These CSOs are based in Beijing and Shanghai and have different legal statuses and backgrounds. A competing values framework was adopted to analyze the relationship between these organizations and external stakeholders, the impact of legislation and public policies on the development of CSOs, and their internal operations and self-regulation systems. It was found that most CSOs are closely connected with the government and that an organization's relationship with a government department affects the operations and development of these organizations substantially. However, few CSOs have a collaborative relationship with the corporate sector (except for foundations), partly owing to a relatively weak sense of corporate social responsibility in China.

The elusive position of the nonprofit sector may be readily discerned from the fact that, while the enforcement of legislation concerning CSOs helps some organizations obtain legal status, it restricts the operations of others. Divergence from the Western model is also evident in the mostly top-down internal governance of CSOs, although there are channels for soliciting views from the lower ranks of the organizational hierarchy. Granted, there is a general absence of systematic assessment of systems to monitor service quality and handle client feedback, and with the ever-changing social context, the inflow of international resources, and the reform impetus of the government, one may foresee a generally improving and growing nonprofit sector. Consequently, it is one thing to suggest that the Chinese experience is different from that of the West; it is quite another to deny the possibilities that are opened up by the hidden but real process of constant negotiation between the nonprofit sector and the public sector in China.

Glossary of Terms

cause marketing. This type of marketing involves the mutually beneficial collaboration between a for-profit corporation and a nonprofit.

centralized registration. The system under which nonprofits are officially registered by the Ministry of Civil Affairs, in cooperation with local civil affairs departments.

Communist Party of China (CPC). The founding and ruling political party of China, also called the Chinese Communist Party (CCP). The CPC is an institution of the state. It has legal power, granted by the national constitution, and stands above the law. It is the world's largest political party, claiming more than 80 million members, or 6 percent of the Chinese population.

corporate citizenship. The process of integrating shared social values into a company's strategies and operating practices. A corporate citizen believes that the success of the corporation is closely related to the health of society. Therefore, the corporation will take all its stakeholders—employees, customers, communities, suppliers, and natural environment—into consideration.

dual oversight. The system by which the Chinese government oversees the operations of nonprofits organizations and nonprofit groups. Dual oversight places nonprofits under the supervision of both the appropriate registration department, and a government department related to the mission of the respective nonprofit. Depending on the jurisdiction of the nonprofit, either the Ministry of Civil Affairs of the State Council or the local Department of Civil Affairs is responsible for registration.

government-operated nongovernmental organization (GONGO). This type of nongovernmental organization has been established by a government, but operates as a nongovernmental organization. By establishing GONGOs, a state can maintain some control of the organization's personnel, mission, and operations, while allowing the organization to qualify for certain forms of international aid and support.

grassroots volunteer organization. A volunteer-driven civic organization that is created by natural, spontaneous processes. Grassroots volunteer organizations in China are typically organized at the local level, and deal with community affairs.

microblog. A form of web log, or "blog," that allows for the exchange of small elements of content, such as short sentences, images, or videos.

microphilanthropy. A new charity model in which the Internet is used as a platform to promote the general public's participation in philanthropy.

Ministry of Civil Affairs. This Chinese department is responsible for social and administrative affairs. It was created in 1978, and falls under the jurisdiction of the State Council of the People's Republic of China.

National Congress. The National Congress of the Communist Party of China (CPC) is held approximately every five years in Beijing, China. The National Congress reviews and changes the Constitution, makes leadership changes every ten years, and selects the Central Committee, a decision-making body. Delegates to the National Congress are selected by grassroots CPC organizations.

netizen. A habitual, or frequent, Internet user.

nonprofit group (Chinese: *shehui tuanti*). Formal or informal group of people joined together to pursue a common nonprofit goal; relatively autonomous, inspired by voluntary altruism; may offer public benefits or member benefits. *Nonprofit groups* are a common term in Chinese political discourse that refer to groups of people working together on a common activity, interest, or goal. Such groups are often unofficial networks organized informally by individuals (Chapter 4).

nonprofit organization (NPO; Chinese: *mingban fei qiye zuzhi*). Nonprofit groups that have achieved a more formal, organized status. In China, nonprofit organizations, also called nonenterprise units, use nongovernmental assets and are formed by enterprise units, civic associations, and other social forces or civic groups.

nonprofit sector. Also called "civil society," or "the third sector," this sphere of social activity exists alongside government and business, and includes all nonprofit groups and organizations.

oversight department. A local government department responsible for overseeing the operations and management of nonprofit organizations and nonprofit groups. The system of dual oversight places nonprofits under the supervision of both the appropriate registration department, and an oversight department that is related to the mission of the respective nonprofit.

people's organization. Nonprofit organizations that send representatives to the Chinese People's Political Consultative Conference, a political advisory body.

private foundation. A nongovernmental, nonprofit organization having a principal fund managed by its own trustees or directors.

publicness. The degree to which a nonprofit's mission serves the public interest. The publicness of NPOs fundamentally requires that the mission of these organizations not be aimed at benefiting a specific group of people (i.e., focused on member benefits), that their operations be transparent, and that their outputs contribute to the overall welfare of society.

public charity. Charity groups that generally derive their funding or support primarily from the general public, receiving grants from individuals, government, and private foundations.

Reform Era. The program of economic reforms in China that introduced capitalist market principles. It was initiated in 1978 by Deng Xiaoping.

state-owned enterprise. A Chinese corporation that is jointly owned and governed by the local government and the national State-Owned Assets Supervision and Administration Commission. These are increasingly being replaced by nonstate-owned enterprises.

References

Anheier, Helmut. 2004. *Civil Society: Measurement, Evaluation, Policy.* Earthscan.

Booth, David. 1987. "Alternatives in the Restructuring of State-Society Relations: Research Issues for Tropical Africa." *IDS Bulletin* 18, no. 4.

Brook, T. and B. M. Frolic, eds. 1997. *Civil Society in China.* Armonk, NY: Sharpe.

Carroll, A. B. 1979. "A Three-Dimensional Conceptual Model of Corporate Performance." *The Academy of Management Review* 4, no. 4: 497–505.

Davis, K., and R. L. Blomstrom. 1966. *Business and Its Environment.* New York: McGraw-Hill.

Deng, Z. 1997. *The State and the Society.* Chengdu, China: Sichuan People Press.

Dunn, E. and C. Hann, eds. 1996. *Civil Society: Challenging Western Models.* London: Routledge.

Frolic, B. M. 1997. "State-Led Civil Society." In *Civil Society in China,* ed. T. Brook and B. M. Frolic, 46–67. Armonk, NY: Sharpe.

Habermas, J. 1989. *The Structural Transformation of the Public Sphere: An Inquiry into a Category of Bourgeois Society.* Cambridge, MA: MIT Press.

He, B. 1997. *The Democratic Implications of Civil Society in China.* London: Macmillan.

Hefner, R., ed. 1998. *Democratic Civility.* New Brunswick, NJ: Transaction.

Held, D. 1987. *Model of Democracy.* Stanford, CA: Stanford University Press.

Korten, D. 1990. *Getting to the 21st Century: Voluntary Action and Perspectives*. West Hartford, CT: Kumarian Press.

Ku, C.-H. 2000. "The Publicness and Autonomy of NPOs in Taiwan (台灣非營利組織的公共性與自主性)." *Taiwan Sociology Research* (台灣社會學研究) 4: 145–89.

Li, Yongjun. 2006. *General Principals to Civil Law*. The Law Press, 307–8.

Lu, H. 2001. "Report on Charity Donation of Enterprises: The Shanghai Corporate Donations Survey (公司捐贈社会公益研究报告:上海企业捐赠社会公益情况的调查)." *Charity* (慈善) 1: 52–4.

Ma, Q. 2006. *Non-Governmental Organizations in Contemporary China: Paving the Way to a Civil Society?* London: Routledge.

Maier, C., ed. 1987. *Changing Boundaries of the Political: Essays on the Evolving Balance between the State and Society, Public and Private in Europe*. Cambridge: Cambridge University Press.

Metzger, T. A. 1998. *The Western Concept of the Civil Society in the Context of Chinese History*. Stanford, CA: Hoover Institution on War, Revolution, and Peace, Stanford University.

Putnam, R. 1993. *Making Democracy Work: Civic Traditions in Modern Italy*. Princeton, NJ: Princeton University Press.

Quinn, R. E. 1988. *Beyond Rational Management: Mastering the Paradoxes and Competing Demands of High Performance*. San Francisco, CA: Jossey-Bass.

Quinn, R. E., M. P. Thompson, and M. R. McGrath. 2002. *Becoming a Master Manager*. 3rd ed. New York: Wiley.

Sajoo, A. B., ed. 2002. *Civil Society and the Muslim World*. London: Tauris.

Salamon, L. M. 1999. *Global Civil Society*. Johns Hopkins Comparative Nonprofit Sector Project.

Salamon, L. M. and H. K. Anheier. 1997. *Defining the Nonprofit Sector: A Cross-National Analysis*. Manchester: Manchester University Press.

Salamon, L. M., H. K. Anheier, R. List, S. Toepler, S. W. Sokolowski, and Associates. 1999. *Global Civil Society*. Baltimore, MD: Johns Hopkins Center for Civil Society Studies, Johns Hopkins Comparative Nonprofit Sector Project.

Shils, Edward. 1991. "The Virtue of Civil Society." *Government and Opposition* 26, no. 1 (Winter).

Sun, L. 1994. "Evolution of the Interaction between State, Civil Ruling Elite and People before and after the Reform in China." *Chinese Social Sciences Quarterly* 6: 37–54.

Vermeer, E. B., F. N. Pieke, and W. L. Chong, eds. 1998. *Cooperative and Collective in China's Rural Development: Between State arid Private Interests*. Armonk, NY: Sharpe.

Wakeman, F., Jr. 1993. "The Civil Society and Public Sphere Debate: Western Reflections on Chinese Political Culture." *Modern China* 19, no. 2: 108–38.

Wang, M., J. He, and G. Liu. 2001. *The Association Reforms in China* (中国社团改革). Beijing, China: Social Science Academic Press.

Wasserstrom, J. N. and E. J. Perry, eds. 1994. *Popular Protest and Political Culture in Modern China*. 2nd ed. Boulder, CO: Westview Press.

Weller, R. 1999. *Alternate Civilities: Democracy and Culture to China and Taiwan*. Boulder, CO: Westview Press.

———, ed. 2005. *Civil Life, Globalization, and Political Change in Asia: Organizing between Family and State*. London: Routledge.

White, Gordon. 2000. "Civil Society, Democratization and Development: Clearing the Analytical Ground." In *Civil Society and the Third Sector*, ed. Zengke He. Social Science Academic Press.

Yang, T. 2011. *Annual Report on China's Philanthropy Development* (中国慈善发展报告). Beijing, China: Social Sciences Academic Press.

Zhao, L. 1998. *NGOs and Sustainable Development* (非政府组织与可持续发展). Beijing, China: Economic Science Press.

About the Contributors

Liqiang Cai, Executive Deputy Director of MPA Education Center, Graduate School of Chinese Academy of Social Sciences. Dr. Cai's research areas include public policy analysis, nonprofit and public governance, and constitutionalism ideology.

Kam-tong Chan, Director of Centre for Third Sector Studies, Hong Kong Polytechnic University. Dr. Chan's areas of research include the third sector, total quality management, and outcome measurement in nonprofit organizations.

Xiufeng Chen, Professor, Executive Director of Center for Social Work Education, Wuhan University of Science and Technology. Dr. Chen's areas of research include foundation, charitable agency, volunteer organization, and private nonprofit organization.

Guosheng Deng, Associate Professor, Director of Center for Innovation and Social Responsibility, School of Public Policy and Management, Tsinghua University. Dr. Deng's areas of research include NGO study, social innovation, and performance evaluation.

Richard L. Edwards, Executive Vice President for Academic Affairs, Rutgers, The State University of New Jersey. Dr. Edwards' research interests include nonprofit and public management, international social work, and social work education.

Li Feng, Executive Director of China Philanthropy Advisors, Deputy Secretary General of Social Entrepreneur Foundation. Dr. Feng's working areas include project development and management, financing, evaluation, and NPO consultation.

Huajun Gao, Executive Vice Dean of China Philanthropy Research Institute. Dr. Gao's areas of research include social security, social assistance, social welfare, and philanthropy.

Chien-Chung Huang, Director of Huamin Research Center, School of Social Work, Rutgers University. Dr. Huang's areas of research include child support, welfare reform, poverty, and nonprofit organization.

Xiaoyong Huang, Associate Dean, Graduate School of Chinese Academy of Social Sciences. Dr. Huang's research areas include world economy, international energy security, and nonprofit organization.

Xiaoguang Kang, Director of NPO Research Center, Remin University of China. Dr. Kang's research areas include nonprofit management, state-society relationship, political development and political stability, as well as political culture.

Li Li, Associate Professor, Institute of Foundation Research, Wuhan University of Science and Technology. Dr. Li's areas of research include social policy, nonprofit organization, public management, and development of the third sector.

Peifeng Liu, Deputy Director of Constitutional Law Education Center, Law School, Beijing Normal University. Dr. Liu's research areas include constitutional law, civic rights theory, and law on nonprofit organization.

Zhenyao Wang, Dean of China Philanthropy Research Institute, Beijing Normal University. Dean Wang's areas of research include China social welfare system, philanthropic research and education, philanthropic consultation and services, and international communication on philanthropy.

Yongguang Xu, Chairman of Narada Foundation and China Foundation Center. His working areas include nonprofit sector, China's charity system development, and philanthropic culture development.

Gaorong Zhang, Deputy Director of Research Department, China Philanthropy Research Institute. His areas of research include philanthropy profession, civil society development, human rights protection, public health, and corporate social responsibility.

Jiangang Zhu, Director of Institute for Civil Society, Sun Yat-Sen University. Dr. Zhu's areas of research include social organization, urban and rural community, social movement, and theory on anthropology.

Index

For Product Safety Concerns and Information please contact our EU
representative GPSR@taylorandfrancis.com Taylor & Francis Verlag GmbH,
Kaufingerstraße 24, 80331 München, Germany

Batch number: 08153793

Printed by Printforce, the Netherlands